Key Wc
A JOURNAL OF CULTURAL MATERIALISM

9
(2011)

edited by
**Catherine Clay
Simon Dentith
Kristin Ewins
Ben Harker
Angela Kershaw
Dave Laing
Stan Smith
Vicki Whittaker**

Key Words: A Journal of Cultural Materialism

Editors: Catherine Clay (Nottingham Trent University), Simon Dentith (University of Reading), Kristin Ewins (University of Salford), Ben Harker (University of Salford), Angela Kershaw (University of Birmingham), Dave Laing (University of Liverpool), Stan Smith (Nottingham Trent University), Vicki Whittaker.

Guest editor for this issue: Daniel G. Williams (Swansea University).

Editorial Advisory Board: John Brannigan (University College Dublin), Peter Brooker (University of Sussex), Terry Eagleton (National University of Ireland Galway and Lancaster University), John Higgins (University of Cape Town), Andreas Huyssen (Columbia University, New York), John Lucas (Nottingham Trent University and Loughborough University), Peter Marks (University of Sydney), Sean Matthews (University of Nottingham), Jim McGuigan (Loughborough University), Andrew Milner (Monash University), Meaghan Morris (Lingnan University), Morag Shiach (Queen Mary, University of London), Dai Smith (Swansea University), Nick Stevenson (University of Nottingham), John Storey (University of Sunderland), Will Straw (McGill University), Jenny Bourne Taylor (University of Sussex), Jeff Wallace (University of Glamorgan), Imelda Whelehan (De Montfort University).

Contributions for prospective inclusion in *Key Words* should comply with the style notes printed on pp. 175–77 of this issue, and should be sent to Catherine Clay, School of Arts and Humanities, Nottingham Trent University, Clifton Campus, Nottingham NG11 8NS, (catherine.clay@ntu.ac.uk).
Books and other items for review should be sent to Professor J. Birkett, Treasurer, Raymond Williams Society, Department of French Studies, University of Birmingham, Birmingham B15 2TT, UK.

Key Words is a publication of The Raymond Williams Society
(website: **www.raymondwilliams.co.uk**).

Contributions copyright © The Author
Issue compilation and *Key Words* © The Raymond Williams Society 2011.

All rights reserved.

Cover design by Andrew Dawson.

Printed by Russell Press, Nottingham.
Distributed by Spokesman Books, Nottingham.

ISSN: 1369-9725
ISBN: 978-0-9531503-5-9

Contents

Editors' Preface	5
Signs, Socialism and Ethics: Eagleton on Language Tony Crowley	8
Terry Eagleton, Postmodernism and Ireland Edward Larrissy	25
Williams and Wittgenstein: Language, Politics and Structure of Feeling Ben Ware	41
***Border Country*: Then and Now** Simon Dentith	58
Raymond Williams in Japan *Essays by contemporary Japanese critics, edited and introduced by Daniel G. Williams*	75
Guest Editor's Introduction: Travelling Williams Daniel G. Williams	76
Soseki Natsume, Raymond Williams, and the Geography of 'Culture' Shintaro Kono	83
Translation and Interpretation: Raymond Williams and the Uses of Action Takashi Onuki	100
'To Feel the Connections': Collectivity and Dialectic in Raymond Williams's *Loyalties* Yasuhiro Kondo	112
The 'Far West' after Industrialisation: Gwyn Thomas, Ishimure Michiko and Raymond Williams Yuzo Yamada	124

Contents

'A Narrative of Unsolved Cases': A Reading of *The Fight for Manod* 134
Yasuo Kawabata

Afterword: Found in Translation 144
Dai Smith

* * *

Debate
A Response to John Lucas and Sean Matthews 148
Dai Smith

Reviews 153

Notes on Contributors 170

Raymond Williams Foundation 174

Style Notes for Contributors 175

Editors' Preface

> The conductress, a West Indian, smiled as he jumped to the platform, and he said, 'Good evening', and was answered, with an easiness that had almost been lost. You don't speak to people in London, he remembered; in fact, you don't speak to people anywhere in England...

Much in this issue of *Key Words* has to do with border crossings. When Matthew Price gets on a London bus in the opening page of Raymond Williams's 1960 novel *Border Country*, he experiences the positive benefits of the crossing of borders by others: the immigrant bus conductress acts as an antidote to the refusal of interpersonal communication which Matthew finds characteristic of England in general and London in particular. This opening vignette figures a certain solidarity – an absence of barriers, perhaps – between those who have had to cross a border to get to England. Of course, in Matthew's case, the border crossed is that between Wales and England, yet in the context of the essays presented in this volume it is perhaps worth noting that *Border Country*'s opening scene is an example of international border crossing. Five of the essays collected here are the result of the willingness of colleagues in Swansea and in Tokyo to cross international borders in order to engage in a transnational discussion of Williams's work. The Editors would like to express their gratitude to Daniel G. Williams and Dai Smith for the opportunity to publish the results of what is clearly a very fruitful international collaboration, one which demonstrates the extent and scope of the ongoing and lively interest in Williams's theory and fiction. Simon Dentith's essay on *Border Country* complements these contributions by exploring the new contexts of reading and reception of Williams's fiction which have emerged since the novel was first published over 50 years ago. Simon Dentith first presented this work as the Raymond Williams Society Annual Lecture on 21 November 2009, and we are pleased to make it available to readers who were not able to be present at that event.

The remaining three contributions focus on questions of language. While this issue is primarily about Raymond Williams's work, his ideas and influence, this section brings two other key thinkers into the dialogue – Ludwig Wittgenstein, and Terry Eagleton, who is perhaps Williams's foremost disciple. Ben Ware's discussion of Williams and Wittgenstein seeks to challenge certain ideological and disciplinary boundaries which have tended to keep these two thinkers apart. For Ware, Wittgenstein is not the conservative thinker some have made him out to be; Ware argues that 'the desire to examine the real human circumstances in which meanings are formed' is common to the thought of Wittgenstein and Williams. Both Ware and Tony Crowley engage with Wittgenstein's affirmation that 'philosophy can in no way interfere with the actual use of language; it can in the end only describe it'. Their aim in so doing is to refute the notion that Wittgenstein's analysis of language precludes an appreciation of its transformative potential. Crowley explores Terry Eagleton's work on language from the perspective of Eagleton's positive engagement with both Wittgenstein and Marx, arguing that 'Eagleton turned to the work of Wittgenstein as a way of returning signification to its basis in social activity'. Like Williams, Eagleton is acutely aware of the ways in which Wittgenstein grounds his discussion of language in the social. Edward Larrissy's essay discusses Eagleton from the perspective of his generally negative engagement with postmodern theory, concluding that, while Eagleton sets himself against some of the worst excesses of postmodern theory, he is nonetheless 'an author of seriously playful philosophical fictions who seeks to ensure that art is pondered and politically responsible'. Larrissy's essay reminds us that sometimes it is a good idea to maintain borders and boundaries – those which separate postmodern and Marxist conceptions of meaning and of human identity, for example. But Larrissy's piece also addresses cross-border issues, considering as it does Eagleton's interest in Irish nationalism and nationality. In all three of these essays, the international scope of the intellectual exchanges described is once again striking – the discussions range over the work of writers such as Herbert Marcuse, Lucien Goldman, Ferdinand de Saussure, Jacques Derrida, Michel Foucault, Julia Kristeva, Mikhail Bakhtin and V.N. Vološinov, as well as Wittgenstein and Marx. The Japanese essays demonstrate the extent to which international intellectual exchange relies on translation: communication happens through language, and these essays have the great merit of showing that the process of interlingual transfer can itself generate new meanings and new readings.

This volume also includes a 'Debate' section in which Dai Smith picks up the threads of a discussion about his biography *Raymond Williams: A Warrior's Tale* (2008) which appeared in *Key Words* 6. The topic under debate is Raymond Williams the novelist. This is most appropriate in a volume which offers readings of *Border Country*, *The Fight for Manod* and *Loyalties*, as well as a comparative analysis of the fiction of Williams, Gwyn Thomas and the Japanese novelist Ishimure Michiko. It is to be hoped that these international perspectives and comparisons will contribute to an ongoing discussion of Williams 'then and now'.

This discussion will continue in 2012 in the pages of *Key Words* with a special issue on *The Long Revolution*, first published 50 years ago in 1961, and much debated in the course of the last half century. The dialogue also continues in conferences, such as the event sponsored by the Raymond Williams Society taking place at the University of Brighton in Hastings in

Editors' Preface

September 2011 on the theme of 'Raymond Williams and Robert Tressell in Hastings: Celebrating 50 Years of *The Long Revolution* and the Centenary of *The Ragged Trousered Philanthropists*'. It is also encouraging to note that a younger generation of scholars working in the cultural materialist tradition continues to engage productively with Williams's work and his legacy. The 2010 Raymond Williams Society Postgraduate Essay Competition produced a range of excellent submissions and a winning entry from Simon Machin, a PhD student in the Department of English, Roehampton University, entitled 'Why, comrade?: Raymond Williams, Orwell and Structure of Feeling in Boys' Story Papers'. The abstract of this essay is available via the web site of the Raymond Williams Society (http://www.raymondwilliams.co.uk/) along with details of the next competition and other forthcoming events.

Signs, Socialism and Ethics: Eagleton on Language
Tony Crowley

Introduction: Against the Grain

The nature, range and copiousness of Terry Eagleton's contribution to contemporary literary, critical and cultural theory has provoked a number of hostile reactions. In his introduction to *The Eagleton Reader* for example, Stephen Regan registers (and vehemently rejects) the 'scandalous' claims that 'Eagleton keeps changing his mind' and that his work has simply surfed 'wave after wave of cross-channel theory'.[1] Likewise David Alderson, in the first book-length study of Eagleton's oeuvre to date, cites Judith Butler's attempted put-down (in response to a review of Gayatri Spivak's *Critique of Postcolonial Reason* in the *London Review of Books*): 'surely, neither the *LRB* nor Eagleton believes that theorists should confine themselves to writing introductory primers such as those he has chosen to provide'.[2] It is perhaps a comment on the state of theoretical debate in the humanities that a major public intellectual should be criticised for changing his position in response to new developments in the field. Or that it can be taken as ground for apparent rebuke if a thinker seeks to communicate new and complex intellectual trends in an open, readable and persuasive manner (particularly given the opacity of much contemporary theory). Be that as it may, my aim in this essay will be to demonstrate that there has been one theoretical issue with which Eagleton has been occupied since the start of his publishing career and with which he continues to engage. Moreover I will attempt to show that his approach has been both consistent and innovative and I will argue that in this regard he has made an important contribution to a much-neglected area of socialist thought. The issue in question, one which underpins his writing from *The Body as Language* (1970) to *The Meaning of Life* (2007), is the identification of language as a constitutive and distinctive factor in human species-being and the political and ethical consequences which follow from this recognition. In this respect, like many others, Eagleton's work may be compared with that of Raymond Williams, his mentor and later colleague, for whom an understanding of the central role of language to any account of the human was also a constant and pressing critical issue.

In one sense Eagleton's concern with language makes him a thinker typical of his age, since it is a commonplace of recent intellectual historiography to note that twentieth-century critical thought was dominated by an interest in language. Such a claim does not bear too much detailed examination since it is difficult to see how critical thinking in the seventeenth, eighteenth and nineteenth centuries can be viewed as not being preoccupied with questions of language and signification, which makes claims for a distinctive twentieth-century 'turn' to language appear somewhat exaggerated. From the Renaissance on, language lay at the centre of much of the advanced theorising in areas of knowledge which are now grouped together as the humanities. The scope of this work stretched from speculation on the relationship between language and world to that between signs and consciousness, from the importance of interpretation to the origin of language, from the insight that groups of languages were related to each other to the understanding that individual languages bore the specific historical traces of their users, from the concern with rules for social use to the discovery of universal laws. Yet even after the so-called 'linguistic turn' is put into historical context, the assertion that there was a new type of focus on language in the twentieth century is accurate in two senses. First, it is evidently the case that the study of language in its own right developed in such a way as to ensure that language held a dominant position in the disciplined field of modern knowledge; it even gained the much sought-after status of 'science' through its institutionalisation in linguistics. Second, it is also true, partly as a result of the specialised study of language *per se*, that an attention to language was characteristic of many of the new, or relatively new, disciplines of knowledge which appeared and/or were consolidated in the twentieth century (from English literature to sociology, psychoanalysis to anthropology). But despite the fact that Eagleton's attention to the significance of language fits a general historical trend, his account is radically idiosyncratic in relation to the dominant modes of the study of language in the twentieth century (Saussurean structuralism and Chomskyan linguistics). Indeed his specific emphasis on the philosophical and political signifcance of language puts his work at a distance from even the most socially cognisant of the more recent approaches – including critical discourse analysis and social semiotics. For while research in these fields has yielded important insights into the ideological and power-laden operations of language in society, Eagleton has been concerned with an analysis of the function of language at a more fundamental level. Largely derived from a reading of Marx and Wittgenstein, his distinctive account presents a singular understanding of the role of language in human life which construes it as central to our species-being: the key to our transformation of the natural and historical worlds. This, it will be argued, is significant both as a contribution to the study of language, but also to socialist cultural and political theory.

Marx's Linguistic Animal: Free in History

Given that Eagleton's work on language is based on Marxist presuppositions, it is important to note Marx's own account of the significance of language. Marx appears to have had little trouble with the idea of human nature, a stance which places him in stark opposition to many contemporary theorists.[3] Human beings, he argued, are unique amongst the biological species in that they are at one and the same time animal – they belong to nature – and yet they differ from other forms of natural life in that through praxis they both change nature and create themselves.

> The practical creation of an *objective* world, the *fashioning* of inorganic nature, is proof that man is a conscious species-being, i.e. a being which treats the species as its own being or itself as a species-being. It is true that animals also produce… But they produce only their immediate needs or those of their young; they produce one-sidedly, whereas man produces universally; they produce only when immediate physical need compels them to do so, while man produces even when he is free from physical need and truly produces only in freedom from such need.[4]

Not confined by their species-being to the satisfaction of their immediate physical needs, human beings create, through their practical activity, a social realm in which 'the realized naturalism of man and the realized humanism of nature' are achieved.[5] For Marx this is not a question of what human beings *should* do, nor is it a denial of the fact that most human beings in history have spent – and do spend – much of their time doing little but satisfying their basic physical needs (for water, food, shelter), it is simply a constitutive human capacity. It is certainly the case that within particular social formations, 'labour, *life activity, productive life*',

> appears to man only as a *means* for the satisfaction of a need, the need to preserve physical existence. But productive life is species-life. It is life-producing life. The whole character of a species, its species-character, resides in the nature of its life-activity, and free conscious activity constitutes the species-character of man.[6]

The reduction of this human capability, the production of a situation in which 'life itself appears only as a *means of life*', is one of the primary bases upon which Marx forms his critique of capitalism. For though it cannot do away with the 'free conscious activity' which constitutes human species-being – indeed it requires it – capitalism prevents the realisation of such activity as a goal in itself since the division of labour forces most human beings to expend their creative practical powers in behaviour which enables them simply to satisfy their fundamental needs. Contrast this with Marx's delineation of a realm which is beyond necessity but grounded in it (since being human perforce entails fulfilling our bodily requirements). That 'true realm of freedom' consists in 'the development of human powers as an end in itself', a process in which human beings will 'govern the human metabolism with nature in a rational way, bringing it under their collective control instead of being dominated by it as a blind power', and doing so 'with the least expenditure of energy and in conditions most worthy and appropriate for their human nature'.[7]

In *The German Ideology* Marx sets out the basis of the historical materialist conception of history in terms of five premises.[8] The first is our basic need to sustain ourselves biologically: 'men must be in a position to live in order to be able to "make history" [which] involves before everything else eating and drinking, a habitation, clothing and many other things'. The second is that the fulfillment of this first necessity, through our action upon material reality, produces new needs. The third is the sexual reproduction of the species itself. The fourth is the fact that this general process of the creation of the self and 'fresh life' takes place through social relationship – the 'materialistic connection of men with one another' and constantly takes new forms. And the final but crucial premise, which distinguishes the human mode of being from all others, is that,

> man also possesses 'consciousness', but, even so, not inherent, not pure consciousness. From the start the 'spirit' is afflicted with the curse of being 'burdened' with matter, which here makes its appearance in the form of agitated layers of air, sounds, in short, of language. Language is as old as consciousness, language *is* practical consciousness that exists also for other men, and for that reason alone it really exists for me personally as well; language, like consciousness, only arises from the need, the necessity, of intercourse with other men... Consciousness is, therefore, from the very beginning a social product and remains so as long as men exist.[9]

It is important to recognise that Marx does not argue that these are evolutionary stages on the way to the achievement of human status, but rather considers them as 'aspects' of social activity, of 'the primary historical relationships', 'which have existed simultaneously since the dawn of history and the first men and which still assert themselves in history today'.[10] As Williams notes, it is crucial to retain the five different 'aspects' as simultaneous elements of a single process of human self-creation in order to avoid the dangers of giving any one of them priority and thus lapsing into either crude materialism (human beings began by working upon the material world and at some point took up language as a medium which allowed them to communicate) or idealism (it is consciousness which distinguishes the human species from all others).[11] Yet although Marx's general account of the constitutive 'aspects' of human historical being refuses the idea that it is language alone which distinguishes human beings from other species, he also makes it clear that language has a central function in the 'free conscious activity' by which we labour upon and transform reality. Indeed for Marx language appears to be a form of labour in its own right: the practical, active form of consciousness which we share with others (because we derive it from others) and which enables us to shape the world.

Language, Meaning, Practice

An emphasis on language as a form of distinctive human praxis can also be found in the writings of the other major thinker whose work has been a consistent reference point in Eagleton's thought: Ludwig Wittgenstein, the reluctant professor of philosophy who attempted to put an end to his own discipline not once but twice.[12] Wittgenstein's insistence on grounding language in a 'form of life' is an attempt to address and debunk dominant metaphysical positions and it is used by Eagleton to develop Marx's brief comments on the practical significance of semiotic production in the creation of history. As will become clear, the work of both Marx and Wittgenstein is fundamental not only to Eagleton's critique of a number of forms of idealism, but also to his articulation of an ethical position from within socialism.

It will be useful to contrast the view of language which Eagleton develops with that of Ferdinand de Saussure's ambitious and influential attempt to theorise language (not least because Saussure's theory appears to share the accentuation on the social basis of signification postulated by both Marx and Wittgenstein) and the poststructuralist critique which grew out of it. For Saussure, for example, it is language that creates meaningful consciousness rather than consciousness which creates meaningful language: 'no ideas are established in advance and nothing is distinct, before the introduction of linguistic structure'.[13] Yet despite this apparent agreement, the understanding of the social realm which underpins Saussurean structuralism differs greatly from that proposed by historical materialism. Thus the *Course in General Linguistics* makes it clear that language is to be understood as 'social in its essence and independent of the individual', 'something which is in each individual, but is none the less common to all', 'a collective phenomenon' and, for that very reason, 'out of the reach of any deliberate interference by individuals'.[14] Influenced in part by Durkheim's notion of the 'social fact', the Saussurean science of language treats the social and the individual as two strictly demarcated and indeed oppositional spheres, hence the rigid methodological distinction between 'langue' and 'parole' (best translated as 'linguistic structure' and 'practice or use'). This leads Saussure to view society as a collective in which language at one and the same time 'belongs to all its users [as] a facility unreservedly available throughout a whole community', but which is nonetheless not amenable to change in practice.[15] In this 'static' account of language, linguistic structure is composed of signs which are inseparable unities made up of signifiers and signifieds and signification itself depends upon the stability of linguistic structure (built on the principles of arbitrariness and difference) and the fixed nature of the sign. In any given linguistic community then, in order to create meaning, all of its members 'will reproduce – doubtless not exactly, but approximately – the same signs linked to the same concepts'.[16] Such a view of a community which shares – with minor deviations – a fixed semiotic code which it derives from the past and transmits to the future (and which therefore lives in a sort of eternal present), is in all probability indebted to the model of the homogeneous and unchanging nation proclaimed by nineteenth-century cultural nationalism. For Saussure, like the cultural nationalists who made language the key to the definition of the nation, the stability of a language is explicable by the fact that it is anchored in time and in a conservative community whose inertia guarantees minimal change. From this perspective, the unified and determinate language is matched only by the undifferentiated and durable collectivity of the nation.[17]

The linguistic determinism upon which Saussure's science of semiotics is based took many forms in the twentieth century – from the Sapir-Whorf hypothesis in anthropology to everyday perceptions of the nature and function of dictionaries – but the idea that a language is constituted by elements which are fixed in terms of their signification is common to them all. It might appear self-evident that historical materialists would find such determinism deeply suspect – likewise the Saussurean notions that speech communities are unified and homogeneous, that they are 'naturally inert' and 'conservative', and that language is 'unreservedly available' to all members of a given group. Be that as it may, however, the most well-known challenge to the type of linguistic determinism characteristic of the work of Saussure and his followers did not primarily come from historical materialism but from the philosophical approach which became known as poststructuralism – a movement whose methods (if not always its political consequences) Eagleton recognised as significant. For it was poststructuralism, primarily through the early work of Derrida, which unpicked the contradiction at the heart of Saussure's work: if meaning is possible only through linguistic structure, and if structure itself was composed by difference rather than positive terms, then how is it possible at any given moment to say what the signified of a specific signifier is? To put it in Saussure's terms, if 'the content of a word is determined in the final analysis not by what it contains but by what exists outside it', then how do we know which of the differences 'outside' the sign – the constitutive differences of the system itself – determines its signification?[18] Moreover, given the commonplace observation that we know that the same word can be used in all sorts of different contexts to signify different meanings, how can signification have the sort of stability which the Saussurean model entails? If a sign is iterable, but its signification seems to shift every time it is used, then where does that leave the structuralist account of language?

Rather a lot was made of Derrida's critique of Saussure in the last third of the twentieth century, including some overblown claims about the significance of indeterminacy – that it undermined the possibility of knowledge, that interpretation became either impossible or a mode of domination, that signs don't have fixed meanings, that concepts such as 'truth' were no longer tenable and so on. In fact at times it seemed as though the denunciation of the quest for the transcendental signifier which would ground all signification and make meaning possible again – God, Civilisation, History, the Self, Identity – was itself functioning as the transcendental signifier. But Derrida's critique, and the use to which it was put by poststructuralism, was an important development and one which could be cast as a potential source of liberation from forms of hierarchical authoritarianism which depended precisely upon the idea that modes of knowledge were indeed determinate, given and absolute. Or, to put the case more prosaically, it offered a way of challenging those who simply 'knew' – on the basis of their status as custodians of tradition, truth, common sense and so on – the 'real' meanings of words, the 'proper' interpretation of texts, the 'truth' of the world itself. In that sense, based on its fundamental contestation of determinacy, poststructuralism was an iconoclastic form of anti-authoritarianism and it was all the more welcome for that. For a Marxist, however, the idea that indeterminacy is radical *per se* has to be treated with caution. Granted that Derrida's revelation of the fundamental instability of signification disturbs forms of authoritarianism and the metaphysics which lie behind them, it is nonetheless the case that the ways in which indeterminacy was used in some of the more popular examples of postmodernist discourse led simply to another form of metaphysics. The claim that *everything* is indeterminate amounts to nothing other than a revelation of the truth about meaning – which sounds suspiciously like a statement of metaphysics.

In order to mount a challenge to the type of all-encompassing scepticism to which the doctrine of indeterminacy led (and given the historical context its practical effect was often more a question of cynicism than scepticism), Eagleton turned to the work of Wittgenstein as a way of returning signification to its basis in social activity. Meaning, he proposes, 'may ultimately be undecidable if we view language contemplatively, as a chain of signifiers on a page'. But 'it becomes "decidable", and words like "truth", "reality", "knowledge" and "certainty" have something of their force restored to them, when we think of language rather as something we *do*, as indissociably interwoven with our practical forms of life'.[19] To understand the influence of Wittgenstein here consider his discussion of what counts as a definition. Rather than seeking some transcendental meaning of the word 'definition', Wittgenstein's argument is that whether a particular set of words will count as a definition 'will depend on the circumstances under which it is given, and on the person I give it to'.[20] That is to say, it will depend on what happens in practice in a given situation. And although that is not something which is decidable in advance, nor is a particular set of contextual conditions iterable, as part of a practical activity the act of definition can undoubtedly be achieved (as indeed can describing reality, telling the truth, speaking with certainty, coming to agreement and so on). What is the basis of such an act? There is none since definition isn't based on anything – it is something which happens, which takes place and takes effect, in practice. As Eagleton notes, 'to say that there are no absolute grounds for the use of such words as truth, certainty, reality and so on is not to say that these words lack meaning or are ineffectual'.[21] The question is not so much that of attempting to identify what an absolute foundation for the use of words would be, since that would be to fall into the metaphysical trap which the popularisers of indeterminacy have set (either there must be an absolute basis for meaning to be determined or there is no such thing as meaning). Rather the issue is that of noting on what basis signification is achieved: the open, contested and not predetermined realm of human practice. As Wittgenstein puts it: 'the *speaking* of language is part of an activity, or of a form of life', which is why 'the meaning of a word is its use in the language'.[22] Meaning does not reside in the language itself, nor is meaning undecidable; meaning is what human beings create through historical use – practical sign-based intercourse as part of a form of life.

Discourse and History

For Wittgenstein, 'philosophy may in no way interfere with the actual use of language; it can in the end only describe it'. The reason for this is that '[philosophy] cannot give [language] any foundation either' and thus 'it leaves everything as it is'.[23] This argument for the linguistic status quo is a warning against those who would seek to ground language transcendentally; since there is no foundation except practice, there is no possibility of intervening in language from a philosophical standpoint to argue that one word or set of words is preferable to another. Yet as Eagleton notes, Wittgenstein's claim that his aim is simply to 'bring words back from their metaphysical to their everyday use' must make an historical materialist pause.[24] For the return to 'ordinary language' in order to banish metaphysics – the shift away from the philosophical tendency to grasp the 'essence' of a word to an analysis of the use of words in our everyday language games – only works if our 'ordinary language' itself is not metaphysical, and that appears to be an assumption on the part of Wittgenstein based primarily on his antipathy to the practices of professional philosophers. But if indeed, as Wittgenstein claimed, his work was 'a battle against the bewitchment of our intelligence by means of language', it is hard to see why this struggle only needed to be conducted against the language of philosophy.[25] For although Wittgenstein's view of language allows for argument and contestation (there is no reason why a particular definition has to be accepted – it depends on the circumstances and the [re-]action of the persons involved), the idea of resorting to 'ordinary language' seems to suggest that there is a more or less given realm of language which can be consulted in order to avoid the misleading disputatiousness of philosophical thought. To a Marxist with any sense of the ways in which language is used to reify, fetishise and mystify past and contemporary history, this is a deeply unconvincing claim. To combat such matter-of-factualism, Eagleton turns to the writings of Bakhtin and, to a lesser extent, Vološinov. Though he tends to conflate the two thinkers and to emphasise the contribution of Bakhtin (not surprisingly given that Vološinov published only two texts – *Marxism and the Philosophy of Language* and *Freudianism: A Marxist Critique* – after which he disappeared in a Stalinist purge), both writers are important in the later development of Eagleton's reflections on language.

For Eagleton, Bakhtin's work is significant not least in that it provides a potential 'foundation for a material theory of consciousness'. This is consequential in that it enables Eagleton to develop a critique of another idealist approach to language, that of phenomenology. Articulated most profoundly in the work of Husserl, phenomenology theorises meaning as the internal experience of a self-present subject – a matter of individual consciousness. Noting that such a position reduces language to a secondary status, a system for ascertaining meanings which exist in their purest form within the consciousness of the subject, Eagleton re-articulates Wittgenstein's emphasis on the social basis of signification. Whereas Husserl brackets off the social in order to trace the origin of meaning in inner subjectivity, for Eagleton it is the social which must be prioritised. Using Wittgenstein's 'private language argument', Eagleton asserts that 'we can only have the meanings and experiences in the first place because we have a language to have them in [...] our experience as individuals is social to its roots'.[26] This reversal of emphasis, in accordance with the fifth of Marx's premises of historical materialism, entails that the individual subject's consciousness is always already social precisely because it is constituted through language. It is a point which Marx reiterates in his remark that 'even the language in which the thinker is active' is 'a social product'.[27] Language, practical consciousness, can only exist for me precisely because it already exists for others. In other words, if I can use signs in a meaningful way, it is not because I am particularly gifted in finding the right signs to express my consciousness, it is simply because I have learned a language as part of my practical intercourse with others. On this point in fact, Wittgenstein and Bakhtin agree, since as Eagleton remarks, Bakhtin claims that 'human consciousness *was* the subject's active material, semiotic intercourse with others, not some sealed interior realm divorced from these relations'.[28] But the difference between the two thinkers lies in Bakhtin's assertions about the nature of the discourse from which consciousness is derived. For Bakhtin, discourse appears to be of its nature dialogical and relativising, heteroglot and decentring, challenging and mocking. Thus rather than the simply given, apparently consensual and non-metaphysical 'ordinary language' of Wittgenstein, Bakhtin sees discourse – language in practice – as radically unstable and conflictual: 'no living word relates to its object in a *singular* way' since any utterance 'finds the object at which it was directed already as it were overlain with qualifications, open to dispute, charged with value'. Words in use are plunged into a 'a dialogically agitated and tension-filled environment of alien words, value judgments and accents'.[29]

Bakhtin's discourse – a dialogical realm of qualification, dispute, value, tension, judgment and accentuation – does not sound much like Wittgenstein's world of 'ordinary language' precisely because Bakhtin's conception of history sees it as a site of conflict and contestation. Despite this theoretical position, however, Bakhtin's sense of history is notoriously difficult to pin down in other than general terms. For example, the heteroglossia which forms such a central component of his thought appears at some points to be produced by the collapse of over-arching verbal-ideological systems of cultural hegemony (Hellenic Greece, Imperial Rome, the late middle ages and Renaissance in Europe), and at others to be an ever-present feature of language itself.[30] Such reticence may well be, as some commentators have noted, a tactic to avoid the ever-watchful censors of Soviet orthodoxy. But a more explicit understanding of history – one which Eagleton perhaps over-generously ascribes to Bakhtin – can be discovered in the work of his colleague Vološinov.[31] For it is in *Marxism and the Philosophy of Language* that the link back to Marx's thinking on language is made clear. Take for example, Vološinov's assertion that 'the individual consciousness not only cannot be used to explain anything, but on the contrary, is itself in need of explanation from the vantage of the social, ideological medium [of language]'.[32] This is not simply a return to the fifth of Marx's premises for historical materialism, but also an explicit *Marxist* critique of the phenomenological position. Yet it is important to note that Vološinov does not simply argue for the primacy of language with regard to consciousness (a point made later by Wittgenstein as we have seen), since he also makes a distinctive claim about the nature of both language and therefore consciousness itself. For Vološinov, 'the domain of ideology coincides with the domain of signs. They equate with one another. Wherever a sign is present, ideology is present too'.[33] The basis of this assertion derives directly from Marx's argument that language, as practical consciousness, is a crucial component in the social intercourse of organised groups of human beings in their creation of the social world. Depending on the way in which a human community is organised materially, members of that group may have differently oriented social interests and if they do, it follows that they will accent signs according to those interests and that therefore signs must be ideological. Thus with specific reference to social life under the historical conditions of capitalism, Vološinov remarks that 'class does not coincide with the sign community [...] thus various different classes will use one and the same language. As a result, differently oriented accents intersect in every ideological sign. Sign becomes an arena of the class struggle'.[34] Two important things follow from this proposition. First, since language is ideological, consciousness must likewise be ideological since 'consciousness takes shape and being in the material of signs created by an organised group in the process of its social intercourse', and thus 'the logic of consciousness is the logic of ideological communication, of the semiotic interaction of a social group'. Consciousness may well be formed by Wittgenstein's 'ordinary language', it is just that 'ordinary language' turns out to be 'the ideological medium of social life'. It follows that 'if we deprive consciousness of its semiotic, ideological content, it would have absolutely nothing left'.[35] Second, given that signs are contested by differently organised interest groups, they are of their nature indeterminate – or as Vološinov puts it, multiaccentual. That is to say, precisely because signs are subject to the pressures of social struggle, they retain their dynamism and creativity; but it is precisely their indeterminacy which enables them to be used – in practice – in determinate (uniaccentual) ways. If they weren't contested and accented by different social interests, then the possibility of fixing signification in the ways dreamt of by determinists would remain open.[36] As it is, the only signs whose meaning is wholly uniaccentual are those which have dropped out of use.

Tony Crowley

Signs, Socialism and Ethics

I have attempted thus far to demonstrate how Eagleton's work has consistently been concerned with the thought of Marx and Wittgenstein on language. It remains to be argued, however, why Eagleton has shown such a sustained interest in language – given that with only a few exceptions, language has not been a central issue in the socialist tradition.[37] In order to do that it is necessary to begin by reiterating the general characteristics of a historical materialist perspective on language. There are three key aspects. First, although it must take material form, language is not determined by the constraints of immediate biological need. Second, it is a form of practical activity through which human beings create both a social world and themselves as individual beings. Third, language and the social consciousness which derives from it, allows for reflection and judgment. For Marx these characteristics make language liberating: it is the medium by which we escape from the limits of our animal being; it enables us to objectify the world; and it allows us to engage actively and critically in the making of reality. But there is another side to this story and it is this which explains Eagleton's insistent return to language as a focus of interest. For if there is a central thesis which runs through his work, one which recurs in various forms, it is that language is at one and the same time 'an ambivalently creative and destructive power'.[38] Language lies at the heart of our humanity and our historicity, it opens up the world and allows us to intervene in it, but there is a cost for such creative powers which must be acknowledged. Consider these claims taken from one of the earliest and one of the most recent of Eagleton's writings. First, from *The Body as Language* (1970):

> Through [language] man comes to individualise himself and objectify his world in a single, dialectical action; by establishing a 'distance' between himself, others, the material world and his own animal nature, he is able thereby to enter into creative relationship with each [...] yet the opening of this distance is at the same time, inescapably, the first step in man's estrangement – from others, the products of his world, the constraints of his own sensuous being [...] Language is the matrix of individual self-achievement, but thus of human division; it provides the basis for man's transformation of the world, but opens also the potential of abstraction and alienation; it allows man freely to transcend his biological limits, but so leads him to violate the creative constraints of his sensuous life.[39]

More recently from *The Meaning of Life* (2007):

It is also true that human beings, not least because they have language, are capable of objectifying their own existence [...] Language, in other words, allows us not only to get a fix on ourselves, but to conceive of our situation as a whole. Because we live by signs, which bring along with them the capacity for abstraction, we can distance ourselves from our immediate contexts, free ourselves from the imprisonment of our bodily senses, and speculate on the human situation as such. Like fire, however, the power of abstraction is an ambiguous gift, at once creative and destructive. If it allows us to think in terms of whole communities, it also allows us to lay them waste with chemical weapons.[40]

There is an intellectual consistency here which bears testimony to a major preoccupation with the significance of language over the course of a life's work (so much for Eagleton's propensity to change his mind with every faddish import).[41] More importantly, these statements capture the essence of Eagleton's argument: not simply that language is central to our historicity, but that an understanding of the duality of language is necessary to a comprehension of our history.

For Eagleton language is a crucial part of the process by which human beings enter into relationship with material reality, with their animal nature, and with others. But since relationship requires objectification, the potential price we pay is that of alienation. If language facilitates the human transcendence of animal being, it does so precisely by the creation of 'distance' or a gap which functions as the basis of our ability to make history. In his early work Eagleton is clear on the cost to be paid for the achievement of historical subjectivity: 'all human alienation [...] is rooted in that potentially destructive disjunction, within and between men, and between men and their world, of linguistic "subjectivity" and animal or material "objectivity"'.[42] This is not to say that language produces alienation, but that language as practical consciousness creates objectification and it is that which serves as the possible ground for alienation. The realisation of objectification as alienation, say the treatment of the material world or other people simply as means to my ends, is a question of praxis under given historical conditions. Language opens up the possibility of free, conscious and active creativity, but it also allows for the possibility of free, conscious and active destruction. Both options are realisable; the question of which of these possibilities occurs is a practical matter which cannot be determined in advance.

It happens to be the case that at the moment the vast majority of human beings suffer under an economic and political order which uses the potential afforded by human labour – understood in the general sense outlined earlier to include language – for destructive and vicious purposes. The term which

Eagleton uses to describe the consequences of that situation, one which appears in his writings repeatedly, is 'tragedy'.[43] And the search for the ways in which that state of affairs might be rectified lies in the field of politicised ethics – specifically in the quest for the circumstances which would allow for the achievement of human virtue. On what basis is such politicised ethics to be grounded? The answer, which will no doubt have the anti-essentialist postmodernists laughing up their sleeves, is that it has to be founded upon a theory of human nature. But for Marxists this necessary foundation cannot be human nature in the sense of an essence which must be conformed to (the conservative version), or liberated (the Romantic version). Rather it is human nature in the sense outlined by Marx: that is, the dual aspect of our existence as animal beings in a material world (which guarantees a certain constancy) and as agents who are able to change the historical conditions of our being (which means that we have the capacity to transform ourselves). Like language, which is rooted in our bodily being and the consistent material world (our 'form of life' in Wittgenstein's terms), and yet able to transgress previously established formal structures, politicised ethics must be limited by the common facts of our bodily existence *and* predicated upon the possibility of rupturing the conditions of the past.

For Marxism the political project has to be geared to the overthrow of capitalism and the establishment of socialist relations of production in order to liberate the resources and capacities which capitalism itself has helped create. The aim of socialism is necessarily then the achievement of the material conditions whose purpose will be 'the absolute working-out of [human] creative potentialities, with no presuppositions other than previous historical development, which makes this totality of development, i.e., the development of all human powers as such the end in itself, not as measured on a *predetermined yardstick*'.[44] Yet as Eagleton notes, the very fact that there is no predetermined yardstick – no human nature in the sense of a fixed essence against which we can measure our accomplishments – means that any assertion of the desirability of the development of *all* human powers is 'a dangerous illusion'.[45] Some human powers, as recent history has made us all too aware, will need to be curtailed: the capacity to destroy the natural environment or to wage war are two all-too-pertinent examples. This creates a difficulty since, although it is clear that the political project of socialism must indeed be the transformation of the relations of production of capitalism, the complex question remains as to which human powers are to be developed and which are not. For even given the attainment of a society in which the basic human material needs are met and in which 'the free development of each is the condition of the free development of all', it is not clear by what mechanisms the free development of each and all is to be regulated and ensured.[46] If 'happiness or well-being, can consist only in each individual realising her productive "species being" in and through the equivalent self-realisation of every other', then the issue in particular historical circumstances will precisely be that of deciding what is to count as well-being and mutual self-realisation and how they are to be achieved.[47] Those questions are properly the concern of a form of socialist ethics based on an acknowledgment of the 'ambivalently creative and destructive power' which we have as animal, historical and linguistic beings in a finite material world.[48] It is a mark of the distinctive achievement of Terry Eagleton's work – rooted in a sustained, tenacious and (given historical conditions largely characterised by defeat) courageous adherence to the basic principles of Marxism – that he has spent the past 40 years reminding us of these issues, and that he has placed the study of language and indeed ethics back squarely within the remit of socialism.

Notes

1   Stephen Regan (ed.), *The Eagleton Reader* (Oxford: Blackwell, 1998), 9.
2   David Alderson, *Terry Eagleton* (Houndmills: Palgrave Macmillan, 2004), 2.
3   For a detailed rejection of the idea that Marx's historical materialism entailed a denial of the concept of human nature, see Norman Geras, *Marx and Human Nature: Refutation of a Legend* (London: Verso, 1983).
4   Karl Marx, *Early Writings* (Harmondsworth: Penguin/New Left Review, 1975), 329.
5   Marx, *Early Writings*, 350.
6   Marx, *Early Writings*, 328.
7   Karl Marx, *Capital*, vol. 3 (Harmondsworth: Penguin/New Left Review, 1981), 959.
8   Karl Marx, *The German Ideology* (Moscow: Progress Publishers, 1964), 39–42.
9   Marx, *The German Ideology*, 41–2.
10 Marx, *The German Ideology*, 41.
11 Raymond Williams, *Marxism and Literature* (Oxford: Oxford University Press, 1976), 28–9.
12 The concern with the work of Wittgenstein is testimony to the early and enduring influence of the Catholic theologians Lawrence Bright and Herbert McCabe, whose own thinking was shaped by Wittgenstein's later philosophy. McCabe was a Dominican monk based in Cambridge and Oxford and a close personal and intellectual friend of Eagleton.
13 Ferdinand de Saussure, *Course in General Linguistics* (London: Duckworth, 1983), 110.
14 Saussure, *Course in General Linguistics*, 19.
15 Saussure, *Course in General Linguistics*, 74.
16 Saussure, *Course in General Linguistics*, 13.
17 Saussure's debt to the conservative element in cultural nationalist thought has hardly been noticed, but it is evident in his explanation of why 'a linguistic revolution is impossible': 'of all institutions, a language affords the least scope for such an enterprise. It is part and parcel of the life of the whole community, and the community's natural inertia exercises a conservative influence upon it'. Saussure, *Course in General Linguistics*, 74.
18 Saussure, *Course in General Linguistics*, 114.
19 Terry Eagleton, *Literary Theory*, 2nd ed. (Oxford: Blackwell, 1996), 127.

20 Ludwig Wittgenstein, *Philosophical Investigations* (Oxford: Blackwell, 1958), §29.
21 Eagleton, *Literary Theory*, 125.
22 Wittgenstein, *Philosophical Investigations*, §§23, 43.
23 Wittgenstein, *Philosophical Investigations*, §124. As noted earlier, Saussure took much the same line as Wittgenstein on this point. For Saussure languages are stable because they are constrained by the complementary forces of arbitrariness and tradition and on that basis there is little point the linguist or anyone else attempting a 'linguistic revolution'.
24 Eagleton's most extensive discussion of Wittgenstein's work appears in 'Wittgenstein's Friends', *New Left Review*, I/135 (1982): 70.
25 Wittgenstein, *Philosophical Investigations*, §109.
26 Eagleton, *Literary Theory*, 53. Though he does not mention Wittgenstein explicitly, Eagleton evidently has the 'private language argument' in mind here. He continues: 'there can be no such thing as a private language, and to imagine a language is to imagine a whole form of social life'. This comment echoes Wittgenstein's own assertion that 'to imagine a language means to imagine a form of life'. Wittgenstein, *Philosophical Investigations*, §19.
27 Marx, *Early Writings*, 350.
28 Eagleton, *Literary Theory*, 102
29 Mikhail Bakhtin, *The Dialogic Imagination* (Austin: University of Texas Press, 1981), 276.
30 For an account of the way in which Bakhtin's central concepts – monoglossia, polyglossia, heterglossia, monologism and dialogism – change in the course of his work, see Tony Crowley, 'Bakhtin and the History of the Language', in *Bakhtin and Cultural Theory*, eds D. Shepherd and K. Hirschkop (Manchester: Manchester University Press, 1989).
31 Eagleton comments that for Bakhtin dialogism 'is a sharp, unremitting struggle between antagonistic class idioms and interests' ('Wittgenstein's Friends', 83). This is surely an overstatement of a case which has to be read into Bakhtin's work. If Bakhtin's reticence was indeed a tactic then to a limited extent it was partially successful since he spent a good deal of his life in Stalinist-imposed exile whereas Vološinov wasn't heard of again after 1929.
32 V.N. Vološinov, *Marxism and the Philosophy of Language* (New York and London: Seminar Press, 1973), 12.
33 Vološinov, *Marxism*, 10.
34 Vološinov, *Marxism*, 23.
35 Vološinov, *Marxism*, 13.
36 It is worth noting that one of the recurrent features of science-fiction, from Orwell's *Nineteen Eighty-Four* to Margaret Atwood's *The Handmaid's Tale*, is the fantasy of a determinate language whose uniaccentual signs prevent its users from thinking otherwise. As in these examples, the protagonists in such fiction are often characters who can remember when language was not uniaccentual, whose memory, because of their transitional historical position, retains the use of words from the time before.
37 The lack of a fully-developed socialist account of language is a puzzling fact. Even Williams, for whom language was always a central issue, did not produce an extended theoretical account, although part one, chapter two of *Marxism and Literature* is an important contribution to such a project.
38 Terry Eagleton, *The Body as Language: Outline of a New Left Theology* (London: Sheed and Ward, 1970), 23.
39 Eagleton, *Body as Language*, 23.
40 Terry Eagleton, *The Meaning of Life* (Oxford: Oxford University Press, 2007), 22.
41 Lest it be said that these texts, almost 40 years apart, are atypical, the same claim is made in one of Eagleton's major theoretical interventions when he asserts that 'one aspect of this unfathomable capacity for self-transgression on the part of the linguistically productive

animal, is the power to extend its body into a web of abstractions which then violate its own sensuous nature'. *The Ideology of the Aesthetic* (Oxford: Blackwell, 1990), 199.
42 Eagleton, *Body as Language*, 28.
43 Eagleton's concern with tragedy is another way in which his work overlaps with that of Williams. It is an open question, however, and this is wholly distinct from the emphasis of Williams's work, whether Eagleton ultimately sees the possibility of the end of tragedy in historical or theological terms.
44 Karl Marx, *Grundrisse* (Harmondsworth: Penguin/New Left Review, 1973), 468.
45 Eagleton, *Ideology of the Aesthetic*, 221.
46 Karl Marx and Frederick Engels, *The Communist Manifesto* (Harmondsworth: Penguin, 2002), 244.
47 Terry Eagleton, 'Deconstruction and Human Rights', in *The Eagleton Reader*, ed. Stephen Regan (Oxford: Blackwell, 1997), 225.
48 Eagleton, *Body as Language*, 23.

Terry Eagleton, Postmodernism and Ireland
Edward Larrissy

Terry Eagleton devoted considerable thought to the nature of postmodernism during the heyday of the postmodernist debate in the eighties and nineties, and always expressed strong reservations about it.[1] It is worth noting that these reservations do not imply any hostility to formal experimentation, or to the registering of alienation in its postmodern form. Rather, he seeks to show how there might be a politically and morally engaged art which was very much of our time. His position is consistent with those he adopts in dealing with other subjects, and may, as we shall see, be illuminated by reference to those works where he does so. Of all these other subjects, the most illuminating for understanding his work is that of Irish literature, for it was during this period that Eagleton became a major figure in Irish studies, and his thinking on postmodernist relativism was developed alongside his critique of revisionism in Irish historiography.

The History and Theory of Postmodernism

Eagleton's book, *The Illusions of Postmodernism* (1996), is something of a summation of his views, and for this reason it makes a good starting-point, especially as it covers a wide range of phenomena: contemporary art and writing, historiography, philosophy, literary theory and criticism.[2] It thus enacts, as much as it states, the notion that contemporary cultural manifestations exhibit a homogeneity, even an essence. This very imputation is itself one which many of those who value something they call postmodernism would seek to reject. Theorists of postmodernism emphasise plurality and difference even in pre-postmodern cultural artefacts, but most of all, of course, in postmodern ones. There is, then, a certain irony, at least from their point of view, in identifying the essential characteristics of postmodernism. Eagleton's decision to treat it as a widely-spread but intelligible *Zeitgeist*, stuck in its historically limited view, is a characteristic piece of polemical effrontery: a humorously disrespectful placing of a young Turk who fails to recognise his own pomposity, ignorance and transience. The exercise could almost be distilled into a joke about 'pure postmodernism'. But like most of Eagleton's polemical moves, this one is founded on principle, and one which he never seeks to cover in obscurity: he adheres to the belief that it is possible to explain and understand cultural phenomena from a broad historical perspective, and that Marxism offers the best explanatory and analytic instruments. Specifically, the strange characteristics of the 'postmodern subject' – a mixture of feeling determined and at the same time free-floating and contingent – correspond to 'the experience of advanced capitalist societies' (*IP*, 89, 90). Not 'late' capitalist societies, though: in one of a number of differences of emphasis from Jameson, Eagleton notes that 'we have no idea just how late they are' (*IP*, 90). In fact, he rejects teleological Marxism of the Trotskyist kind, while insisting that history provides the knowable conditions for a limited range of possible future developments but not for others (*IP*, 106–7). An example would be the way in which the increasing socialisation of production in advanced capitalism provides a necessary, but not sufficient, condition for socialist reorganisation of industry. Such a reorganisation is not inevitable, however. On the other hand, the conditions simply do not exist for a return to feudalism.

The belief in historical explanation, and the belief that Marxism remains the most powerful and effective explainer, are separable. Because Eagleton discerns in postmodern thought a tendency to scepticism about the possibility even of the former, he devotes much of his time to the amused dismissal of the supposedly radical tenets – or sentiments – upon which this scepticism is loosely based. He discerns, in fact, two related and overlapping prejudices: one against 'grand narratives' (to use Lyotard's influential formulation) and another against 'essentialising'. Both of these can be further reduced to a prejudice against generalisation and in favour of particularity and irreducible variousness. Eagleton's inability to take such prejudices seriously, his air of playful derision, are utterly appropriate: after all, he has participated in enough colloquia, symposia and seminars to know upon what slender consideration such prejudices are often advanced. Furthermore, the objection to generalisation goes to the very root of thinking and making propositions; that, at any rate, is a kind way of putting it. A more trenchant thought is that, taken with sufficient seriousness, it would render both thinking and uttering impossible. This is why Eagleton's use of simple examples is entirely appropriate: the questions involved are fundamental: 'there [is] no way of constructing the concrete without general categories. Devotees of particularism should try doing without them for a while, an experiment which would need to include never opening their mouths' (*IP*, 50). In other words, to utter any noun-substantive is to give at least formal assent to the notion that a particular thing is one of a kind; but if one does not wish to do this, then one had better stop uttering. The use of simple examples, of course, is routine in academic philosophy ('This desk in front of me here'; 'If I say "Good morning!"'), though it seems to be a cause of scandal to sophisticated literary theorists.

What Eagleton does, then, to put the matter more technically, is to address first the fundamental philosophical questions about universals and the hermeneutic circle as a way of clarifying the serious problems which confront any particularist theory. Starting with fundamentals in this way has a useful side-effect, as well. For the historicising of grand philosophical positions can seem to reduce the pursuit of truth to the blindness of ideology. But Eagleton is not prepared to abandon truth-claims that easily: it is harder to historicise away questions to do with the relation of universal and particular than those to do with the categories of understanding. He then proceeds to bring these and parallel considerations to bear on the sort of theorising with which historians and literary critics are more familiar.

Chief among these is the idea that 'grand narratives' can no longer enjoy assent. It is most important for Eagleton to rebut this notion for the reason that it would seem to make large-scale historical interpretation, signally including that proposed by Marxism, difficult or impossible. Although it is now habitual to quote Lyotard's phrase when discussing these matters, it is the legacy of deconstruction in general that has been the most encouraging medium for certain types of new historicist particularism, at least in the field of literary studies. It seems to me to be slightly misleading, in fact, that the name of Foucault is so routinely associated with new historicism. For, important though his influence is, it was accepted into a climate where Derrida also was regarded as an unavoidable master of thought, however difficult it might be to reconcile the outlooks of the two philosophers. A convenient way of gauging the co-existence of these influences might be to examine the introduction to a book by one of Eagleton's students, Francis Barker, which, on the face of it, might seem to have more to do with Foucault. In the Preface to *The Tremulous Private Body*, after a lengthy acknowledgement of the influence of Foucault, a well-warranted acknowledgement of Derrida is offered, in which Barker proclaims his adoption of the language and themes of the latter, even though he refers briefly to disagreements between the two thinkers.[3] In fact, as most people are prepared to concede, the new historicism has always been an appropriately various phenomenon; and this is to leave on one side postcolonial criticism, where the influence of deconstruction has been pervasive. Students of the early modern period may seem to look more to Foucault, but in Britain the work of Willy Maley, as well as that of Barker, owes as much to deconstruction. Critics of the Romantic period, especially in America, have often avowed the influence of Derrida. Marjorie Levinson, for instance, has referred to herself as a 'deconstructive materialist', and Alan Liu, in his major book *Wordsworth: The Sense of History*, has adopted this designation for himself and his work.[4] The method in these cases appears to be one which claims broad, though not clearly specified, Marxian co-ordinates, but which is also acutely conscious of the difference, deferrals and aporias of the texts, both literary and non-literary, that they address. My own work on Blake and Yeats was cast in this mould. There are differences within the field of 'deconstructive materialism'. Levinson appears to be less of a sceptic than Liu, who, in the epilogue to his book is constrained to admit that, in his opinion, 'No one can know the differential relation between history and literature, or any other register of mind, with full certainty. This is why, after all, I say "I believe." I treat not of certainty but of credibility.'[5] Understood very strictly, this seems reasonable; after all, who would claim to possess 'full certainty' about very much? Yet the choice to utter this credo constitutes a telling and appropriate piece of rhetoric. In any case, it may serve to remind us of the extent to which it is deconstruction which has encouraged the current climate of hostility to grand narratives. This has the advantage for our argument that it permits a clear exposition of the grounds of contention.

It is well known that deconstruction has potentially corrosive effects on the attempt to construct large-scale histories, or indeed to promote any coherent set of truth-claims with wide application. A bold and easily grasped formulation of the considerations which may lead to these effects is to be found in the work of Jean-Jacques Lecercle, in particular in his elaboration of Derrida's concept of the remainder, which itself is merely another formulation of the supplement, in his book *The Violence of Language*: it has a number of aspects, including some which align it with Kristeva's semiotic chora.[6] That which concerns me here, though, is the way it gives sharp relief to the problem of interpretation from a deconstructive point of view. The remainder can be conceptualised in the following way: for every interpretation of the text in support of which n pieces of evidence are offered, it is always possible to find at least one piece of evidence which does not support this interpretation: hence the formula $n + 1$, where 1 is the remainder.[7] The textual presumptions of much theory treat history as a text, and assume that it is vulnerable to the consequences of the formula. As we shall see, Eagleton thinks the consequences of deferring to this kind of argument are sufficient in themselves to render the argument untrustworthy.

Postmodernist Particularism and Irish Historical Revisionism

Eagleton's absorption in Irish history and literary history has gone hand in hand with a critique of revisionism in the historiography of Ireland. Now admittedly, many exponents of this tendency are unlikely candidates for the description 'postmodernist', or are even hostile to postmodernism, appearing to espouse a rigorous but undogmatic search for evidence about what really happened. But one of the interesting things about Eagleton's work is that it implies a deep historical connection between postmodernism and the sorts of debunking that occur in historical revisionism. The history of Ireland, and events such as the plantations, the Cromwellian massacres, the penal laws, and the Irish Famine are seen by revisionists as having been misrepresented by a nationalist historiography, motivated by simplistic narratives of Irish victimhood, which was dominant in the 26 counties between 1922 and the seventies, and which still enjoys a degree of unjustified esteem. The undermining of nationalist simplifications is achieved by the advancing of evidence which is intended to convey a more complicated and nuanced, and a less one-sided, history, and is accompanied by a rhetoric of evidential rigour. Revisionism in Irish historiography is paralleled by strong positivistic tendencies in the wider world of contemporary historical research. In the case of both postmodernism and neo-positivism we are confronted, Eagleton seeks to remind us, by a scepticism about general interpretation which in fact rests on frail and ill-considered philosophical foundations. Rather than isolating postmodernism, then, we should see it, in part, as a major component in a re-focusing, towards particularism, of the relationship of general and particular. And there is a concomitant failure to give due significance to value as an important element in deciding even what is supposed to constitute an historical event: to put it another way, some kind of broad framework is necessary even to allow one to name a particular fact. Eagleton insists that we should not renounce the ideal of constructing a rational, connected, coherent and ethically cogent view of human experience and history. As far as he is concerned, there is only one ultimate choice: to accept the rational appeal to such understanding, or to renounce it in favour of particularism. The apparent half-way house of the micro-narrative is only a modified form of particularism, and the tenets on which it claims greater probity suffer from the same weaknesses.

In the face of the undoubted threat posed by Lecercle's remainder, Eagleton effectively says: 'Make your choice: do you wish to be cowed by the ease with which counter-examples can be adduced? In that case you should logically be bound for a life of surreal disconnection.' If the fact of the remainder is held to undermine all interpretation, no interpretation is well-founded, and that covers the tales you tell your therapist and your partner, as much as the ideology of the American Republican Party. No society in fact can or does operate without at least a variety of interlocking grand narratives, even if it may be harder to say that it possesses only one of them. In any case, it must be asked how genuinely corrosive is the logic of the supplement, or the remainder. For while issues of truth or evidential validity are certainly indefeasible for major historical and social interpretation, it may be asked whether, when it comes to judging on the larger scale, words such as 'adequacy' would not be better guides. At the same time, the question of what constituted countervailing evidence to the interpretation would itself be intrinsically contestable. What value-system says that the new fact really is to be judged a piece of countervailing evidence? In seeking to convert somebody to a world-view, probability is as strong an ally as truth, even though they should seek to go hand in hand.

One of the kinds of grand narrative to which Eagleton has been understanding, perhaps to the surprise of some, is the kind produced by nationalism. His remarks on this have been preponderantly made in the context of the study of Irish culture, but they have a general resonance for an academy which is deeply suspicious of nationalism. He has pointed out, although admittedly it is fairly routine for a Marxist to do so, that there is a progressive moment in nationalism when it is harnessed in the service of liberation from a dominant and exploitative power. Indeed, in his essay 'Nationalism, Irony and Commitment', he offers a rather neat formulation: being defined in terms of national identity may be constraining in relation to a full humanity, rather like being defined by class or gender; but it is something you should go 'not around, but somehow all the way through it and out the other side.'[8] Of course, this kind of Marxist concession makes nationalism sound like the bandit you allow into the resistance as a temporary ally, all the time plotting to hang him when the war is over. In recent years, Eagleton has gone further than this and, without expressly retracting that point of view, has expressed a strong appreciation of the specificity of one national tradition, that of Ireland. In this he runs counter to some of the dominant trends of postcolonial theory. This will become clearer by contrasting Eagleton's work with what is perhaps the most influential book on nationalism of recent years, and one which can easily be shown to suffer from the weaknesses of generalised postmodernism.

Apart from being cited in many important books and articles, Benedict Anderson's *Imagined Communities* appears on myriad reading lists for modules on postcolonialism.[9] After the last few centuries, it is surely possible to reflect that this highly original and vivacious little book, which sees the nation as an imagined community, is the most ambitious tribute to the imagination ever penned or capable of being penned, although it has nothing explicit to say about that mesmerising faculty. The book is in many ways valuable in its stress, with a little help from Lucien Febvre, on the development of monoglot print-cultures as a decisive factor in the rise of nationalism. And in undermining the idea of nation, Anderson makes effective use of such well-worn examples as that of the essenceless Scotland.[10] Yet its witty, late-enlightenment debunking in the end seems too arid, decadent and frail a bloom in the face of the irrational power that could produce a Hitler or send the insurgents of the Easter Rising to their deaths.

Anderson, with an appearance of judiciousness, builds into his thesis a preliminary investigation of the 'cultural roots' of nationalism. He considers 'the religious community' and 'the dynastic realm' as forebears, but adds to them a discussion of the development of modern concepts of time which allow the imagining of simultaneity across the monoglot community of the nation, via such media as newspapers.[11] The argument thus becomes circular: the origins are in part explained by means of the concomitants. As for the other cultural roots, they do not go back past the middle ages, since with equal circularity the book has already assumed that it is not necessary to go back any further. Indeed, one of the problems with the book centres upon a flawed underestimating of ancient societies. Not that it is very explicit about that underestimating. But the logic of the book can only fit with the idea that these societies were marked by a decentred and chaotic diversity of language and tradition, which was brought into a semblance of order by the advent of monoglot print culture. This is an expression of modern prejudice, rather like the notion that ancient Britons grunted and wore furs. The study of ancient societies, say that of Ancient Britain or Ireland, suggests, on the contrary, considerable similarity of place-names over a large area; customs, such as fairs, which brought the clans of a loose language-and-tradition community together from over a wide region; religious organisation; and a mystical concept of the relationship between the land and that larger community which included such notions as the omphalos and the idea of pre-eminent or high kingship. The Olympic games and other customs transcending the boundaries of the city-state suggest strong parallels in Ancient Greece. The usual response to this kind of objection is that, of course, the modern nation is a completely different entity, and it is anachronistic to make the comparison. Different, indeed; but if one has the temerity to set about finding the cultural roots of this troublesome entity one had better be serious about it.

As for the imagined community itself, Anderson seeks to epitomise its irrationality in a strikingly empiricist manner: 'It is *imagined* because the members of even the smallest nation will never know most of their fellow-members, meet them, or even hear of them, yet in the minds of each lives the image of their communion.'[12] So much for working-class solidarity, then, since presumably no member of the working class has ever met most of the others. In fact, this reasoning bears a very strong resemblance to one that is attributed to Margaret Thatcher about there being no such thing as society. And that is no accident. For it exhibits that inability to bring the general and the particular into focus which, as we have seen, is also shared by contemporary historians of different political affiliations.

Granted that the nation-state is a modern phenomenon, one nevertheless needs to gauge the various kinds of irrational appeal it is able to harness – and with that due respect for the irrational that cultural critics are, apparently, eager to extend to the unconscious but not to a patriotic vision-poem. The sense of the pre-modern, and the various kinds of appeal it was able to muster, needs to be richer than one finds in Anderson's neat selection. And that might enable a sense of how discursive remnants of this complex pre-modern survive into the modern nation-state. It is in this connection that Eagleton's remarks on the nation, to be found in his 'Revisionism Revisited' (in *Crazy John and the Bishop*), are so suggestive, for they offer a way of thinking about the nation that is at least ready to accord due weight to its powerful associations, and also – a different point – to those aspects of nationalism which share in the ideals of modernity, while at the same time not permitting any leeway for racism or fascism. At one point in this essay he offers an appropriately dialectical formula:

> 'modernising the nation' is both a tautology and an oxymoron. It is a tautology in the sense that modernity and the nation-state belong together in any case; it is an oxymoron to the extent that the nation represents at the same time a pre-modern residue within that state.[13]

All Eagleton's work on Ireland indicates that the 'pre-modern' cannot be dismissed, but also has to be understood dialectically. It is the bearer, into the modern age, of deeply-held suspicions about modernising rationality and the free market. It also embodies an ethos of integrating the individual into a large social project founded on a tradition and on struggles which span the generations. These very phenomena, though, are also double-edged and may equally be linked with reaction and mumbo-jumbo. At the same time, they may ally themselves with modernity: the free market becomes the patriotic destiny of the nation.

The Case of Irish Literature

Now for Eagleton, the attraction of Ireland as a subject is that it violently lays bare such contradictions in the idea of nation, even as it is the locus of nationalist idealism. Furthermore, the history of an oppression unparalleled in Europe (one which no Czech or Hungarian peasant in the Austrian Empire could possibly envy) sharpens the political and ethical questions inherent in the history of national liberation struggles. And, most of all, the linguistic struggle and the recent nearly total displacement of Irish by English have added point and self-consciousness to what would in any case have been a battle of signs. Eagleton's first move, in *Heathcliff and the Great Hunger*, is to demonstrate how Nature in Ireland is not just written over with place-name lore and tradition, but is inscribed in a language which instantiates conflict.[14] The result is a literature which is not only wedded to artifice, rather than to the natural, but is also challengingly and appropriately prone to semiotic deferral and disruption: pre-modernist texts that look proto-modernist; modernist texts that look almost postmodern. When he discusses Irish modernism, Eagleton comes up with the description 'The Archaic Avant-Garde', in order to link its artifice, self-consciousness and parodic tendencies to the kind of doubleness we have been discussing in the idea of the nation: a significant aspect of Irish modernism links up with the pre-modern as a way of making strange and subverting the modern. [15]

However, we are being offered two different, albeit overlapping, models of the origins of Irish textual self-consciousness. One derives it from the strange-making powers of the pre-modern; and another (the *Heathcliff* argument) accords it a structural place in the conflicted social relations of Ireland. The element of overlap is where it is implied that it would be natural for an Irish writer, formed in these relations, to adopt procedures and/or themes that could be represented as pre-modern. Thus, it is really only the argument about contemporary social relations which possesses probity as an historical thesis, for only a particular contemporary history can decide what counts in the pre-modern, or what can be revived, or even perhaps what can be glimpsed there. Here is one index of a certain essentialising of Irish textual self-consciousness. (Whatever one thinks about this, one may wonder why Eagleton has not had more to say about James Clarence Mangan. Even on Eagleton's own terms, Mangan operates where pre-modern traces and contemporary conflicts overlap. On the one hand, the fact that Mangan 'detested Nature' goes well with his combination of artifice and nationalism, while on the other, he 'produced "translations" from exotic languages of which he was entirely ignorant'.)[16]

Eagleton's critics have noticed this bold, essentialising aspect of his Irish theories. One sometimes encounters criticism of Eagleton's grasp of empirical detail, but often alongside the concession that he has elaborated models that are both suggestive and productive. The latter point is certainly supported by the influence of the *Heathcliff* thesis. A book such as Seamus Deane's *Strange Country* (1997), for instance, influential enough in itself, bears obvious signs of indebtedness to Eagleton's leading ideas, especially in its crucial identification of the problem of representing Ireland, and its association of this problem with the mismatch between Ireland's actual state in the late-eighteenth century, and the kind of modernity to which she could with benefit aspire. Eagleton's Heathcliff (the character) is also a sign for the meaning of Irish Gothic, a topic which has been the subject of growing and detailed attention. In fastening on the hypothesis of Heathcliff as fugitive from the Irish famine, Eagleton also opens up the wider topic of the appropriateness to Irish experience of the prime Gothic topos of the accursed inheritance, a topos handled in Irish literature well before the famine: it is central to *Castle Rackrent,* and dominates

Melmoth the Wanderer. As recently as 2011, Christina Morin has mounted a detailed argument for the inseparability of the Irish Gothic from the Irish 'national tale'.[17] Yet such an argument is already implicit in Eagleton's book.

However, questions about the Gothic also unavoidably provoke reference to British literature of the eighteenth and nineteenth centuries, and Eagleton's handling of the relationship between Britain and Ireland again reveals an unexpectedly essentialising bent, as epitomised by a 2004 review in the *London Review of Books* of Paul Murray's *From the Shadow of Dracula*, which includes this remark: 'While England had *Middlemarch*, [the Irish] had *Melmoth the Wanderer*.'[18] Now the subsequent discussion makes it clear that he wishes to qualify the remark, which reads like a parody of his own *Heathcliff* thesis. But in fact, the qualification only goes so far, as if to defend his *Heathcliff* argument by boldly differentiating it from parodies of his position: the Irish understand 'realism', and advert to it, but do otherwise. However, what is erased in this account is the profundity and detail of the relationship between Irish and British literature. To separate *Melmoth* from the tradition of Walpole, Radcliffe and 'Monk' Lewis is not a legitimate exercise in literary history. Furthermore, it actually weakens the point about the legacy of a dark and bloody history, and removes a central piece of background for the anti-Catholic prejudice of *Melmoth*. Again, to read the Edgeworths without situating them in relation to the 'Midlands Enlightenment' in England, to which they enjoyed close links, removes a central context for the idea of 'improvement'. It should be added that the choice of *Middlemarch* to epitomise the realist tendencies of British fiction is also tendentious. The British Gothic romance is not 'realist' in the Lukácsian sense implied; but neither is the work of Dickens.

Modernism and Postmodernism

Eagleton's assault on relativism, whether 'revisionist' or 'postmodernist' leads him to over-essentialise Irish tradition. In doing so, he also over-identifies it with traits which were to be foregrounded in modernism: a transformative modernism, harnessing innovative technique to the struggle to represent new truths. At the same time, Eagleton is especially interested in those aspects of modernism which can indeed be seen as precursors of postmodernism: in other words, offered the choice of examining a modernism that seeks to be true to the thing, on the one hand, or a modernism of poetic artifice on the other, Eagleton chooses the latter. Now this choice is relevant to the question of his attitude to postmodernism. The point may be best made with a reminder that Eagleton's own literary writings are also characterised by artifice, parody and textual self-consciousness. Linda Hutcheon, in her book *The Politics of Postmodernism*, offers a reading of Eagleton's novel *Saints and Scholars*, in the context of a discussion of fictions that 'denaturaliz[e] [...] the conventions of representing the past in narrative – historical and fictional – [...] in such a way that the politics of representing are made manifest.'[19] Eagleton is introduced as 'a Marxist critic who has accused postmodern fiction of being ahistorical'.[20] This novel represents the unlikely gathering of Bakhtin, Wittgenstein, a fictional character (Leopold Bloom), and one who is supposed to be dead (James Connolly) in a cottage in the west of Ireland. The novel's metafictionality is buttressed by many 'parodic intertextual echoes'.[21] Hutcheon rightly sees a crucial event in the novel as being the point at which Wittgenstein 'tries to convince Connolly that the limits of his language are the limits of his world', at which point the latter asks if, in that case, we should 'languish in the prison-house of language'. This reference to Jameson's book is a reminder of the Marxist critique of self-reflexive language and narrative, one in which Eagleton shares. Hutcheon proceeds, at this point, to suggest that he is attempting to reconcile 'seemingly opposing positions'.[22] But is he? The truth seems rather to be that he is operating consistently in a manner that is fully, albeit adventurously, at one with the ideals of a critical socialist modernism, of the kind that Brecht sought to defend from Lukács's championing of Balzac and Tolstoy, and from the critique of modernist writers which was later to find developed expression in *The Meaning of Contemporary Realism*.[23] The self-reflexivity and metafictionality of Eagleton's novel is in part to be seen as a demonstration of the way in which the sharpening of innovative aesthetic instruments in the postmodern world can yet be harnessed self-consciously by a truth-telling Marxism, not only to reflect the experience of that world, but to representing different viewpoints and their blindnesses along with the concomitant production of sign and discourse. Such a view is suggested by his essay, 'Capitalism, Modernism and Postmodernism', and the general position is there summed up:

> From the avant-garde, postmodernism takes the dissolution of art into social life, the rejection of tradition, an opposition to 'high' culture as such, but crosses this with the unpolitical impulses of modernism [...] An authentically political art in our own time might [...] draw upon both modernism and the avant-garde, but in a different combination from postmodernism.[24]

Specifically, this authentic political art would learn from the commitment of the avant-garde, while picking up the contradictions of modernism and casting them in a new light (these contradictions being to do with an attempt to comprehend history via concrete means, such as myth or imagism, while fleeing politics, which were seen as vitiated by a reductionist rationality).

When one considers this passage alongside *Saints and Scholars,* it becomes clearer that Eagleton's position towards postmodernism is in fact closely parallel with that taken towards modernist experimentation by Brecht and Benjamin, as in the pithy formulation in the latter's essay, 'The Author as Producer': 'Before I ask: what is a work's position *vis-à-vis* the production relations of its time, I should like to ask: what is its position *within* them?'[25] Eagleton's own words on Brecht and Benjamin are very clear and instructive:

> The truly materialist vision of Benjamin's redemptive hope will come not through his mentor Lukács but through his friend Bertolt Brecht. For nothing is quite so striking as the way in which the *Origin [of German Tragic Drama]* recapitulates, even before they had been properly initiated, all the major themes of Benjamin's later championship of Brechtian drama. Baroque allegory lays bare the device [...] *writing* comes to receive all its material weight [...] Objects in such spectacles are always strictly coded, in a discourse as far as Jacques Derrida himself would wish from the speaking voice [...].[26]

We have reached the point of recognising how these words figure, for Eagleton, some of the value-terms that could guide contemporary writing, but we have done so by way of a discussion of Irish literature. This is because, for him, much Irish writing is unusually likely to exemplify the tendencies prized by Benjamin.

While the book on Benjamin adumbrates the possibility of a formally radical and innovative socialist literature, the Brechtian and Bakhtinian emphases Eagleton now develops are not radically at odds with his earlier work. In particular, the idea of the author as producer looks back to the theorising of literary production which Eagleton undertook in *Criticism and Ideology* (1976).[27] There are differences. When Eagleton discusses literary form in *Criticism and Ideology*, despite the abstract diction of his discourse about ideology, he tends to employ relatively well-worn literary-critical terms, such as organicism and symbolism, and to use them with a broad brush, while anchoring them in that analysis of ideological blindness and distortion where, for him, Macherey is the chief mentor. Motif is rapidly translated into theme, and vice versa. The Benjamin book, on the other hand, offers a view of the foregrounding of the device which emphasises its role in obtrusively producing ideology. This might all add up to saying that Eagleton's concern with Benjamin has led to a greater appreciation of the qualities of modernism, and of those pre-modernist works, like the *Trauerspiel,* into which modernism can offer a renewed insight. By contrast, there is much on the nineteenth century in *Criticism and Ideology*, and much, as Stephen Regan points out, that remains indebted to the concepts Raymond Williams developed to understand it.[28] A significant staging post between these two positions is offered by Eagleton's essay on John Bayley, 'Liberality and Order' (1978), in which he takes a nineteenth-century novelist, Thomas Hardy, and pays particular attention to the problematising of verisimilitude and the textual variety and dissonance to be found in his work:

> With blunt disregard for formal consistency, he is ready to articulate form upon form – to mingle realist narration, classical tragedy, folk-fable, melodrama, 'philosophical' discourse, social commentary, and by doing so to betray the laborious constructedness of literary production.[29]

And these days, when Eagleton writes about a nineteenth-century novel, it is as likely as not to be an example of the Anglo-Irish novel: part of a lineage 'for which [...] realism [...] had never been less than profoundly problematic'.[30]

If to be a postmodernist was simply to prize metafictionality and formal inventiveness in writing, then Eagleton would be a postmodernist. But his deep antipathy towards ethical relativism, and his adherence to a Marxist form of modified human universalism, renders the description wide of the mark. One may gather a clear idea of this disagreement from *The Illusions of Postmodernism*. There, however, it is a matter of arguing the point with a generalised adversary, with a tendency. But Eagleton has also engaged in detailed argument with a specific representative of the adversary in the matter of ethics. I refer to his paper on 'Deconstruction and Human Rights', given as one of the Oxford Amnesty Lectures (1992), where he discusses deconstruction's turn to the ethical.

Eagleton notes Derrida's desire to address such matters as 'gift and promise, obligation and responsibility'.[31] These might seem like fundamentals of moral behaviour, yet Eagleton does not pause to give Derrida any credit. This is because he seeks to show that deconstructionist ethics is, in effect, acting out a sham engagement with moral fundamentals. He quotes de Man on how ethics has 'nothing to do with the will [...] of a subject', and Hillis Miller on the derivation of ethics from imperatives for which 'there is absolutely no foundation in knowledge'.[32] This means that obligation and responsibility become a matter solely of language. Such reasoning, though Eagleton does not say it, out-Nietzsches Nietzsche, for despite the latter's description of morality as 'the sign-language of the emotions',[33] not only did he leave emotions in the formula, he also tied them to the 'form of life'. For Eagleton, the 'form of life' would raise the question of the political. But deconstruction resists the inclusion of the political in the ethical. As Hillis Miller says, 'an ethical act that is fully determined by political considerations or responsibilities is no longer ethical'.[34] Eagleton does not have much trouble demonstrating the narrowness and unorthodoxy of such a view, nor in suggesting that Marxism is the inheritor of a more coherent view of the political animal: a tradition of civic virtue, which goes back at least as far as Aristotle.

Above all, then, postmodernism in general is accused of an abrogation of ethical seriousness. The accusation is cogent, shrewd, well-supported and adroitly argued. Yet there is something almost idealistic about the virtue tradition. By this I do not mean to go back on my implication that it offers a coherent and defensible ethic, capable of being re-worked in the manner that Eagleton advocates. Rather, I want to suggest that it might have to be brought into some relationship with a hard-headed estimate of the important part played in life by lack of virtue. Such an estimate would have to consider the question whether or not Foucault had a point about power. It was partly impatience with Marxism's eagerness to tie power-relations to the economic structure which led a generation of intellectuals to seek instruction from Foucault in the hope of finding something more detailed about specific institutions and localised practices. But Eagleton enters persuasive strictures on Foucault's 'self-causing and self-sustaining [...] autonomous and self-referential' power.[35] Nevertheless, there is a case for considering the possibility that power, like sexuality, enjoys a degree of relative autonomy with respect to the larger social organisation. Relevant questions might include the brutally simple one about individual power and ambition, as well as about group behaviour and small-scale power-games. The enquiry might have to extend as far as the universal and essential role of deception and lying in social life, in politeness and diplomacy, and in actual struggles. It would also have to consider the important fact of self-deception. Possibly all of these activities could be said to have their own poetics. But unless such an enquiry also recognised that power can make very good use of truth, and (a different point) that the pursuit of truth can be in a meaningful sense disinterested and self-sacrificing, it would constitute another form of one-sidedness. Furthermore, the venerable point that the criminal needs the law is relevant in this context.

Nevertheless, the attraction of Eagleton's position lies in its balance and roundedness as a contribution to cultural and moral understanding in our time. While he trips up on some of the Irish detail, he makes a powerful case for the continuing relevance of a virtue tradition, while rejecting vacuous universalism in favour of a view of the human subject in concrete historical conditions. At the same time, far from turning his back on experimentation in the arts, Eagleton is himself an author of seriously playful philosophical fictions who seeks to ensure that art is pondered and politically responsible.

Edward Larrissy

Notes

1. At least since the publication of 'Capitalism, Modernism and Postmodernism', *New Left Review* I/152 (1985): 60–73. Reprinted in *Against the Grain: Essays 1975–1985* (London and New York: Verso, 1986), 131–47.
2. Terry Eagleton, *The Illusions of Postmodernism* (Oxford: Blackwell, 1996). Subsequent page references are given in the text after the abbreviation 'IP'.
3. Francis Barker, *The Tremulous Private Body: Essays on Subjection* (London and New York: Methuen, 1984), x.
4. Marjorie Levinson, *Wordsworth's Great Period Poems: Four Essays* (Cambridge: Cambridge University Press, 1986), 10; Alan Liu, *Wordsworth: The Sense of History* (Stanford: Stanford University Press, 1989), 39.
5. Liu, *Sense of History*, 501.
6. Jean-Jacques Lecercle, *The Violence of Language* (London and New York: Routledge, 1990). Derrida receives only one mention in this book. But that appears to be an indication of the taken-for-granted character of his influence; for Lecercle avows that his methodology is deconstructive (266).
7. The formula $n + 1$ is specifically advanced as a way of showing how linguistics attempts to deal with exceptions to a rule, where n is the number of features supporting the rule, and 1 is an exception: namely, by suggesting that the exception can be brought within a reformulation of the rule (*Violence of Language*, 22). Lecercle, however, believes that since exceptions are sufficiently many, and since new ones keep being generated, they constitute a kind of condition of language, to which he gives the term the remainder. But he conceives his book as being about the philosophy of language, as well as about linguistics, so the formula also bears the interpretation I place upon it.
8. Terry Eagleton, 'Nationalism, Irony and Commitment', in *Nationalism, Colonialism and Literature*, ed. Seamus Deane (Minneapolis: University of Minnesota Press, 1990), 23.
9. Benedict Anderson, *Imagined Communities: Reflections on the Origin and Spread of Nationalism,* 2nd revised ed. (London: Verso, 1991).
10. Anderson, *Imagined Communities*, 89–90. Here there is a discussion of the venerable co-existence of English-speaker and Gael-speaker in Scotland, and of the hostility between Lowland and 'Gaeltacht' (sic – revised Irish spelling!). But he could have made profitable use of the ancient saying that there were 'Four Peoples' in Scotland: Picts, Britons, Gaels and Angles. (At p. 89 he quotes Seton-Watson calling the English-speakers 'Saxons'.) Indeed, with the Norse perhaps this should be Five Peoples.
11. Anderson, *Imagined Communities*, 9–36.
12. Anderson, *Imagined Communities*, 6.
13. Terry Eagleton, *Crazy John and the Bishop and Other Essays on Irish Culture*, Field Day Essays 5, gen. ed. Seamus Deane (Cork: Cork University Press, 1998), 314.
14. Terry Eagleton, *Heathcliff and the Great Hunger: Studies in Irish Culture* (London and New York: Verso, 1995), 1–9.
15. Eagleton, *Heathcliff*, 273–319.
16. Eagleton, *Heathcliff*, 5; and Terry Eagleton, *Figures of Dissent: Reviewing Fish, Spivak, Žižek and Others* (London: Verso, 2003), 240.
17. Christina Morin, '"Gothic" and "National"? Challenging the Formal Distinctions of Irish Romantic Fiction', in *Ireland and Romanticism: Publics, Nations and Scenes of Cultural Production*, ed. Jim Kelly (Basingstoke: Palgrave Macmillan, 2011), 172–87 (183).
18. Terry Eagleton, 'Running out of Soil', review of Paul Murray, *From the Shadow of Dracula*, *London Review of Books* 26, no. 23 (2 December 2004): 28–30 (28).

19 Linda Hutcheon, *The Politics of Postmodernism* (London and New York: Routledge, 1989), 59.
20 Hutcheon, *Politics of Postmodernism*, 59.
21 Hutcheon, *Politics of Postmodernism*, 60.
22 Hutcheon, *Politics of Postmodernism*, 60.
23 Bertolt Brecht, 'Against Georg Lukács', *New Left Review* I/84 (1974): 39–53. These writings were originally written in 1938 for *Das Wort,* but not published.
24 Terry Eagleton, 'Capitalism, Modernism and Postmodernism', *Against the Grain,* 46–7. This essay was first published in *New Left Review* I/152 (1985).
25 Walter Benjamin, 'The Author as Producer', *Understanding Brecht*, trans. Anna Bostock (London: New Left Books, 1973), 87.
26 Terry Eagleton, *Walter Benjamin, or Towards a Revolutionary Criticism* (London and New York: Verso, 1981), 22–3.
27 Terry Eagleton, *Criticism and Ideology* (London: Verso: 1976).
28 Stephen Regan, Introduction to Part III, in his edited *The Eagleton Reader* (Oxford: Blackwell, 1998), 165.
29 Terry Eagleton, 'Liberality and Order: The Criticism of John Bayley', *Against the Grain*, 40–1. This essay was first published in *New Left Review* I/110 (1978).
30 Eagleton, *Heathcliff,* 225.
31 Terry Eagleton, 'Deconstruction and Human Rights', in *Freedom and Interpretation*, ed. Barbara Johnson (New York: Basic Books, 1993), 123.
32 Eagleton, 'Deconstruction and Human Rights', 122, 125.
33 Friedrich Nietzsche, *Beyond Good and Evil: Prelude to a Philosophy of the Future*, trans R.J. Hollingdale ([1886], Harmondsworth: Penguin, 1973), 91.
34 Eagleton, 'Deconstruction and Human Rights', 124.
35 Terry Eagleton, *The Ideology of the Aesthetic* (Oxford: Blackwell, 1990), 390.

Williams and Wittgenstein: Language, Politics and Structure of Feeling

Ben Ware

I

Looking back through the pages of Raymond Williams's major works it is striking not to find any references to the writings of the philosopher Ludwig Wittgenstein. Given that both thinkers attach supreme importance to language and to its role in structuring how we see the world, one might have expected to discover, at the very least, a passing mention. Why, then, this rather strange silence on Williams's part?[1] In one sense, this question is perhaps not too difficult to answer. During the 1950s and 1960s – the period in which Williams was laying down the foundations for the project he would eventually term 'cultural materialism' – the general consensus amongst both liberal and Left intellectuals was that Wittgenstein's philosophy was inherently conservative. In his 1959 work, *Words and Things*, Ernest Gellner thus wrote that Wittgenstein's thought 'is conservative in the values which it in fact insinuates [...] It refuses to undermine any accepted habits, but, on the contrary, concentrates on showing that the reasons underlying criticisms of accepted habits are in general mistaken.'[2] In *One-Dimensional Man* (1964), Herbert Marcuse adopted a similar line of attack. According to Marcuse, Wittgenstein's philosophy, with its emphasis upon linguistic analysis and its rejection of the 'vocabulary of "metaphysics"', 'militates against intellectual non-conformity'.[3] Rather than striving to imagine the world otherwise, this philosophy restricts itself to reaffirming established modes of language and thought. As Marcuse puts it:

> Paying respect to the prevailing variety of meanings and usages, to the power and common sense of ordinary speech, while blocking (as extraneous material) analysis of what speech says about the society that speaks it, linguistic philosophy suppresses once more what is continually suppressed in this universe of discourse and behaviour. [...]
>
> The self-styled poverty of philosophy, committed with all its concepts to the given state of affairs, distrusts the possibility of a new experience. Subjection to the rule of the established facts is total – only linguistic facts, to be sure, but the society speaks in its language, and we are told to obey. The prohibitions are severe and authoritarian: 'Philosophy may in no way interfere with the actual use of language'.[4]

Whilst it is unclear whether or not Williams was familiar with these criticisms of Wittgenstein, a remark which he makes about ordinary language philosophy, in his 1971 essay 'Literature and Sociology', suggests clear affinities with Marcuse. In the context of a discussion of the work of Lucien Goldmann, Williams argues that, within the humanities, there is a strong tendency for British thinkers and writers to be constantly 'pulled back towards ordinary language: not only in certain rhythms and in choices of words, but also in a manner of exposition'.[5] Although Williams acknowledges some positive aspects of this 'habitual manner', he emphasises what he takes to be its negative consequences: 'a willingness to share, or at least not too explicitly to challenge, the consciousness of the group of which the thinker or writer [...] is willingly or unwillingly but still practically a member'.[6] This group, as Williams points out, is ('especially in places such as Cambridge') 'in effect and detail a privileged and at times ruling class'.[7] Consequently, the pull back towards ordinary language is, at the same time, a pull towards the dominant consciousness: 'a framing of ideas within certain polite but definite limits'.[8]

What Williams (like Marcuse) is here criticising is not only the privileged position from which ordinary language philosophy speaks, but also its inherent quietism: its unwillingness to challenge the prevailing world-view. Whilst Williams's essay does not refer specifically to Wittgenstein, there can be little doubt that it is the latter's philosophical legacy which is being placed under intellectual and ideological scrutiny. For Wittgenstein, 'the propositions of ordinary language, just as they stand, are in perfect logical order';[9] and thus 'what we do [in philosophy] is to bring words back from their metaphysical to their everyday use' (PI 116). For Williams, however, the return to ordinary language is itself indicative of a deeper crisis of thought and of politics; and it is out of this crisis that there emerges a 'search for alternative traditions' and 'alternative methods' – a search which is evidenced most clearly in what Williams describes as 'the long reach for theory'.[10]

Whilst it will not be my intention in the present essay to put forward a defence of ordinary language philosophy, I would like to begin by addressing the charges of conservatism and quietism which have been (and, to some extent, continue to be) levelled against Wittgenstein. My aim, in so doing, will be to open up a space within which to explore some hitherto unacknowledged affinities between Wittgenstein and Williams.

II

The philosopher J.C. Nyíri argues that Wittgenstein 'belonged to a constellation of conservative thinkers', and that his 'conservative attitudes' (which he expressed in relation to language, art, literature and social practices) 'crystallized into a kind of conservative theory' in both the *Tractatus* and the *Philosophical Investigations*.[11] As evidence, Nyíri cites the following pieces of biographical data: 'Wittgenstein's admiration for Dostoevsky', 'his dislike for any language that [had] not "grown organically"', 'his often voiced disparaging judgment of modern art [and] architecture', 'his distaste for modes of thinking "characterized by the word 'progress'"', and his understanding of his times as 'an age without culture'.[12] According to Nyíri, these attitudes and tastes point to a clear set of 'family resemblances' between Wittgenstein and certain renowned conservative thinkers – most notably, Oswald Spengler, Paul Ernst and Moeller van den Bruck.

In addition to locating him within the force field of conservative thought, Nyíri also contends that Wittgenstein's philosophy solves one of the key theoretical problems of conservatism; namely, how to uphold 'absolute standards' and 'fixed truths' in a world in which all 'absolute standards have perished historically, are a thing of the past, and fixed truths do not exist at all'.[13] For Nyíri this paradox is solved by Wittgenstein's later concepts of 'following a rule' and 'forms of life'. 'The following of a rule is', as Nyíri states, 'a custom, an institution, embedded in the agreements, in the correspondences of behaviour within society [...] Rule-following is, in the last analysis, blind: it cannot be explained or justified.'[14] Because language and thinking (as rule-governed phenomena) both rest upon 'agreements' and 'regularities' in the behaviour of individuals within society, Nyíri argues that 'any given form of life [...] cannot actually be criticized': 'the given form of life is the ultimate givenness'.[15] From this he concludes that 'any human being must, in order to be a human being, be constrained by some form of life'; and, moreover, that such forms of life are 'network[s] of tradition' which 'cannot be consciously transcended' or 'judged'.[16]

Nyíri's analysis of Wittgenstein's position is, I want to argue, radically mistaken; and therefore his claim that 'Wittgenstein's conceptual analyses can [...] be regarded as a [...] foundation of conservatism'[17] is one which cannot be upheld. Whilst Nyíri is correct to emphasise that, for Wittgenstein, rule-following involves training, custom, use, institution, technique, practice and so on,[18] he is wrong to suggest that (i) rules 'cannot be explained or justified';[19] and (ii) that rules act as the immovable *foundations* upon which 'all order [...] and communication by means of language' rest.[20] Arguing against this latter conception of rules, Stanley Cavell eloquently remarks: '[Wittgenstein] wishes to indicate how inessential the "appeal to rules" is as an explanation of language. For what has to be "explained" is, put flatly and bleakly, this':

> We learn and teach words in certain contexts, and then we are expected, and expect others, to be able to project them into further contexts. Nothing insures that this projection will take place (in particular, not the grasping of universals nor the grasping of books of rules), just as nothing insures that we will make, and understand, the same projections. That on the whole we do is a matter of our sharing routes of interest and feeling, modes of response, senses of humour and of significance and of fulfilment, of what is outrageous, of what is similar to what else, what a rebuke, what forgiveness, of when an utterance is an assertion, when an appeal, when an explanation – all the whirl of organism Wittgenstein calls 'forms of life.' Human speech and activity, sanity and community, rest upon nothing more, but nothing less, than this. It is a vision as simple as it is difficult, and as difficult as it is (and because it is) terrifying.[21]

According to Cavell, what we do and what we say thus rests not on a fixed and uncontested set of rules (which can be grasped from an independent and objective vantage point), but on our involvement with and our dependence upon everyday human practices.[22] Immersed, as we normally are, in our 'whirl of organism', the appeal to foundations does not strike us as necessary. What matters, as Cavell points out, are shared 'routes of interest and feeling'[23] and 'the attunement of one human being's words with those of others'.[24]

Nyíri's account of 'forms of life' is also deeply problematic. In the *Philosophical Investigations* (contra Nyíri) Wittgenstein does not speak of 'the given form of life', nor of 'the ultimate givenness'; rather, he writes: 'What has to be accepted, the given, is – so one could say – *forms of life*' (*PI*, 192). Acceptance, however, does not preclude criticism, nor should it be taken to imply support for the status quo. As Terry Eagleton neatly observes in his essay 'Wittgenstein's Friends': 'There is no reason why what has to be accepted are *these particular* forms of life, and indeed little reason to believe that Wittgenstein himself was in the least content with his own society'.[25] Wittgenstein's alleged quietism – the notion that, for him, existing forms of life and language are immune to criticism – is often linked to the following remark in the *Investigations*:

> Philosophy can in no way interfere with the actual use of language; it can in the end only describe it.
> For it cannot give it any foundation either.
> It leaves everything as it is. (*PI*, 124)

For critics such as Nyíri (and, indeed, Marcuse) this remark is understood as stating that philosophy *ought not* to interfere with 'the actual use of language.' It is therefore taken as lending support to what Marcuse describes as 'the prevailing universe of discourse and behaviour'.[26] This interpretation, however, misses both the point and the context of Wittgenstein's statement. In the *Investigations*, Wittgenstein readily accepts that 'a reform [of language] for particular purposes, an improvement in our terminology to prevent misunderstanding in practice, is perfectly possible' (*PI*, 132); yet this is *not* the issue with which he is concerned. What concerns Wittgenstein – and, indeed, what he takes to be the *task* of philosophy – is to uncover the types of confusions which we routinely fall into when we engage in philosophical questioning. Such confusions are manifestations of our 'failure […] to command a *clear view* of the use of our words' (*PI*, 122). They arise, according to Wittgenstein, 'when language is like an engine idling' (*PI*, 132) or when it '*goes on holiday*' (*PI*, 38). Underlying these confusions are bewitching (*PI*, 109) and disquieting (*PI*, 112) pictures (*PI*, 115) of language, which hold us captive (*PI*, 115) and lead to feelings of dissatisfaction (*PI*, 105) with ordinary, everyday words. Being in the grip of these 'metaphysical' (*PI*, 116) pictures is akin to suffering from an 'illness' (*PI*, 255); and it is the role of philosophy, as Wittgenstein conceives of it, to treat this illness. Put simply, then, the purpose of the *Investigations* is *therapeutic* (*PI*, 133); and Wittgenstein's particular therapeutic method consists not in advancing philosophical doctrines and 'theses' (*PI*, 128, 109), but in providing a 'perspicuous representation' (*PI*, 122) of the use of our words. Giving a clear presentation of our words-in-use is of 'fundamental significance' (*PI*, 122) because philosophical problems require us to '[look] into the working of our language […] [they] are solved, not by reporting new experience, but by arranging what we have always known. Philosophy is a battle against the bewitchment of our intelligence by means of language' (*PI*, 109).

This method gives rise to an anxiety which is expressed, in the *Investigations*, by one of Wittgenstein's interlocutors: 'Where does our investigation get its importance from, since it seems only to destroy everything interesting, that is, all that is great and important? (As it were all the buildings, leaving behind only bits of stone and rubble.)' The response given to this question is that 'What we are destroying is nothing but houses of cards and we are clearing up the ground of language on which they stand' (*PI*, 118). The role of philosophy, thus understood, is largely a negative or critical one: it destroys metaphysical structures of air (*Luftgebäude*) – which we were tempted to imagine as 'great and important' buildings – and, in so doing, it succeeds in 'the uncovering of one or another piece of plain nonsense and bumps that the understanding has got by running its head against the limits of language' (*PI*, 119). Giving full voice to this clarificatory aim at *Investigations* §464 Wittgenstein writes: 'My aim is to teach you to pass from a piece of disguised nonsense to something that is patent nonsense.'

To go back, then, to the remark at *Investigations* §124 ('Philosophy does not interfere with the actual use of language [...] It leaves everything as it is'), and to place it within the context of the philosophical perspective just outlined, we might suggest the following interpretation: what this statement means is simply that it is not the role of philosophy to attempt to *change* anything in language. 'We are not', as Wittgenstein observes, '*striving after* an ideal, as if our ordinary vague sentences had not yet got quite an unexceptional sense, and a perfect language awaited construction by us' (*PI*, 98). Instead, we must begin with our ordinary, everyday language – not because we are committed to 'leaving everything as it is', but because *this* is the very 'ground' (*PI*, 118) upon which we stand. Cora Diamond provides an insightful gloss on this point, when she remarks: 'The point of attention to ordinary language is not that it is in any way sacred; rather, attention to ordinary language is capable of transforming our problems and our sense of where we are with them.'[27]

Understood in this way, there is nothing in Wittgenstein's view of philosophy which supports linguistic conservatism or which speaks against a transformation of our existing forms of life. Indeed, we might argue that in order to overcome the kinds of philosophical confusions which hold us captive, a change in our current orientation towards the world is *exactly* what is required. In the *Investigations*, Wittgenstein sounds this note when he speaks of the need to rotate 'our whole investigation' around 'the fixed point of our real need' (*PI*, 108). A similar point is made in the penultimate section of the *Tractatus*, when Wittgenstein invites his reader to 'throw away' the book's nonsensical sentences as a precondition for 'seeing the world aright' (*TLP*, 6.54, Pears and McGuinness). It is, however, in the *Remarks on the Foundations of Mathematics*, that we find most clearly expressed the idea that a change in our social mode of life is needed in order to bring about a change in our philosophical thinking. As Wittgenstein puts it:

> The sickness of a time is cured by an alteration in the mode of life of human beings, and it [is] possible for the sickness of philosophical problems to get cured only through a changed mode of thought and of life, not through a medicine invented by the individual. Think of the use of the motor-car producing or encouraging certain sicknesses, and mankind being plagued by such sickness until, from some cause or other, as the result of some development or other, it abandons the habit of driving.[28]

This point, it would seem, is a genuinely materialist one: the sickness of philosophical problems, which are rooted in the sickness of a time, cannot be cured by the intellectual endeavours of individuals; rather, what has to change is something deep within society as a whole.[29] In a passage in his private manuscripts of 1947, Wittgenstein reiterates this idea when he writes: 'It is not by any means clear to me, that I wish for a continuation of my work by others, more than *a change in the way we live*, making all these questions superfluous. (For this reason I could never found a school).'[30]

III

It is at this point that I would like to draw attention to some concrete affinities between Wittgenstein and Williams. For Wittgenstein, as I have suggested, philosophy begins with the feeling of lostness ('A philosophical problem has the form: I don't know my way about' (*PI*, 123)), which arises as a consequence of the 'exile of words'.[31] Overcoming this linguistic estrangement involves a turning back to the ordinary and to the social – to an examination of what Wittgenstein describes as the 'hurly-burly'[32] of everyday words and actions. It is this same desire to examine the real human circumstances in which meanings are formed that animates Williams's work, both early and late. In the introduction to *Culture and Society 1780–1950*, Williams thus characterises the focus of his project as: 'the study of actual language: that is to say [...] the words and sequences of words which particular men and women have used in trying to give meaning to their experience'.[33] In the introduction to *Keywords*, written almost two decades later, he summarises the book's chief interest as follows: 'words in *everyday* usage [...] the vocabulary we share with others [...] when we wish to discuss many of the central processes of our *common life*'.[34] For Williams, then, as he famously puts it in *Marxism and Literature*, 'A definition of language is always, implicitly or explicitly, a definition of human beings in the world'.[35]

For both Williams and Wittgenstein, language does not consist in the reproduction and exchange of mere dead signs; rather, it is an active and living process. In *Politics and Letters*, Williams emphasises this point when he remarks that 'Language is a continuous social production in its most dynamic sense'.[36] This view stands in opposition to the idea of language as a fixed and objective 'system', existing independently of actual social relationships. Linguistic 'signs are', as Williams puts it elsewhere (following Voloshinov), 'living evidence of a continuing social process into which individuals are born and within which they are shaped, but to which they then also actively contribute, in a continuing process'.[37] Like Williams, Wittgenstein stresses the social, active and variable nature of language. In the *Investigations*, he gives expression[38] to the temptation to imagine a 'sublime' connection between meanings and words:

You may say to me: 'You understand this expression, don't you? Well then – I'm using it in the sense you are familiar with.' As if the sense were an atmosphere accompanying the word, which is carried into every kind of application. (*PI*, 117)

In the section of his 1944 manuscripts upon which the above remark is based, Wittgenstein writes that 'meaning' is not 'a halo that the word carries round with it and retains in any sort of application'.[39] Rather, as he points out in both his early and later writings, the meaning of a word (or sentence) is inextricably bound up with its significant use in our language.[40] Putting the point succinctly in the *Blue Book*, he writes: 'if we had to name anything which is the life of the sign, we should have to say that it was its *use*'.[41]

In *Keywords* Williams makes an important point about the issue of meaning and use, which is worth drawing attention to here. He says that 'the problem of meaning can never be wholly dissolved into context. It is true that no word ever finally stands on its own, since it is always an element in the social process of language [...] Yet it can be useful to pick out certain words, of an especially problematic kind, and to consider, for the moment, their own internal developments and structures.'[42] The purpose of this kind of historical semantics, as Williams suggests, is to recognise not only linguistic 'community between past and present', but also the persistence of 'radical change, discontinuity and conflict'.[43] Despite clear differences in both aims and method, there is, I would contend, no fundamental incompatibility between this way of looking at language and the one advocated by Wittgenstein. The latter's point – that the meaning of a word (or sentence) depends upon the circumstances of its use – is not to be understood as a doctrine or thesis, but rather as a grammatical *reminder* (*PI*, 127) – a warning against the potential dangers of looking for meaning in the psychological realm. Importantly, at *Investigations* §43, Wittgenstein remarks that 'For a *large* class of cases – though not for all – in which we employ the word "meaning"', we merely 'can' define meaning as use – the implication here being that we are not *obliged* to do so,[44] and thus that, on Wittgenstein's account, a project such as Williams's looking at the 'internal developments and structures' of certain words would not necessarily be ruled out.

We can, I believe, go even further than this. Wittgenstein's approach to linguistic meaning not only fails to conflict with Williams's, it also significantly connects with it in a number of ways. In *Zettel* Wittgenstein states that words have meaning 'in the *stream* of thought and life'; and that we can see life as a '*weave*' in which 'one pattern [...] is interwoven with many others'.[45] With these remarks Wittgenstein makes the point that our life with words is both infinitely changeable and, at the same time, intimately bound up with ongoing social relationships. The metaphor of the *stream* evokes fluidity and movement; whilst *weave* suggests a dense network of (historical and social) fibres (the warp of our past and the woof of our present) which produce a fabric or 'pattern' which, as Wittgenstein writes, is 'always [in]complete and is varied in a multiplicity of ways'.[46] For Wittgenstein, then, language is never static and meanings are never fixed, simply because what we say is always fully integrated into the complex 'mesh [of] life'.[47] Williams echoes this point when he speaks of 'semantic openness, corresponding to a still active social process, from which new meanings and possible meanings can be generated'.[48] To this emphasis upon change and open-endedness, however, Williams adds the crucial point that our words are always shot through with tangled ideological significances – always, that is to say, indicative of competing 'social values and conceptual systems'.[49] As he observes in *Politics and Letters*:

> Signs [...] take on the changed and often reversed social relations of a given society, so that what enters into them is the contradictory and conflict-ridden social history of the people who speak the language, including all the variations between signs at any given time.[50]

It is this emphasis upon the historical and political dimensions of meaning which, I would argue, is one of Williams's most important legacies, and one which any Wittgensteinian investigation of linguistic practices would do well to absorb.

IV

In the opening section of this essay, I suggested that Wittgenstein and Williams appear to move in opposing directions on the issue of ordinary language; and that this, along with the general perception of Wittgenstein as a conservative thinker, might have been a reason why Williams failed to engage with a work such as the *Investigations* in his own writings. In conclusion, I would like to point to another, seemingly clear (one might say 'standard'), contrast between Wittgenstein and Williams; however, in so doing, my aim will be to illuminate a further point of possible connection between the two thinkers.

On a cursory reading, at least, one of the most significant differences between Wittgenstein and Williams is their opposing attitude towards theory. In a December 1930 discussion of 'ethical value' with the Viennese logical positivist Moritz Schlick, Wittgenstein remarks:

> 'If I were told anything that was a *theory*, I would say, No, no! That does not interest me. Even if this theory were true, it would not interest me [...] it would not be the exact thing I was looking for. What is ethical cannot be taught. If I could explain the essence of the ethical only by means of a theory, then what is ethical would be of no value whatsoever [...] For me, a theory is without value. A theory gives me nothing.'[51]

In *Philosophical Investigations*, Part 1 section 109, this rejection of philosophy as a theoretical discipline is reiterated: 'And we may not advance *any kind of theory*. There must not be anything hypothetical in our considerations. We must do away with all *explanation* and description alone must take its place.'[52] In his essay 'Literature and Sociology', it appears to be precisely this kind of view that Williams is working against. Here he argues that there is a paradox within sociology and literature that 'presents itself [...] most evidently as a problem of style': 'The basic form of the paradox', Williams writes, 'is this: that *we need theory*, but that certain limits of existence and consciousness prevent us from getting it, or at least making certain of it; and yet the *need for theory* keeps pressing on our minds.'[53] The reference to 'limits' here relates to the fact that '[a]n idea of theory suggests laws and methods, indeed a methodology. But the most available concept of laws, and from it the most available organized methods, come in fact [...] from studies that are wholly different in kind' to the humanities; namely, 'from the physical sciences'. Like Wittgenstein, Williams rejects taking science as any kind of model for his own work ('the pursuit of the falsely objective');[54] this leads him, however, not to the belief that 'everything lies open to view [and] that there is nothing to be explained' (*PI*, 126), but rather to the opinion that 'the only *real* interest is theory and practice' – which, in Williams's case, translates into a rigorous attentiveness to the 'active processes through which social groups form and define themselves'.[55]

The conception of Wittgenstein as simply an anti-theorist – or, as some have argued, an end-of-philosophy philosopher – is, however, somewhat crude and misleading.[56] Throughout his life, Wittgenstein maintains an ambivalent attitude towards the activity of philosophising: although he expresses a profound hostility towards the (metaphysical) idea that the *essence* of language and thought can be grasped independently of one's own concrete situation in the world, he concludes his 1929 'Lecture on Ethics' by acknowledging that he 'cannot help respecting deeply' the 'tendency of the human mind' to want '*to go beyond* the world and that is to say beyond significant language'.[57] I thus think that it is useful to see Wittgenstein, especially in his later writings, not as a *dogmatic* anti-theorist, nor as someone whose intention it is to ride roughshod over the conceptual arguments of others, but rather as one who invites his readers to look closely at their use of particular words and to *clarify*, where necessary, precisely why they are using certain words in certain contexts.

The idea of clarity – stressed in the previous sentence – provides us with the ground upon which to establish a further link between Wittgenstein and Williams. In the *Investigations*, clarity (or, more specifically, arriving at '*a clear view* of the use of our words' (*PI*, 122)) is intimately allied with what Wittgenstein refers to as 'the understanding that consists in "seeing connexions"' (*PI*, 122). An example of what 'seeing connexions' entails is given by Wittgenstein, early in the *Investigations*, when he asks us to consider many of the things we call 'games': 'What is common to them all?—Don't say: "There *must* be something common, or they would not be called 'games'"—but *look and see* whether there is anything that is common to all.—For if you look at them you will not see something that is common to *all*, but similarities, relationships, and a whole series of them at that' (*PI*, 66). As Wittgenstein then goes on to conclude:

> And the result of this examination is: we see a complicated network of similarities overlapping and criss-crossing: sometimes overall similarities, sometimes similarities of detail. I can think of no better expression to characterise these similarities than "family resemblances"; for the various resemblances between the members of a family; build, features, colour of eyes, gait, temperament, etc. etc. criss-cross and overlap in the same way. (*PI*, 66–7)

Shifting the focus from language games to literature and art, it is this idea of 'seeing connexions' and, in particular, of discerning 'a complicated network of similarities overlapping and criss-crossing' that Williams touches upon with his concept of 'structure of feeling'. The concept of structure of feeling, first formulated by Williams in his 1954 study *A Preface to Film*, co-authored with Michael Orrom,[58] is one that the author returns to again and again throughout his oeuvre. Notoriously, Williams's definition of this concept shifts – on occasion, extremely radically – between texts: on the one hand, it corresponds to the 'dominant social character of a period' or is used, simply, as a general, descriptive phrase;[59] on the other hand, it is intimately related to 'emergent' or 'embryonic' social formations – as Williams writes in *Marxism and Literature*:

> structures of feeling can be defined as social experiences in *solution*, as distinct from other social semantic formations which have been *precipitated* […] It is a structured formation which, because it is at the very edge of semantic availability, has many of the characteristics of a pre-formation, until specific articulations – new semantic figures – are discovered in material practice.[60]

Cutting through these descriptive ambiguities, however, there is what we might refer to as a generic understanding of structure of feeling, where the highly personal phrase points to an attempt, on Williams's part, to *see what is common* (*PI*, 72). This is evident, for example, as early as *The Long Revolution*, when Williams speaks of structure of feeling as:

> [A] *common* element that we cannot easily place [...] a particular sense of life, a particular community of experience hardly needing expression, through which the characteristics of our way of life [...] are in some way passed, giving them a particular and characteristic colour. [...] [I]t is as firm and definite as 'structure' suggests, yet it operates in the most delicate and least tangible parts of our activity.[61]

In his 1971 'Literature and Sociology' essay, Williams stresses the aesthetic dimensions of the concept, writing that structure of feeling is intended 'to indicate certain *common characteristics* in a group of writers [...] in a particular historical situation'. Specifically, structure of feeling is linked to 'fundamental changes of form' in literary works – changes which 'normally precede those more recognizable changes of formal idea and belief which make up the ordinary history of consciousness'.[62] In *Politics and Letters*, these ideas are re-affirmed when Williams describes structure of feeling as follows:

> a structure in the sense that you could perceive it operating in one work after another which weren't otherwise connected [...] yet it was one of feeling much more than thought – a *pattern* of impulses, restraints, tones, for which the best evidence was often the actual conventions of literary or dramatic writing.[63]

What emerges, then, from this cluster of (key) quotations is the clear idea of structure of feeling as 'a network of similarities' (*PI*, 66) and relationships (one might say, 'family resemblances' (*PI*, 67)) between certain authors and texts in a particular period. It is, as Williams puts it, indicative of a 'common' set of aesthetic 'characteristics'; it also acts as a kind of invisible thread which links together seemingly disparate or unconnected works. Understood in this way we can, I would argue, see Williams's concept as providing – within the domain of 'actual [...] literary analysis' – an illustration of what Wittgenstein describes, in the *Investigations*, as 'the understanding which consists in "seeing connexions"' (*PI*, 122): a mode of understanding which, as Marie McGinn observes, involves 'seeing a *pattern* or form in what is there before our eyes, but which we had previously neglected or overlooked'.[64]

Establishing this kind of connection between structure of feeling and certain ideas in Wittgenstein's later work need not entail us passing over the political resonances of Williams's concept (for example, his insistence, in *Marxism and Literature* and *Politics and Letters*, that structure of feeling is always 'distinct from the official or received thought of a time');[65] nor should it lead us to sidestep some of the fundamental theoretical and philosophical problems involved in its exposition (for instance, the concept's ambiguous relation to the 'more formal' concept of ideology, or the extent to which – as 'thinking and feeling in an embryonic phase before it can become fully articulate'[66] – it might be seen as analogous with what Wittgenstein describes in the *Tractatus* as the *ineffable*).[67] Whilst an analysis of these theoretical and philosophical problems goes beyond the scope of the present paper, it should, however, be noted that, in conversation with his New Left interlocutors, Williams himself acknowledges the disquietudes which the concept of structure of feeling leaves him with. He says that the 'deliberately contradictory phrase' is one with which he has 'never been happy', and one that he returns to, again and again, without any real sense of 'theoretical satisfaction'.[68] The phrase '*theoretical* satisfaction' is, I think, of particular importance here; for it indicates how – on Williams's *own* later view – the lasting significance of the concept of structure of feeling might be seen to rest on it being grasped in an anti-doctrinal (that is to say, 'Wittgensteinian') sense, rather than in a standardly critical-theoretical sense. The *ideal* of such a theoretical articulation had, for Williams, from *Preface to Film* to *Marxism and Literature*, seemed at times an irresistible temptation; however, in *Politics and Letters*, it is to the more ordinary and 'straightforward notion'[69] (i.e. seeing connections, resemblances, and linkages in the actual forms and conventions of writing) that he returns. Whilst never referring directly to Wittgenstein's writings, one gets the sense, in these later dialogues, of Williams engaged in a markedly *therapeutic* practice: working to untie 'knots'[70] in his thinking and to liberate himself from a theoretical *picture* that had once held him captive (*PI*, 115).

Notes

1 Fred Inglis attributes this silence to 'Williams's general habit of writing and thinking in disregard of the bibliography of his day'. See Fred Inglis, *Raymond Williams* (London: Routledge, 1995), 221. Here I do not wish to speculate further on this issue, only to suggest some *possible* ideological motivations for Williams's silence.

2 Ernest Gellner, *Words and Things: A Critical Account of Linguistic Philosophy and a Study in Ideology* (London: Gollancz, 1959), 296.

3 Herbert Marcuse, *One-Dimensional Man: Studies in the Ideology of Advanced Industrial Society* (London and New York: Routledge, 1991), 179.

4 Marcuse, *One-Dimensional Man*, 182. The embedded quotation is taken from Wittgenstein and can be found in Ludwig Wittgenstein, *Philosophical Investigations*, 3rd ed., trans. G.E.M. Anscombe (Oxford: Blackwell, 2001), §124. All subsequent references to the *Investigations* will appear in the text as *PI* followed by a paragraph number. Where a paragraph number is not given, a page reference will be supplied.
5 Raymond Williams, 'Literature and Sociology: In Memory of Lucien Goldmann', *New Left Review* I/67 (1971): 3–18 (4).
6 Williams, 'Literature and Sociology', 4.
7 Williams, 'Literature and Sociology', 4.
8 Williams, 'Literature and Sociology', 4.
9 Ludwig Wittgenstein, *Tractatus Logico-Philosophicus*, trans. David Pears and Brian McGuinness (London: Routledge, 2001), §5.5563 (*cf. PI*, 98). An alternative translation of this remark is given in Ludwig Wittgenstein, *Tractatus Logico-Philosophicus*, German text with an English translation *en regard* by C.K. Ogden (London: Routledge, 2000). All subsequent references to the *Tractatus* will be from the C.K. Ogden translation (unless otherwise indicated) and will appear in the text as *TLP* followed by a proposition number.
10 Williams, 'Literature and Sociology', 4.
11 J.C. Nyíri, 'Wittgenstein's Later Work in Relation to Conservatism', in *Wittgenstein and his Times*, ed. B.F. McGuinness (Bristol: Thoemmes Press, 1998), 45, 48–9.
12 Nyíri, 'Wittgenstein's Later Work', 48–51, 57.
13 Nyíri, 'Wittgenstein's Later Work', 56.
14 Nyíri, 'Wittgenstein's Later Work, 58.
15 Nyíri, 'Wittgenstein's Later Work', 58–9.
16 Nyíri, 'Wittgenstein's Later Work', 59.
17 Nyíri, 'Wittgenstein's Later Work', 61.
18 See *PI*, 199, 202, 206.
19 For Wittgenstein, the business of philosophy is description rather than explanation (*PI*, 109). However, in certain everyday circumstances – if, say, a particular rule was unclear to a person attempting to follow it – then there would be nothing to prevent one offering an explanation – for instance, by giving 'examples' (*PI*, 71). The claim that rules *cannot* be justified – which opens Wittgenstein up to the charge of moral relativism – misses the significance of *Investigations* §289: 'To use a word without a justification does not mean to use it without right.'
20 Nyíri, 'Wittgenstein's Later Work', 58.
21 Stanley Cavell, *Must We Mean What We Say?* (Cambridge: Cambridge University Press, 2007), 52.
22 There is, of course, much more that can be said about Wittgenstein's complex treatment of rules in his later writings. However, Cavell's crucial point is that, for Wittgenstein, we do not need a substantive philosophical account of rule-following in order to be able to *go on*. This is fully in line with Wittgenstein's anti-metaphysical, therapeutic conception of philosophy outlined at PI 89–133. It is also worth noting Wittgenstein's remark in the *Blue Book*: 'For remember that in general we don't use language according to strict rules – it hasn't been taught us by strict rules either.' See Ludwig Wittgenstein, *The Blue and Brown Books*, 2nd ed. (Oxford: Blackwell, 1969), 25.
23 Cavell, *Must We Mean What We Say*, 52.
24 Stanley Cavell, *The Claims of Reason: Wittgenstein, Skepticism, Morality, and Tragedy* (Oxford: Oxford University Press, 1999), 32. For Cavell, we appeal to criteria only when 'attunement is threatened or lost. […] Then we start finding ourselves by finding out and declaring the criteria upon which we are in agreement' (34). Agreement itself, however, cannot be abstracted 'from the life into which it is woven'. On this point, see Cora

Diamond, 'Rules: Looking in the Right Place', in *Wittgenstein: Attention to Particulars*, ed. D.Z. Phillips and Peter Winch (Basingstoke: Macmillan, 1989), 12–34.
25 Terry Eagleton, 'Wittgenstein's Friends', *New Left Review* I/135 (1982): 64–90 (71).
26 Marcuse, *One-Dimensional Man*, 175.
27 Cora Diamond, 'Criss-Cross Philosophy', in *Wittgenstein at Work: Method in the 'Philosophical Investigations'*, ed. Erich Ammereller and Eugen Fischer (London: Routledge, 2004), 215.
28 Ludwig Wittgenstein, *Remarks on the Foundations of Mathematics*, 3rd ed., ed. G. H. von Wright, R. Rhees and G.E.M. Anscombe, trans. G.E.M. Anscombe (Oxford: Blackwell, 1978), 132. This remark appears in the context of a discussion of Cantor's Diagonal Argument, demonstrating the important connection in Wittgenstein's thinking between, on the one hand, questions of philosophy, logic and mathematics, and, on the other, questions of ethics, subjectivity and culture.
29 On this point, Wittgenstein is strikingly close to Marx, who, in his Eleventh Thesis on Feuerbach, famously states: 'philosophers have only *interpreted* the world, in various ways; the point is to *change* it'. Karl Marx, 'Theses on Feuerbach', in *The German Ideology*, 2nd ed. (London: Lawrence & Wishart, 1974), 123.
30 Ludwig Wittgenstein, *Culture and Value*, trans. Peter Winch, ed. G.H. von Wright, revised edition of the text by Alois Pichler (Oxford: Blackwell, 1998), 70 (emphasis added).
31 See Stanley Cavell, *This New Yet Unapproachable America: Lectures After Emerson After Wittgenstein* (Albuquerque, New Mexico: Living Batch Press, 1989), 36.
32 Ludwig Wittgenstein, *Zettel*, ed. G.E.M. Anscombe and G.H. von Wright, trans. G.E.M. Anscombe (Berkeley and Los Angeles: University of California Press, 2007), §567.
33 Raymond Williams, *Culture and Society: 1780–1950* (Harmondsworth: Penguin, 1963), 18.
34 Raymond Williams, *Keywords: A Vocabulary of Culture and Society* (London: Fontana, 1983), 14 (emphasis added).
35 Raymond Williams, *Marxism and Literature* (Oxford: Oxford University Press, 1977), 21.
36 Raymond Williams, *Politics and Letters* (London: Verso, 1979), 176.
37 Williams, *Marxism and Literature*, 37.
38 The interlocutor's voice – what Cavell famously refers to as 'the voice of temptation' – is introduced, in the *Investigations*, in remarks beginning 'You may say to me…', 'We want to say…', 'One would like to say…' and/or with double quotation marks. It is the interlocutor's perspective that the reader is invited to work through and, eventually, overcome.
39 Ludwig Wittgenstein, *Culture and Value* (Chicago: Chicago University Press, 1984), 44.
40 See *TLP*, 3.3, 3.314. Here Wittgenstein reformulates Frege's 2nd principle in *The Foundations of Arithmetic*, which states: 'never […] ask for the meaning of the word in isolation, but only in the context of a proposition'. Gottlob Frege, *The Foundations of Arithmetic* (Evanston: Northwestern University Press, 1980), x. In the later work, Wittgenstein extends Frege's insight, applying it to sentences (and their use within particular 'language games') as well as to words.
41 Wittgenstein, *Blue and Brown Books*, 4. *Cf. PI*, 432.
42 Williams, *Keywords*, 22–3.
43 Williams, *Keywords*, 22–3.
44 On this point, see Rupert Read and Phil Hutchinson, 'Towards a Perspicuous Representation of "Perspicuous Representation"', *Philosophical Investigations* 31, no. 2 (2008): 141–60 (141–2).
45 Wittgenstein, *Zettel*, §§173, 568–9. Emphasis added.
46 Wittgenstein, *Zettel*, §568.

47 Ludwig Wittgenstein, *Philosophical Grammar*, ed. Rush Rhees, trans. Anthony Kenny (Berkeley: University of California Press, 1978), §29.
48 Raymond Williams, *Politics of Modernism: Against the New Conformists* (London: Verso, 2007), 75.
49 Williams, *Keywords*, 23.
50 Williams, *Politics and Letters*, 176.
51 Ludwig Wittgenstein, *Ludwig Wittgenstein and the Vienna Circle, Conversations recorded by F. Waismann*, ed. B.F. McGuinness, trans. J. Schulte and B.F. McGuinness (Oxford: Basil Blackwell, 1979), 116–7. Here it might be argued: 'OK, but what about the early Wittgenstein? Surely the *Tractatus* was concerned with putting forward certain doctrines and theories – for example, the picture theory of language?' Although this paper is concerned primarily with Wittgenstein's post-*Tractatus* writings, I will note here that – along with the likes of James Conant, Alice Crary, Rob Deans, Cora Diamond, Piergiorgio Donatelli, Burton Dreben, Juliet Floyd, Warren Goldfarb, Logi Gunnarsson, Martin Gustafsson, Michael Kremer, Oskari Kuusela, Thomas Ricketts, Rupert Read, Matthew Ostrow – I do not see Wittgenstein, in the *Tractatus*, as attempting to advance metaphysical doctrines or theories; rather, his aim, as in the *Investigations*, is a radically therapeutic one. For more on the literary and aesthetic implications of this point, see my 'Wittgenstein, Modernity and the Critique of Modernism', *Textual Practice* (forthcoming).
52 Emphasis added.
53 Williams, 'Literature and Sociology', 6 (emphasis added).
54 Williams, 'Literature and Sociology', 6. A handful of passages from both Wittgenstein's early and later writings illustrate his rejection of the idea that science can provide a model for philosophy: 'Philosophy is not one of the natural sciences', *TLP*, 4.111; 'Philosophers constantly see the method of science before their eyes, and are irresistibly tempted to ask and answer questions in the way science does. This tendency is the real source of metaphysics, and leads the philosopher into complete darkness.' Wittgenstein, *Blue and Brown Books*, 18; 'It was true to say that our considerations could not be scientific ones', *PI*, 109.
55 Raymond Williams, 'The Uses of Cultural Theory', *New Left Review* I/158 (1986): 19–31.
56 It should be noted that, in the *Investigations*, Wittgenstein nowhere speaks of bringing philosophy to an end; rather, he says at §133 that 'the real discovery is the one that makes me capable of stopping doing philosophy when I want to. — The one that gives philosophy peace, so that it is no longer tormented by questions which bring *itself* into question.' In the 'Big Typescript', we also find the following important remark: 'we'll never get finished with our work [...] because it doesn't have an end'. Ludwig Wittgenstein, 'Big Typescript', in *Philosophical Occasions 1912–1951*, ed. J.C. Klagge and A. Nordmann (Cambridge: Hackett Publishing, 1993), 195. *Cf. Zettel*, §447.
57 Ludwig Wittgenstein, 'Lecture on Ethics', in *Philosophical Occasions*, 44.
58 Raymond Williams and Michael Orrom, *A Preface to Film* (London: Film Drama Limited, 1954). Cited in *The Raymond Williams Reader*, ed. John Higgins (Oxford: Blackwell, 2001), 33.
59 See, for example, *Modern Tragedy* where Williams speaks at different points of a medieval, a bourgeois, and a liberal structure of feeling. Raymond Williams, *Modern Tragedy* (Peterborough, ON: Broadview Press, 2006).
60 Williams, *Marxism and Literature*, 133–4.
61 Raymond Williams, *The Long Revolution* (Harmondsworth: Penguin, 1971), 64 (emphasis added).
62 Williams, 'Literature and Sociology', 12, 14 (emphasis added).
63 Williams, *Politics and Letters*, 159 (emphasis added).

64 Marie McGinn, *Wittgenstein and the 'Philosophical Investigations'* (London: Routledge, 2002), 26 (emphasis added) (*Cf. PI*, 129).
65 Williams, *Politics and Letters*, 163
66 Williams, *Marxism and Literature*, 131.
67 See *TLP*, 4.1212.
68 Williams, *Politics and Letters*, 159.
69 Williams, *Politics and Letters*, 159.
70 See Wittgenstein, *Zettel*, §452.

Border Country: Then and Now
Simon Dentith

This essay explores how our sense of Raymond Williams's first novel, *Border Country* (1960), has been transformed by the ways the world has changed in the 50 years since its publication. This re-evaluation takes into account the mass of new information about the composition of the novel made available by Dai Smith's biography: although it was widely known that Williams had prepared multiple drafts of the novel before it was published, *Raymond Williams: A Warrior's Tale* (2008) certainly makes clear the full extent of the unpublished material. I also address the controversy about Williams's talent as a novelist, most recently and provocatively discussed in the pages of this journal, with John Lucas asserting that 'I doubt [Williams] ever had it in him to be a worthwhile novelist', and that 'the ambition, which I am prepared to believe was quite genuine, simply isn't matched by the one quality which every writer needs: an interest in words, in rhythm, cadence'.[1] But most fundamentally, the essay explores the massive transformations in British society since the novel's time of publication that have necessarily redefined our understanding of it. But I begin by examining the novel in its originating moment; I seek to understand the multiple determinations that acted on it then, in 1960, and more widely, in the late-fifties conjunction of the first New Left, 'Anger', and the scholarship boy.

*

It has long been known that *Border Country* was the product of multiple drafting and redrafting (Williams said as much in *Politics and Letters*), but Dai Smith's biography, *Raymond Williams: A Warrior's Tale*, enables us to trace the evolution of the novel's various incarnations quite precisely – though since this is a matter of incomplete drafts, plans, and re-incorporated material, the story is quite a confusing one to follow.[2] The first version was called *Brynllwyd* and was mostly written in the late 1940s. A differently organised account of some of the same material was written as *Between Two Worlds* (1954–5); while a third substantial version was *Border Village*, completed in April 1957. Between this and the final published novel came the death of Williams's father, Harry, in March 1958; another version called *A Common Theme* was written before *Border Country* itself was published in 1960. In Williams's own account one especially significant factor in this extended pre-publication history was the reluctance of a publisher to bring out a very long novel. Dai Smith's account, by contrast, stresses the important formal evolution that can be traced in the differing versions, in addition to very differing emphases in terms of how much attention is to be given to the successive generations depicted in the novel. In Smith's telling, it is above all the double perspective created by the structure of the novel that is the substantial innovation between *Border Village* and *Border Country* – the way, that is, that the novel is framed by Matthew Price's experience, beginning as it does with Price in London being recalled by the illness of his father, before restarting with the arrival of Harry and Ellen at Glynmawr.

Clearly several factors are at work in this complex history of drafting and redrafting. In one sense it is simply normal: novelists characteristically work through several drafts before getting their work published. But it also resembles the practice of Raymond Williams's contemporary Doris Lessing (linked at this time by apparently shared political positions), who over the years has repeatedly told and retold the story of her upbringing in Rhodesia, both in the Martha Quest novels, in different versions in *The Golden Notebook*, in memoirs and in subsequent novels – though the obvious difference is that Lessing has done so in actual published work, while Williams's various versions remained in his desk drawer. This has meant that the evolutions in Lessing's retrospective self-understanding, as realised in these differing accounts, have been visibly driven by evidently differing agendas, both personal and political. In Williams's case the differing phases of his own self-understanding, of the processes which came to make him what he was, clearly also inform these differing versions. As he himself wrote in 1966 (the quotation now prefaces the Introduction to Dai Smith's biography), 'writing the kind of novel in which I was interested was a long process, full of errors, and the delay meant that I became first known as a writer in other fields'.[3] But two other factors were also clearly decisive: the death of his father between the completion of *Border Village* and the writing of *Border Country*, which in a sense permitted the discovery of the double perspective that characterises the novel; and the fact that in 1958 he published *Culture and Society* to general acclaim, which clearly put him in a much stronger position with his publisher when it came to proposing a novel for publication.

At all events the publication date, 1960, of the final incarnation of the novel is clearly significant, and it is worth recalling it. This was the moment of the first New Left, of Hoggart's *The Uses of Literacy* (1957) and Williams's own *Culture and Society* (1958), and of a very distinctive relationship between intellectuals and wider society; Williams himself in the early 1960s addressed a packed hall of delegates at the conference of the National Union of Teachers. *Border Country* addresses many of the preoccupations of that moment, above all the interrelated questions of class, of educational transition out of the working class, and of generational conflict. Moreover, the novel makes its address in a form (realism) which had a wider resonance in that late-fifties New Left moment. The comparison with Doris Lessing is valuable here also; she was testing realism to destruction contemporaneously with Williams as she was writing *The Golden Notebook* (1962), and she also wrote a notable defence of realism in 1958 in 'A small personal voice', published in *Declaration*, edited by Tom Maschler, an anthology of essays often seen as a kind of manifesto of the generation of 'angry young men'.[4] (*Border Country* is not exactly an 'angry' book, though there are some angry elements in it, as we shall see.) For both Lessing and Williams, realism was the mode of writing which permitted the novelist to retain the double focus both on the individual in all his or her complexity and particularity, and a wider sense of the larger society and its transitions which create that complexity.[5] In Lessing's case this led her to the remarkable formal complexity of *The Golden Notebook*. *Border Country* is formally complex also, though clearly not to the same degree. Realism is the mode, for all the strain that it was under, which seemed most emphatically to serve the purposes of the cultural fraction to which both Lessing and Williams belonged, however briefly they inhabited that same space together. They converged on realism from different starting-points, with Lessing coming from a more orthodox Marxist commitment, but their shared formal commitments led them both to a realism which remained rooted in the shared world of common social experience while seeking to mediate it in formally complex ways.[6] Their different political and aesthetic trajectories meant that they did not inhabit that shared space for long.

It is worth pausing briefly on the significance of realism as an aesthetic category for Williams at this time. A later moment of left cultural politics was given to frankly scholastic debates about the inherent politics of realism, understood as an antonym to modernism. Part of the difficulty with these arguments is that they failed to realise both the potential formal complexity of realism, and also the way that the cultural politics of form can change in differing historical circumstances, a point made powerfully by Fredric Jameson in his afterword to one of the key volumes of the 1970s which made the 1930s German debates on these topics current.[7] For Jameson, in an argument which anticipated his engagement with postmodernism,

> there is some question whether the ultimate renewal of modernism, the final dialectical subversion of the now automatized conventions of an aesthetics of perceptual revolution, might not simply be [...] realism itself! For when modernism and its accompanying techniques of 'estrangement' have become the dominant style whereby the consumer is reconciled with

capitalism, the habit of estrangement itself needs to be 'estranged' and corrected by a more totalizing way of viewing phenomena.[8]

In this light, Williams's publication of *Border Country*, and the chapter on 'Realism and the Contemporary Novel' in *The Long Revolution* published a year later, were two aspects of the same intervention to transform the inheritance of realism, and were by no means a retreat into it from the more experimental forms of modernism, as some commentators have perceived the dominance of realism in 1950s Britain. For Williams, what needed to be transformed was a contemporary novelistic practice which was unable to synthesise two formal possibilities in the novel, focused as it seemed to him either on individual development, or with an alternative practice of external and stiffly realised 'sociological' description. In this project he was later to discover that he had described an aesthetics cognate with that of Georg Lukács, who also found in the classic realist novel a practice which mediated between the individual and the social in comparable terms, though Lukács's Hegelian inheritance, which informed these ideas, was not then available at first hand to Williams. *Border Country* carries with it the classical ambition of realism: the painstaking record of ordinary lives. But it addresses this in a way which seeks to recognise its full complexity, born of the material circumstances that people inhabit (or which inhabit people), and which in the same breath acknowledges people's distinctive individuality.

The formal complexity of the realist novel as Williams inflected it served a central purpose for him also, insofar as it can be seen as a resolution of the particular intellectual problems faced by Matthew Price in the novel, *Border Country*, of which he is the protagonist. Price is an academic social historian who is encountering a writer's block in his work on population movement into South Wales in the nineteenth century. The problem is that he cannot find a form of writing which permits him at once to hold together the relatively abstract and statistical demographic data which he has accumulated, with the lived experience of the people whose life-stories he is recounting. As always with Williams – this is one of his greatest insights as a critic and the one that is sometimes hardest to keep hold of – this formal problem for Matthew Price as a writer is at the same time a crisis of social relationships. For in a society with unequal access to education, the capacity and the skills to create the analytical and synoptic overview are divorced from the life-experience of the people about whom the story is being told. While it is not clear in the novel that Matthew Price ever resolves this dilemma, the novel itself stands as a massive answer to it. Its formal complexity emerges from the torsions of that dilemma, while at the level of content the conflict between Harry and Matthew / Will turns in part on the value of the educational experience that the latter has undergone, which permits him the synoptic view but which tears him out of his environment at the same time.

The practice of Williams-the-novelist, insofar as it embodies a 'solution' to Matthew's dilemma, is also therefore an answer to one of the deforming characteristics recognised by Williams-the-critic, in his accounts of the tradition of realist writing in Britain – the distortions created by an educated narrator looking down on or looking back to a social world from which s/he is in part excluded by that very education. It is a pattern which, elsewhere, he finds in George Eliot's writing, but perhaps most visibly in Lawrence.[9] To return briefly to John Lucas's polemical account of Williams as a novelist: it is not clear that the distortions are absent from the novelistic practice of the 1930s to 1950s, which Lucas promulgates as though Williams were in ignorance of that practice. Certainly the formal distortions in the novel, created by class, understood as both material circumstance and as differential access to education, were not simply solved in the tradition of working-class writing in the thirties which Lucas might also have referred to.[10] The formal complexity of the novel, which holds together the experience of the adult Matthew Price returning to visit his dying father, with an account of that same father's arrival in the village in which Matthew will grow up, provides a formal resolution to the problem: at once a formal and social one, as we have observed. Whether the problem is resolved at the local, textual level – in the 'words, rhythm and cadence', to use Lucas's formulation – remains to be seen.

Williams himself was quite explicit about his ambitions in this area, and there is an evident coincidence between his critical views and his artistic practice at this period. In addition to 'Realism and the Contemporary Novel' in *The Long Revolution*, already noted, there is his reaction to Richard Hoggart's *The Uses of Literacy* (1957), written in something of a hybrid form which some reviewers felt was a kind of novel *in potentia*:

> I am not blaming Hoggart for this variety, but since the condition is general, I am trying to insist on the distinctions we shall have to make. We are suffering, obviously, from the decay and disrepute of the realistic novel, which for our purposes (since we are, and know ourselves to be, individuals *within* a society) ought clearly to be revived. Sound critical work can be done; sound critical observation and analysis of ideas. Yet I do not see how, in the end, this particular world of fact and feeling can be adequately mediated, except in those more traditionally imaginative terms.[11]

The 'realistic novel' in this formulation is what permits the mediation of a 'world of fact and feeling', because it can synthesise the outer with the inner world, and the individual with society. But this is not a matter of simply resuming an established form (as Williams's shorthand allusion to 'traditionally imaginative terms' might suggest); on the contrary the struggle to find a form adequate to the experience is constant, and is simultaneously a social and aesthetic project.

In Williams's own case the struggle was to find ways of representing the people from whom he had emerged; in the famous disclaimer on the copyright page, he says that 'I know this country, but the characters and events of the novel are imagined, and are not intended to describe actual persons and events'.[12] One of the axes of that struggle has already been touched on: it concerns the generational conflict between Matthew / Will and his parents, and concerns the education which they are both intent on encouraging but which simultaneously propels him out of Glynmawr. But this conflict is in turn impossible to understand without a sense of the conflicts within Glynmawr itself – within, that is, the complex social formation of this border village, with economic, personal and cultural affiliations running in multiple and contradictory directions, and bringing with them profound and unresolved tensions. This is a crucial matter when considering the way that Williams seeks to write about the working class, and all that is riding on that representation for him. The contrast with Hoggart's almost contemporaneous account of working-class life is telling, for *The Uses of Literacy* does indeed provide an unduly *Gemeinschaft* representation of the working class. *Border Country*, by comparison, provides a difficult and at times strained account of the tensions and conflicts within its known community; indeed, the point of the novel is in some ways to confront the reader with the unreconciled nature of those conflicts, and not to grant any too readily positive sense of them. If this is *Gemeinschaft*, it is very uncomfortable.

Nevertheless, what I have described so far is perhaps an aesthetic project rather than a realised aesthetic fact, however difficult it may be to grant priority, in biographical actuality, to the 'critical' or the 'novelistic' in Williams's developing thinking in the fifteen years or so after the end of the Second World War, and however difficult it is to point, in a way that brooks no contradiction, to aesthetic success, not only in the case of Williams, but of all writers ever. But it is possible to recognise what is distinctive in *Border Country*, to argue that this is closely related to Williams's sense of what constitutes community and neighbourliness, and to suggest that this aesthetic distinctiveness of the novel has a power which is certainly aligned with his understanding of the nature of working-class life, but which is simultaneously 'aesthetic' insofar as it provides a persuasive sense of that life realised in the local texture of the prose.

Take, for example, a related pair of incidents concerning the character Jack Meredith, a fellow signalman with Harry Price and Morgan Rosser, who also has a small farm near Glynmawr. He is opposed to the General Strike, and is only saved from acting as a scab by the Station Master, Rees. After the

Border Country: Then and Now

strike, he is in turn responsible for ensuring that Harry Price gets re-instated as a signalman, when he refuses to work even a few minutes beyond his agreed time. This is the scene when Harry Price attempts to thank him:

> 'I heard about Friday night, Jack. I want to thank you. I owe you a lot.'
> 'Owe me?' Meredith said, slinging his frail on his shoulder.
> 'It got me back to work. I won't forget that.'
> Meredith looked at him. 'Only your own bloody silliness got you out of it, didn't it?' As he spoke he rubbed his fingers across his broad nostrils, and his small, bloodshot eyes stared.
> 'Aye, well that,' Harry said. 'Perhaps it's always silly to go helping your mates.'
> 'Of course,' Meredith said, and walked to the door. 'People ought to learn to look after themselves for a change.'
> Harry smiled and signed on in the register, for the first time in nearly seven weeks.
> 'Get on home now, Jack. You'll find your sheep on the road, I wouldn't wonder.'
> 'Don't you worry about my sheep,' Meredith said, and he pulled on his cap and opened the door. He turned suddenly, his face under the low peak still set and sour.
> 'Haven't forgotten how to work the box, I suppose?'
> There was the trace of a smile at his mouth as he slammed the door. (136–7)

Despite that concluding trace of a smile, this scene gives a powerful sense of two conflicting personalities, especially that of Meredith and his sheer bloody-mindedness. The scene gives an acute sense of his discordant physical presence (broad nostrils, small bloodshot eyes, a set and sour face) and the way that he refuses to acknowledge Harry Price's thanks – indeed, the whole verbal exchange is characterised by Meredith refusing to take up the conversational cues he is offered, so that the predominant sense is one of awkwardness and unresolved tension. This seems to me to be a characteristic novelistic effect of Williams's fiction: to confront the reader with the sheer recalcitrance of human interactions, the unresolved awkwardness that can characterise them.

This tension between Harry and Meredith, partially resolved, perhaps, in this scene, reappears later in the novel in outright hostility between Meredith and Morgan Rosser. The latter is himself an interesting character, read by Dai Smith as an externalisation or splitting off of Harry Williams's entrepreneurial side. Some years after the end of the General Strike, when Harry Price, Morgan Rosser, and an otherwise unmentioned character, 'Lippy', go off to 'see the trout jumping' – that is, to have a Sunday drink over the border in

England, rather than have to stay in dry Wales. There's a very strange interlude in which Lippy, formerly a flyweight boxer, is egged on to a display of shadow boxing by the drinkers in the pub. Harry characteristically acts as the pacifier and benign authority figure here. But this display provokes Meredith to call Morgan Rosser a liar, and the two men almost come to blows.

> 'Aye, only Rosser's a liar,' Meredith said loudly, 'so what's that count?'
> There was a sudden silence, and Morgan stood up. Meredith looked across at him, holding his glass.
> 'Say that again, Jack.'
> 'I said you was a liar, an underhand dealer, and no bloody good to anybody.'
> Morgan had gone very white, but did not move.
> 'Jack, you're an old mate of mine. But if you wasn't older than me I'd thrash you for that.'
> 'Try it, Rosser. I've dealt with yappy dogs afore.'
> 'We're going,' Harry said. 'Come on, Lippy.' (218)

The scene continues with an appeal to Harry to judge between the two men: he won't; and the three of them leave the pub with the conflict left essentially unresolved. The immediate cause for dispute between Meredith and Rosser concerns some fields attached to Meredith's smallholding and which Rosser arranges, against Meredith's wishes, to be turned over to currant-bush cultivation to serve Rosser's growing jam-making business. As in the previous scene, but more dramatically, the writing here requires the reader to confront the intractable tensions within the community of Glynmawr, realised in this instance in near-violence, and unresolved despite the appeal to Harry Price, beholden to both the antagonists, to mediate. His own explanation of what is happening appears in the scene:

> 'Jack done me a good turn. Years back. He knows I've not forgotten it.'
> Meredith smiled.
> 'I done you no good turn, nor nobody else. One thing I've learned, I'll tell you. That's every man for himself. Nobody else will help you.'
> 'That's what you made out then. That's what's happening now.' (218–9)

So the conflict in this scene is grounded in a set of conflicted economic circumstances, meticulously detailed by Williams in the preamble to this scene, but finally to do with the particular social mix of Glynmawr, which is a small community based in part on small-scale agriculture and which also has a presence of more typically proletarian workers on the railway. Meredith in fact works in both areas, but his primary loyalty is to his small farm. The further social-historical element is the aftermath of the General Strike, alluded to heavily here. It is the defeat of the General Strike which leads to the lesson which Meredith has apparently learnt: 'every man for himself. Nobody else will help you.' But it is also the defeat of the General Strike which has led a disillusioned Rosser to his entrepreneurialism.

The scene that I have just tried to describe thus seeks to typify a whole social history, grounded in a particular political economy, and over-determined by a wider political narrative. But this account can scarcely address its aesthetic success, which must depend on the way that this scene carries conviction as a representation of conflict between people with its own specific trajectory and rhythm of dialogue and gesture. I think that it does, and indeed that it is one of the strengths of Williams's novel writing that he can make scenes of this kind genuinely carry the force of conflict and frustration required of them.

There is nevertheless a striking account of the homogenising power of this community, especially in relation to its distinctive Welshness, in the brief description devoted to the Eisteddfod. It begins with Will wishing to resist this evident enactment of 'community', but ends with him as it were submitting himself to it:

> It was time now for the choirs, and Will knew, looking up, that it was no use at all even trying to stay separate. Each choir moved into position, into dark settled rows, and the set faces turned to the conductor, eyes widened and lips poised; men and women surrendered, asking for movement and control. The drop of the raised hand, and then not the explosion of sound that you half expected, but a low, distant sound, a sound like the sea yet insistently human; a long, deep, caressing whisper, pointed suddenly and sharply broken off, then repeated at a different level, still both harsh and liquid; broken off again, cleanly; then irresistibly the entry and rising of an extraordinary power, and everyone singing; the faces straining and the voices rising around them, holding, moving, in the hushed silence that held all the potency of these sounds, until you listening were the singing and the border had been crossed. When all the choirs had sung, everyone stood and sang the anthem. It was no longer simply hearing, but a direct effect on the body: on the skin, on the hair, on the hands. (207)

The remarkable erotics of this writing underline the sheer force of the way that it figures 'community'. Will's initial resistance to the performance; his resolute keeping of himself separate during the recitations, and the private way he seeks to understand the set piece, from the Book of Job; and then his submission to the communal experience, culminating in the emphatic line 'and the border had been crossed' – all these indicate at least one possibility for interpersonal life, though it should be said that it is scarcely pursued beyond this scene in the novel.

'Community' can thus be represented in differing ways and with radically differing emphases. If this is true of the way that the novel represents the complex and interlocked tensions that make up 'Glynmawr', then a similar case can be made in relation to the family dynamics of the Price household. The novel in one way certainly does hero-worship Harry Price, and there is something perhaps tendentious in the claim, which Harry himself makes and which Will / Matthew can never fully come to terms with, that Matthew's work is a continuation in another context of the work that Harry has done in his own lifetime. But even admitting the hero-worship, the novel gives a remarkably tense and fraught account of family life. I suggested earlier that this is scarcely an 'angry' book, but it is possible to see in it some anger at the repression and enforced silence of the Price household, in some respect echoing the themes of Williams's contemporaries, and the sense of fraught generational transition that they so notably dramatised. Once again, however, this is not a question simply of alluding to a topic in the novel, if that topic is not realised with genuine aesthetic conviction. So we need another example. I've taken the next extract from a scene about two-thirds of the way through the book: Will is seventeen, and is arguing with his parents about the encouragement they have given him to stay on at school:

> 'You wanted me to go on at school. You sent me up to Pugh's for him to persuade me. Why deny it when you did?'
> 'It was for your own good, Will,' Ellen said. 'It was what you'd really want.'
> 'That's what I'm saying. Only it's one law for me and a different one for you. You've got this course mapped out for me, and that was that.'
> 'Don't shout at your Mam,' Harry said.
> 'I'm shouting at you, Dad. Everything in this house is kept under so much it needs shouting.' [...]
> He was answering his mother, and looking at her, but it was his father's response he was waiting for. (239)

I think this stretch of dialogue, for all its rawness (or perhaps because of its rawness, even its naivety), catches a real sense of familial intensity: the generational hostility between father and son, the placatory talk of Ellen, and the actual exclusion of Ellen from the real dynamic or tension in the scene (and of course, there's a lot more to say about that exclusion – about the way that the novel represents Ellen, the displacement onto that character, perhaps, of some of Williams's biographical resentment at his mother's continued disapproval of his wife, Joy). That phrase especially, 'Everything in this house is kept under so much it needs shouting', has a particular force and resentment behind it, in a way that certainly undermines any notion that the novel offers a too-easy or sentimental account of Williams's upbringing.

So *Border Country* undoubtedly corresponds to the general intellectual case that Williams was making in the late 1950s about the realist novel, a case that was cognate with other elements of the first New Left, but which he argued with particular force and distinctiveness. It corresponds also with the case he made tirelessly and continuously about working-class life and culture, starting with his resentment at being told, as an undergraduate, that nobody now knew what 'neighbour' meant, and including this grand statement from 'Culture is Ordinary':

> There is a distinct working-class way of life with its emphasis of neighbourhood, mutual obligation and common betterment, as expressed in the great working-class political and industrial institutions, [it] is in fact the best basis for any future English society. As for the arts and learning, they are [...] a national inheritance [...] available to everyone. So when the Marxists say that we are living in a dying culture, and that the masses are ignorant, I have to ask them, as I asked them then [in the 1940s], where on earth they have lived. A dying culture, and ignorant masses, are not what I have known and see.[13]

However, the actual experience of reading *Border Country*, while it is cognate with this vision – is, indeed, precisely what Williams has known and seen ('I know this country') – does not provide a sentimental account of working-class culture at all. On the contrary, it depicts the particular culture of Glynmawr as riven by conflict and tensions. This is equally true of the family life that the novel recounts. It is the particular aesthetic distinction of the book to represent these tensions in a way that makes them present to the reader in uncomfortable, even uncompromising ways. This nevertheless does not detract from the fundamental affirmation that the book seeks to make, of the country and the people who inhabit it. The contradictions that the book exposes are never fully resolved: the familial tensions persist, and the particular social and political history, which has led from the General Strike to undermining obvious forms of working-class industrial militancy and solidarity, forming indeed one of the central themes of the book, is left unresolved; but these are ultimately subordinate to the affirmation that it makes of a particular phase of working-class life. And this phase of working-class life, the solidarities on which it is based, is at the very heart of Williams's intellectual and political project in the late 1950s and early 1960s.

*

Williams's sense at this time was that such a position was, to use a vocabulary that he would develop later, *emergent*. There is perhaps a certain Whiggishness about such an idea, as there is indeed in the whole notion of the 'Long Revolution'. At all events, he was prepared to pin his hopes on the forms of solidarity that he knew from his upbringing, and which he represented, with all the complexities and contradictions that I have indicated, in *Border Country*. So how do such hopes look now, when a renewed sense of crisis clusters around representations of the working class, when the social formations on which Williams pinned his hopes have been so hollowed out or undermined, and when the very landscape of Pandy and 'Glynmawr' has been transformed?

It is easiest to start with that last and least uncomfortable aspect, the transformations that have been wrought to Pandy / Glynmawr in the last 50 years. In fact such changes had begun even while Williams was writing the novel: the Abergavenny to Hereford line on which his father worked was closed to freight traffic from 1958, and Pandy station was closed as one of the Beeching cuts. The main road has now been made into a trunk road, the bends straightened out, and (Williams himself made a television programme about this) the lorries roar along it without having to slow down for Llanfihangel Crucorney or Pandy (a change to which he also alluded in the opening pages of *The Country and the City*, in 1973). The outpost of the industrial proletariat, created by the presence of the railway station, has disappeared. The small-scale farming persists, as precarious as ever; but tourism now contributes much more significantly to the local economy. It is hard to tell how the forms of community represented in the novel have persisted and been transformed.

The working class more generally has evidently been transformed since the time that Williams wrote his novel, still more from the time of the General Strike, upon which so much hinges in the book and in Williams's thinking. Fifty years after the moment of *Border Country*, the British working class is as ever the subject of widespread and anxious consideration, but in a register which has been completely transformed from that which characterised the late fifties and early sixties. The themes of neighbourliness and solidarity which inform Williams's novel are once again prominent, but have been spoken most characteristically on the right than on the left, often using a vocabulary inherited from the tradition of the romantic critique of capitalism and the market which ironically Williams did so much to resurrect, especially in *Culture and Society*.[14] While the current debate about the working class can be seen as focusing excessively on questions of representation, as for example in Owen Jones's *Chavs: The Demonization of the Working Class* (2011), and Michael Collins's *The Likes of Us: A Biography of the White Working Class* (2004),[15] this does not prevent locating these matters of representation in an attempted political economy of class, in which the dissolution and reconstitution of the working class is to be understood in the context of capital flows, neo-liberalism, and a deliberate reckoning with the forms of labour power.

The following is an account of these transformations in summary form, taken from the Runnymede Trust 2009 publication *Who Cares about the White Working Class?*:

> In Britain, over the course of the 20th century, the proportion of the working population employed as 'manual workers' fell from 75% to 38%. This decline, and the accompanying change in the composition of the working classes, has had important consequences for the *experience* of inequality and disadvantage. To be a 'manual worker' at the beginning of the 20th century was to hold a position shared by three quarters of the working population; by the end of the century, the bulk of their fellow workers were in more privileged jobs. There are important differences, therefore, in being a 'manual worker' between then and now, because the *relative disadvantage* of the category has changed. Even if they performed exactly the same sort of work as their parents, the members of the working classes would be in a very different social position, because of proportional shifts in occupational distributions. But labour-market restructuring has also meant a shift in the *composition* of the working classes, with an increase in more routine and relatively insecure forms of employment, a growth in part-time, casual and flexible jobs, and a decline in traditional 'craft and operative' occupations (in 'heavy' industries), at the expense of routine and semi-routine jobs in services.
>
> These changes have deepened the experience of class disadvantage, and some groups have been hit particularly hard. Since the last quarter of the 20th century, young men in particular have become disproportionately concentrated in low-level manual work, and have seen their relative pay slip behind that of older men. Employment-based class divisions have widened and polarized for all, and this class restructuring has meant that the 'working class', and especially young working-class men, have become relatively more disadvantaged. These shifts have also affected the culture of manual work, and undermined some of the historic claims of working class status. In the past, one of the main ways in which working class men could lay claim to social respect rested in the nature of the jobs they performed. In traditional working class industries (like shipbuilding, iron and steel, mining and the railways), although the work was dirty, dangerous and tough, it also nourished 'heroic' images of men's manual labour. Craft and

shop-floor union strength permitted a sense of working class self respect, based on 'manly independence'. The fracturing of these industries, and the rise of the 'McJob', has undermined such claims to respect, which in any case, were never available to working-class women, who have always had to contend with stigmatized and highly sexualized labels. For both women and men, manual work is increasingly seen as a form of subordinate and dependent labour.[16]

If that gives a broad overview of changes, especially concentrating on the brute demographic facts and their implications, there are a couple of aspects of this account which bear especially strongly on a retrospective reading of *Border Country*. The book is undoubtedly suffused with a sense of 'working class self respect', but it could scarcely be said that this is based upon a notion of 'manly independence', or indeed a heroic sense of manual labour. Insofar as there is such a sense, it clusters around the labour that Harry Price (and to some extent his father) performs outside his job as a signalman – there's a powerful scene in which he exerts himself in catching a swarm of bees; his labour for the bowling club (especially pulling the roller) is emphasised; and there's an interesting scene in which his father is portrayed digging the vegetable patch. And certainly a lot of the pathos around his dying concerns his physical decay. But in general the novel does not concentrate on a heroic sense of manual labour; where the general changes indicated by Wendy Bottero in the passage above press most heavily on the novel they concern the comment that 'craft and shop-floor union strength permitted a sense of working class self respect'. Williams of course was interested in a lot more than 'self respect', important though that may be. It is the erosion of forms of working-class solidarity, based (in Williams's words from 'Culture is Ordinary') upon 'neighbourhood, mutual obligation and common betterment, as expressed in the great working-class political and industrial institutions', that presses particularly upon our reading of the novel now, and lends it a particular pathos. We seem to be in the extraordinary position of the emergent element in a whole social formation passing to the residual without ever going through the phase of being dominant.

Perhaps Williams's own experience of 'neighbourhood', as realised at least in *Border Country*, was always too atypical of working-class life to be capable of the wider generalisation that he wished for it; or rather, it is precisely more typical working-class neighbourhoods, reliant on heavy or manufacturing industry, that have been most put under pressure by the social transformations of the past 50 years. In addition to the brute demographic changes indicated above, we can add of course the massive political defeats of the Labour and Trade Union movements, and the all-but-complete erosion of social housing initiated above all by the right-to-buy policies of the 1980s.

The story that many working-class people tell about these changes, we know, is one about immigration or race. Race is largely absent from *Border Country*, though the editorial introduction to this edition of *Key Words* alludes to the suggestive moment which opens the novel: Matthew Price finds in the easy friendliness of a West Indian bus conductress an antidote to the stuffiness of England, and by extension a reminder of that friendliness in the Welsh community that he has left. Dai Smith in his biography stresses the submerged question of Welshness as one that was always present for Williams, even though it emerged much more fully later in his career. The national question, therefore, in the context of the 'break-up of Britain', can be seen as already present in the novel, and the novel's insistence, from its title onwards, of 'border crossing' as an essential way of understanding the constitution of individuals and communities, becomes more salient in the light of the history subsequent to its publication.[17] Nevertheless, the sense of community that the novel seeks largely to create as a political value in the Britain contemporary to it, is now necessarily accompanied by a sense of loss.

It may be, however, that that sense of pathos created by benefit of hindsight is too premature, and that we can revert to the sense of contradictions within working-class life, so prominent in *Border Country*, to come up with a harder-edged perspective on the novel and its current situation. I am struck again by the terms of Jack Meredith's exchange with Harry Price: "'One thing I've learned, I'll tell you. That's every man for himself. Nobody else will help you.' 'That's what you made out then. That's what's happening now.'" I suggested earlier that the novel finally subsumes such complexities within its more widely affirmative account of working-class life, though it is careful not in any sense to resolve them by a narrative outcome that reconciles Meredith to his neighbours, or which softens the entrepreneurialism of Morgan Rosser. Reading with hindsight has this striking advantage: what appear as latencies or possibilities in a text's originating moment appear illuminated, strengthened, and made more salient by the subsequent social history; the rhetorical economy of a text, which weights one outcome against another and allows one value to predominate over another, is radically disturbed in the light of the text's unanticipated futures. We can therefore see some of the changes in the political economy of the working class as extensions of the attitudes adumbrated by Williams but seen as subordinate by him to the more politically benign realities that he saw to be central. Certainly the notion of 'every man for himself' was one that was consciously promoted in the 1980s, and the right-to-buy policy undoubtedly played to a spirit, if not exactly of 'manly independence', then one of individual rights over social good. So the history of the British working class over the last 50 years certainly could be told as a story in which attitudes recognised by Williams are ones which have become greatly more prevalent, and the entrepreneurialism indicated by the characterisation of Morgan Rosser has perhaps been a part of that story, whether or not characterised by disillusion with the failures of working-class solidarity and the Labour Party or other parties of the left. The aesthetic distinctiveness of *Border Country*, then, is in part based on its capacity to give vivid realisation to the implicit tensions and contradictions within the working-class and family life that it depicts. The dissolution and reconstitution of the British working class over the last 50 years exaggerates this effect, making more salient, as we read the novel with hindsight, those places where the actual subsequent history has exploited attitudes and possibilities that Williams allows to be visible but keeps socially subordinate.

Williams's assumption, in the late fifties and early sixties, that a future British socialism would be built on the basis of existing social, communal and political forms of working-class life has seemed impossible to sustain. Nevertheless, as the destruction wrought by neo-liberalism continually destroys actually existing communities and solidarities, the novel's capacity to provide a sense of what 'community' means, in recognisably realist terms, gives the novel a force that can be recognised beyond the pathos that surrounds it. In contradiction to some of the more sentimental accounts of the 'white working class', the account that the novel provides is one of genuine community that is, for all that, riven by contradiction; this has its own 'realistic utopianism' in the present context – a formulation that acknowledges the capacity of reading from the past to bear its own testimony to other social possibilities than the *pensée unique* of the present. To find in *Border Country* a utopianism based on complexity rather than simplification is in the spirit of Williams;[18] it is the obverse of the historicist gesture which equally correctly sees in the novel a particular response to its own moment.

Notes

1 John Lucas, 'Debate: Raymond Williams Novelist?', *Key Words: A Journal of Cultural Materialism* 6 (2008): 16–22.
2 Raymond Williams, *Politics and Letters* (London: New Left Books, 1979), 277–85; Dai Smith, *Raymond Williams: A Warrior's Tale* (Cardigan: Parthian, 2008).
3 Smith, *A Warrior's Tale*, 1.
4 Tom Maschler, ed. *Declaration* (London: MacGibbon and Kee, 1957).
5 Williams's case about realism is made most fully in the chapter 'Realism and the Contemporary Novel', in *The Long Revolution* (London: Chatto and Windus, 1961), 274–89.
6 The sometimes unexamined Popular Front assumptions about the cultural value of the great bourgeois realist novel are apparent in 'A small personal voice'. Williams's distance from these traditional Communist Party assumptions is apparent, though Francis Mulhern

has argued that such assumptions are a partially hidden intertext for the arguments of *Culture and Society* (1958), whose publication immediately preceded *Border Country*, but whose composition was mostly contemporaneous with it. See Francis Mulhern, 'Culture and Society: Then and Now', *New Left Review* 55 (January / February 2009): 31–45.
7 Ernst Bloch, et al., *Aesthetics and Politics*, with an afterword by Fredric Jameson (London: New Left Books, 1977).
8 Fredric Jameson, 'Reflections in Conclusion', in *Aesthetics and Politics*, 196–213, at 211.
9 See Raymond Williams, *The English Novel from Dickens to Lawrence* (London: Chatto and Windus, 1970).
10 I discuss some of these issues in 'Tone of Voice in Industrial Writing in the 1930s', in *British Industrial Fictions*, ed. H. Gustav Klaus and Stephen Knight (Cardiff: University of Wales Press, 2000), 99–111. An excellent survey of this fiction is to be found in Andy Croft, *Red Letter Days: British Fiction in the 1930s* (London: Lawrence and Wishart, 1990).
11 Raymond Williams, 'Fiction and the Writing Public', *Essays in Criticism* VII, no. 4 (1957): 422–8 (427–8).
12 Raymond Williams, *Border Country* (London: The Hogarth Press, 1988 [1960]). All subsequent references in the text are to this edition.
13 Raymond Williams, 'Culture is Ordinary' (1958), in *Resources of Hope*, ed. Robin Gable (London: Verso, 1989), 8.
14 See for example Phillip Blond, *Red Tory: How Left and Right have Broken Britain and How We Can Fix It* (London: Faber and Faber, 2010); Roger Scruton: *England: An Elegy* (London: Chatto and Windus, 2000); and for a response to these, and to the current Conservative notion of the Big Society, see Jonathan Rutherford, 'The future is conservative', *Soundings* 47 (Spring 2011), 54–64.
15 Owen Jones, *Chavs: The Demonization of the Working Class* (London: Verso, 2011); Michael Collins, *The Likes of Us: A Biography of the White Working Class* (London: Granta Books, 2004).
16 Wendy Bottero, 'Class in the 21st Century', in *Who Cares about the White Working Class?*, ed. Kjartan Páll Sveinsson (London: Runnymede Trust, 2009), 7–15 (8–9).
17 Tom Nairn, *The Break-up of Britain: Crisis and Neo-nationalism* (London: New Left Books, 1977). Nairn unsurprisingly writes more strongly on the Scottish than the Welsh situation, but the various crises around the national question to which he alluded have in different ways deepened since he wrote.
18 See Williams's comment that 'a higher socialist form will not only have to meet as complex difficulties as these; it will have to be more complex' (*Politics and Letters*, 433).

Raymond Williams in Japan

A series of articles by contemporary Japanese critics, edited and introduced by Daniel G. Williams, with an afterword by Dai Smith

Introduction: Travelling Williams
Daniel G. Williams

It gives me great pleasure to introduce the following series of five articles on Raymond Williams by Japanese scholars. They derive from three events held in Swansea and Tokyo. The papers by Shinatro Kono and Takashi Onuki collected here were first delivered on 16 October 2009 at a one-day conference entitled 'Raymond Williams in Transit: Wales – Japan', arranged by CREW (The Centre for Research into the English Literature and Language of Wales) at Swansea University, and supported by the JSPS/MEXT Grant-in-Aid for Scientific Research. Their papers were supplemented at the event with a comparative account of Welsh and Japanese coalfield societies by Swansea historian Chris Williams, and a discussion of the role of Wales in the imaging of industrial society in contemporary Japanese animator Miayzaki's film 'Laputa: Castle in the Sky' by Gwenno Ffrancon of the Department of Media Studies at Swansea University. The papers by Yasuhiro Kondo and Yuzo Yamada were presented on 25 September 2010 at a follow-up event held at Japan Women's University, Mejiro Campus, entitled 'Fiction as Criticism / Criticism as a Whole Way of Life', which also included papers on Williams's fiction by Tony Pinkney, Dai Smith and Daniel G. Williams. Yasuo Kawabata, who was primarily responsible for arranging that event, kindly agreed to contribute a recent paper on *The Fight for Manod* to this special issue of *Key Words*. The conference on 25 September was preceded by a symposium on 23 September entitled 'Raymond Williams in the 1950s' at which Hideaki Suzuki, Fuhito Endo, Takashi Onuki and Shintaro Kono presented papers. The events in Japan were hosted by the Raymond Williams Kenkyukai (The Society for Raymond Williams Studies in Japan), with the support of the Faculty of Humanities at Japan Women's University, and the JSPS/MEXT Grant-in-Aid for Scientific Research.[1]

These essays, and the events from which they developed, illustrate the truth of Edward Said's observation that 'like people and schools of criticism, ideas and theories travel – from person to person, from situation to situation, from one period to another'.[2] What happens, Said asked, to a theory developed in one geographical location and within one field of study when

> in different circumstances and for new reasons, it is used again and, in still more different circumstances, again? What can this tell us about the theory itself – its limits, its possibilities, its inherent problems – and what can it suggest to us about the relationship between theory and criticism, on the one hand, and society and culture on the other?[3]

In broad terms, these are the questions indirectly addressed in this series of essays. What form does Raymond Williams's writing take in Japan today? What aspects of his work are selected for analysis? Which dimensions of his thought are seen to have relevance? Drawing on the work of Masao Miyoshi, Edward Said argued in *Culture and Imperialism* that despite the country's 'staggering financial resources', Japan was lacking in any 'international cultural power' due to the impoverished nature of Japanese 'verbal culture – dominated by talk shows, comic books, relentless conferences and panel discussions'.[4] There's more than a touch of Said's characteristic high-cultural elitism informing his analysis here. The remarkable and distinct phenomenon of *manga* cannot be easily dismissed as 'comic-book culture' in the sense in which that phrase is used in the United States or Britain. As Asada Akira has noted, there were forms of *manga* that contributed to student unrest in the 1960s, and deviant *manga* for girls challenging sexual norms in the 1970s, while today gender and ecological issues can be found reflected in *manga*, as well as extreme forms of masculinism and ultra-nationalism.[5] Said's overall diagnosis of Japan as a country which witnesses 'an absolute disparity between the total novelty and global dominance in the economic sphere, and the impoverishing retreat and dependence on the West in cultural discourse' was only partially reinforced by the Japanese contributors to the three events that formed a basis for this collection of essays, for they also noted that such generalisations inevitably glossed over the real complexities of culture and society.[6] A wide variety of themes and approaches are contained within this collection, and though I cannot claim any expertise in Japanese politics or culture, I will attempt to make a few generalisations of my own by way of introduction. What follows is drawn from my involvement in the events which formed a basis for this special issue, and my discussions and interviews with the participants.

Firstly, it is striking that several of the pieces collected here draw on Williams's own etymological approach in order to analyse the layers of meaning, and semantic residues, within words. Onuki and Kono explore the different meanings of 'action' and 'culture' respectively, and draw on the multiple forms that these words take in Japanese to develop some of Williams's own insights. The appeal of Williams's work for Onuki was that 'his writing is not based on technical terminology but on common vocabulary. The keywords of his seminal text also play vital roles in our everyday lives: words such as "action", "communication", "experience", "feeling", and "structure".[7] *Keywords* is also a key text for Kono, who notes that:

> It is the most accessible book, and at the same time the most difficult text to really understand its implications. As I've shown in relation to the word 'culture' in my article, to have more than one language is really an

advantage in thinking about the social significance of the transformations of words, because one is forced to be conscious of multi-layered meanings in a given word. In my teaching I ask Japanese students to read *Keywords*, and ask them to think about the meanings of a given word both in English and Japanese.[8]

Asada Akira noted some time ago that Japanese literary criticism was 'always crucial to the definition of collective meanings in the wider culture'.[9] The contemporary literary scene in Japan is characterised by 'a return to interiority' according to Akira, following a familiar sense of political disillusion after the more militant 1960s.[10] Onuki argues that since the 1990s

> English literary studies in Japan have been in a state of crisis due to their over-professionalization. Some scholars are using post-structuralist theories quite efficiently; others feel alienated by this trend and try to avoid such theories by analyzing literary texts as if they were philologists or historians. In any case, it can be said that English literary scholars lost their influence on ordinary people, who could not understand the writings produced by either of these groupings and, naturally, came to be disinterested in it.[11]

Kono picks up the narrative in relation to our current moment:

> Around the turn of the century and into the twenty-first century, as stark economic inequalities and exploitation under neoliberalism and globalisation become apparent, there seems to be a renewed call for new political criticism. In fact, there emerged in Japan a new generation of rather radical and oppositional critics with some anarchist tendencies. I'm not sure what will result from these moves, but it is at least certain that we need literary/cultural theory which addresses the present situation. In this context, structuralism and poststructuralism emerge as something that poses serious limitations.[12]

In a narrative that is all too familiar, and perhaps in need of questioning, it seems that the older role of criticism, and its connections to 'collective meanings in the wider culture', has broken down. Williams seems to offer a model of social commitment and, in a context where poststructuralist approaches have been dominant, offers an alternative basis for literary study in Japan's English departments. Kondo selects Williams's early *Reading and Criticism* as a text to which we should return at this juncture for 'though Terry Eagleton regarded it as the typical manifestation of "Left Leavisism", the very foundation of Williams's radical critique of not only literature but also culture and society are to be found here'.[13] Kono, Onuki and Kondo referred to the fact that though Raymond Williams's name was known in Japan, he was very rarely read. They suggested that part of the reason for this lay with the attack mounted on Williams's humanism by Terry Eagleton in *Criticism and Ideology* (1976) – a text which had a considerable following and influence on the left in Japan.[14] Williams was consequently seen as a voice from the 'Left-Leavisite' past. In seeking to (re-)engage the world of literary criticism with that of the 'collective meaning of the wider culture' the new generation of critics represented in the essays that follow are returning to Williams and reading his works anew.[15]

If Williams's emphasis on the materiality of language is of particular significance in the pieces that follow, then so too is his fiction. It is clear from the writings of Kawabata, Kondo and Yamada that Williams's fiction is seen as a central dimension of his oeuvre in Japan. Despite Williams's insistence that his novels were central to his work, English critics have been reluctant to take the fiction seriously. Dai Smith's 2008 biography *The Warrior's Tale* has shifted the focus decisively towards the fiction, reflecting a broader tendency in Wales to give this aspect of Williams's writing its due.[16] It is therefore also interesting that Williams's location as a Welsh writer is an issue of particular interest to Yamada and Kondo. Kawabata (a senior academic who was the primary organiser of the events in Japan which formed the basis for this collection) explores the struggle to articulate a Utopian vision in *The Fight for Manod* (1979), and sees the difficulties that characters have in finding a new language for their new environment reflected in the teasing appearance of unsolved mysteries in Williams's fictions. In connecting Williams's notion of 'complex seeing' to Fredric Jameson's recent writing on the dialectic, Yasuhiro Kondo creates a theoretical context in which to explore the complex relationships between the main protagonist, Gwyn, and his true and adopted fathers, Norman and Bert, in *Loyalties* (1985). Both Kono and Yamada offer comparative readings of Williams's writings, bringing his work into illuminating dialogue with Japanese writers Soseki Natsume and Ishimure Michiko respectively.

As Yamada makes clear in his article, and as Kono revealed in an interview, personal experiences lie behind both the comparative nature of their essays, and their attraction to Williams's work. Kono notes that

> there was a great resonance between the experience of Williams as someone who was born in the Welsh border country and went up to Cambridge to read literature, and my experience of being brought up in the western part of Japan and going up to Tokyo to complete my education. This resonance is, as I've found out, not only personal but historical and general. Paradoxically, it is Williams's 'Welsh experience' that makes him general – even universal.[17]

The use of this kind of experience as the basis for comparative analysis has been pursued under the controversial banner of 'postcolonialism' in recent years. Raymond Williams was one of the first critics to describe Wales as being both part of an imperial British state and a 'post-colonial' nation, 'conscious all the time of its own real strengths and potentials, longing only to be itself, to become its own world but with much, too much on its back to be able, consistently, to face its real future'.[18] Japan has been described by Gavan McCormack as a 'client state', as 'one that enjoys the formal trappings of Westphalian sovereignty and independence, and is therefore neither a colony nor a puppet state, but which has internalized the requirement to give preference to "other" interests over its own'.[19] In relation to Japan and Wales, where neither of the subjects of comparison are unambiguously 'postcolonial', Joe Cleary's approach to Ireland is useful. Cleary notes that while questions relating to 'geo-cultural location and constitutional statute' are important in the postcolonial debate, they are not the decisive issues.[20] For if

> colonialism is conceived as an historical process in which societies of various kinds and locations are differentially integrated into a world capitalist system, then it is on the basis of the comparative conjunctural analysis of such processes that debate must ultimately be developed.[21]

The point then is not to adduce whether Japan or Wales are 'just like' each other (they are obviously not), or whether they are like any other more unambiguously 'colonial' situation, but to 'think of the ways in which specific national configurations are always the product' of the 'dislocating intersections between local and global processes' that characterise the workings of capitalism.[22] Yamada's notion of the 'far West' regions of Britain and Japan seems a fruitful model for developing such readings, as is Kono's highly suggestive analysis of the multi-layered conceptions of culture created by the mobility and social transformations of modernity. Their essays seem to substantiate an emergent, comparative, way of thinking.

Following the symposium 'Raymond Williams in the 1950s', Shintaro Kono and I raced over to Bunkamura Orchard Hall in Tokyo to witness the opening concert of jazz pianist Keith Jarrett's 'Japan Tour 2010'. In a recent interview, when asked about his recording of American classical composer Lou Harrison's *Piano Concerto*, Jarrett recalled:

> That was actually supposed to be a documentary recording, but it became an official New World release because Naoto Otomo and the New Japan Philharmonic knew what to do with the drum part. Everybody else that played this piece was informed by the way classical percussionists always

worry that they shouldn't protrude from the texture. And there's the koto drummer tradition over there. At first I couldn't figure out why the hell this music had finally come to life, and it occurred to me that they have a drum tradition we don't have. Over there, if a classical percussionist sees forte or whatever Lou might have written on their part, they go for it. Over here, they would diminish the attack. The first time I played it was with Dennis Russell Davies and the American Composers Orchestra, and I expected it to be really good. But I almost didn't even notice the drums in the 'Stampede,' and that's the biggest thing in that movement![23]

The passage can be seen as a lesson in the way in which cultural works are affected by the contexts of their reception and performance. While rhythm and drumming are often the weakest aspects of the Western classical tradition, the drum tradition in Japan allowed for new dimensions of Harrison's composition to become apparent. I think it can be argued, in conclusion, that something similar happens to the writings of Raymond Williams in this collection of essays by Japanese scholars. New elements of Williams's writings are brought to the fore in these essays, as his political commitment and cultural vision create the bass lines on which the five Japanese critics collected here improvise a rich superstructure of ideas and insights.

Notes

1. Tony Pinkney has written a report on the events in Tokyo on the Raymond Williams Society website: http://www.raymondwilliams.co.uk/ [accessed 15 December 2010].
2. Edward Said, *The World, The Text and the Critic* (Cambridge MA: Harvard University Press, 1983), 226.
3. Said, *The World*, 230.
4. Edward Said, *Culture and Imperialism* (London: Vintage, 1994), 400.
5. Asada Akira, 'In the Place of Nothingness', *New Left Review* 5 (September/October 2000), 39.
6. Said, *Culture and Imperialism*, 400. A discussion of Said and Japan can be found in Daisuke Nishihara, 'Said, Orientalism, and Japan', *Alif: Journal of Comparative Poetics* 25 (2005), 241–53.
7. Interview with Takashi Onuki. 24 September 2010.
8. Interview with Shintaro Kono, 24 September 2010.
9. Akira, 'In the Place of Nothingness', 34.
10. Akira, 'In the Place of Nothingness', 36.
11. Interview with Onuki.
12. Interview with Kono.
13. Interview with Kondo, 25 September 2010.
14. Terry Eagleton, *Criticism and Ideology* (London: Verso: 1976).

15 In this respect the contemporary interest in Raymond Williams may be seen to parallel novelist Kenzaburo Oé's interest in the most socially committed of all Welsh poets, R.S. Thomas. See Oé's novel *Somersault*, trans. Philip Gabriel (London: Grove Press, 2003).
16 Dai Smith, *Raymond Williams: A Warrior's Tale* (Cardigan: Parthian, 2008).
17 Interview with Kono.
18 Raymond Williams, 'Welsh Culture', in *Who Speaks for Wales: Nation, Culture, Identity*, ed. Daniel Williams (Cardiff: University of Wales Press, 2003), 9.
19 Gavan McCormack, 'Obama vs. Okinawa', *New Left Review* 64 (July/August 2010): 25.
20 Joe Cleary, *Outrageous Fortune: Capital and Culture in Modern Ireland* (Dublin: Field Day Publications, 2006), 45.
21 Cleary, *Outrageous Fortune*, 45.
22 Cleary, *Outrageous Fortune*, 46.
23 Ethan Iverson interviews Keith Jarrett, 'Do the Math' website http://dothemath.typepad.com/dtm/interview-with-keith-jarrett.html [accessed 15 December 2010].

Soseki Natsume, Raymond Williams, and the Geography of 'Culture'
Shintaro Kono

Travelling Culture

This essay[1] is an attempt at exploring the relevance of Raymond Williams in Japan, and for the study of Japanese modernity, by comparing his work with that of the Japanese novelist Soseki Natsume. Before proceeding, it will be helpful to elucidate what the word 'culture' might signify in a Japanese context, for the word followed a curious trajectory when it was translated into Japanese – a trajectory that will reveal some aspects of modernity in general.

There is no one word in Japanese that corresponds squarely to the word 'culture'. Basically, we have different words for the various meanings that the word 'culture' has in English. For the sake of simplicity, let's look at some definitions of the word and see which translation corresponds to which definition.

> 1-a. the arts and other manifestations of human intellectual achievement regarded collectively (a city lacking in culture).
> 1-b. a refined understanding of this; intellectual development (a person of culture).
> 2. the customs, civilization, and achievements of a particular time or people.
> 3. improvement by mental or physical training.
> 4-a. the cultivation of plants; the rearing of bees, silkworms, etc.
> 4-b. the cultivation of the soil.
> 5. a quantity of micro-organisms and the nutrient material supporting their growth.

In Japanese, the most general term for 'culture' is *bunka*. It covers various meanings, but of the five definitions from the dictionary, *bunka* corresponds to the definitions 1-a and 2. Depending on the context, *bunka* can also mean 1-b. But for definition 1-b, which has highly charged implications in the Arnoldian tradition, we have the word *kyouyou*, which can signify 'culture' in this meaning, and 'education' or 'sophistication', again according to the context. For definition 3, we have *shuuyou* or *kunren*, the former being exclusively for the cultivation of human personality and the latter a general term for training or discipline.

In addition to the current usages of the word, it is important to introduce the etymology of the word *bunka*. According to *Nihon gogen dai-jitenn* (*A*

Dictionary of Japanese Etymology),[2] the word *bunka* has been in the Japanese language since it was imported from Chinese. In the Meiji period (in the late nineteenth century), it was employed as an equivalent of the word 'civilisation'. At present, 'civilisation' is normally translated as *bunmei*, a word that was also present in the Japanese language well before the Meiji Restoration. The result was that we had both *bunmei* and *bunka* as the translations of 'civilisation' at that time. Around the turn of the twentieth century, however, with the proliferation of German philosophy in Japanese society, *bunka* began to be used as the translation of the German word *kultur*. At that dividing moment of *bunka* and *bunmei*, culture and civilisation, it is highly important to note that the division involved a certain evaluative hierarchy quite different from the division wrought, for instance, by F.R. Leavis in *Mass Civilisation and Minority Culture* (1930). And this difference derives directly from, as it were, each country's geopolitical configuration of modernity. Generally speaking, the word civilisation, or *bunmei*, has not had the negative connotation suggested by Leavis, but when the word culture, or *bunka* or *kyouyou*, was used with positive connotations, it has always been in relation to the concept of 'culture' in the West. Indeed, culture, or *kyouyou*, has never ceased to be something Western, and continues to be so today. As we will see, such a geopolitical configuration in the word 'culture' informs Japanese modernity at large. Nowhere is this more clearly shown than in Soseki Natsume's *Sanshiro*.

Soseki Natsume and *Sanshiro*

Kin'nosuke Natsume, later known by his pen name Soseki Natsume, was born into a wealthy family in Ushigome, Shinjuku, Tokyo in 1867. In his school days Natsume excelled in English and he entered the English Department of Tokyo Imperial University (now the University of Tokyo) in 1890. During his college days, he met Shiki Masaoka, a prominent haiku poet, and learned haiku. After graduating from the university, he was sent by the Japanese government to England, first to Cambridge and then to London. His London years were miserable, spent alone in his flat reading Dickens or Thackeray, and he descended to being on the verge of a nervous breakdown. In fact, his mental condition had not been very good before he went to England, and it is said that this was due partly to his difficulties in his married life and partly to his scepticism and discomfort as a Japanese writer dedicating his time to the study of English literature. Rumour of his condition moved the Japanese government to call him back to Japan in 1903, where he was appointed to a teaching position at Tokyo Imperial University, as successor to Lafcadio Hearn. His job there was not without trouble, and he again suffered from nervous depression, which is said to have led him to write his first novel, *I Am a Cat*. Before his death in 1916, he wrote fourteen novels, ten shorter fictions, essays, haiku and poems and the Japanese one-thousand-yen bills bear his impression today. In this essay, I want to focus on *Sanshiro*, Soseki's seventh novel published in book form in 1909.

Sanshiro is a story about the eponymous hero going up from Kumamoto, a prefecture in the Kyushu Island in western Japan, to study at university in Tokyo. Kumamoto is at the western end of Japan, and the journey from there to Tokyo is roughly 870 miles. As it is a story of a young man encountering a new environment and growing up, the novel can be described as a *bildungsroman*, but taking into account the fact that the duration of the story is only four months and the emphasis is on describing the everyday world of a young scholar in Tokyo, it could be called a novel of manners, or a 'condition of Japan' novel.

Whatever the case may be (the genre of this novel will be dealt with as a crucial problem in its own right later in this essay), the first part of the novel, in which Sanshiro takes a ferry and a train to go up to Tokyo, is worth focusing upon. Here, we see at work 'culture' in the overdetermined senses described above. Sanshiro's journey is not just a spatial movement, but an imaginary journey between what Sanshiro himself later calls 'three worlds':

> Three worlds took shape for Sanshiro. One of them was far away and had the fragrance of the past, of what Yojiro called the years before Meiji fifteen. Everything there was tranquil, yes, but everything was drowsy, too. [...] He felt a twinge of remorse when it occurred to him that he had buried his dear mother there as well. Only when her letters came did he linger awhile in this world, warm with nostalgia.
>
> In his second world stood a mossy brick building. It had a reading room so vast that, standing in one corner, he could not discern the features of people in the other. There were books shelved so high they could not be reached without a ladder, books blackened with the rubbing of hands, the oil of fingers, books whose titles shone with gold. There was sheepskin, cowhide, paper of two hundred years past, and piled on all of these, dust. It was precious dust, dust that took twenty, even thirty years to accumulate, dust more silent than all those silent days and months. [...]
>
> Sanshiro's third world was as radiant and fluid as spring, a world of electric lights, of silver spoons, of cheers and laughter, of glasses bubbling over with champagne. And crowning everything were beautiful women. Sanshiro had

spoken to one of them, he had seen another twice. This world was for him the most profound.³

One of the three worlds is his native region, Kumamoto, whose warmth is left behind by the modernity represented by the other two worlds. The other two worlds are the two faces of the metropolis, Tokyo, which Sanshiro encounters in the novel. One is represented by the university, 'a mossy brick building' and books thick with dust. This is Tokyo as the centre of culture and education; that is, as the centre of *kyouyou*. Here, as mentioned above, *kyouyou* is imbued with Western culture, as represented by hardbound books, most of which are presumably in English or German. And the other face of Tokyo is the Tokyo which is 'as radiant and fluid as spring'; that is, Tokyo as a place of commercialised culture. Here, we might do well to remember the distinction that F.R. Leavis made between minority culture and mass civilisation. In the case of *Sanshiro*, however, mass civilisation, represented by drinking bouts or women, is quite as fascinating as minority culture, or the world of university. Furthermore, the presence of the first world, that is, his home country, complicates and even undermines Leavis's dichotomy. In terms of temporality, Kumamoto is definitely past, and the latter two worlds, which are located in Tokyo, belong to the present or the future. Sanshiro's journey is spatial and temporal, real and imaginary at the same time, and it is a movement from the periphery to the centre, the centre not only of Japan but of the world: that is to say, the West.

Not only that: the railway Sanshiro takes also leads to the Japanese Empire. Here, it is interesting that the hierarchy of empires, that is, of the Japanese Empire and the various Western empires, is represented in sexual as well as racial terms. The narrative of *Sanshiro* begins in Kyoto, where he meets a woman who got on the train there. She is described as follows:

> She was very dark, almost black. The ferry had brought him from Kyushu, and as the train drew closer to Hiroshima, then Osaka and Kyoto, he had watched the complexions of the local women turning lighter and lighter, and before he knew it he was homesick. Then she had entered the car, and he felt he had gained an ally of the opposite sex. She was a Kyushu-color woman.⁴

From the conversation between this woman and an old man in the same compartment, Sanshiro learns that she has a husband who is in Dalian (or *Dairen* in Japanese). Dalian, China, was a territory leased to Japan as the result of the armistice treaty between Japan and Russia; in other words, as a result of an imperial war.⁵

The train stops at Nagoya, Aichi, and there the woman asks Sanshiro to escort her to her inn. There, it happens that the innkeeper misunderstands their relationship and they are obliged to stay in the same room. Sanshiro, still sexually immature at the age of 23, rolls a futon sheet and makes a partition between him and the woman, and goes to sleep. (Whether he had a sound sleep or not, the novel doesn't tell.) When they part at the station, the woman says to him, 'You're quite a coward, aren't you?'[6]

This episode with the Kyushu-coloured woman makes a sharp contrast with the next scene, in which Sanshiro encounters a high-school teacher, Hirota. Throughout the novel, Hirota occupies a privileged place as someone who possesses real culture, or *kyouyou*, which transcends the West-oriented and philistine culture then and since prevalent in Japan. And at the same time, Hirota is immune from nationalistic feelings as the simple reversal of such snobbism. That he occupies such a position is foretold by an incident at Hamamatsu, Shizuoka. There, waiting for the train to start, Sanshiro and Hirota witness a group of 'Westerners' loitering around on the platform. It is important that their nationality is not specified and they are generalised as 'Westerners'. It is, so to speak, a case of inverted Orientalism. Sanshiro is attracted to them:

> Foreigners as colorful and attractive as these were not only something quite new for Sanshiro, they seemed to be of a higher class. He stared at them, entranced. Arrogance from people like this was understandable. He went so far as to imagine himself travelling to the West and feeling very insignificant among them.[7]

Hirota, seemingly reading Sanshiro's thoughts, states:

> 'We Japanese are sad-looking things next to them. We can beat the Russians, we can become a first-class power, but it doesn't make any difference. We've got still the same faces, the same feeble little bodies. [...] – Oh yes, this is your first trip to Tokyo, isn't it? You've never seen Mount Fuji. We go by it a little farther on. It's the finest thing Japan has to offer, the only thing we've got to boast about. The trouble is, of course, it's just a natural object. It's been sitting there for all time. We certainly didn't make it.' He grinned broadly once again.

Sanshiro had never expected to meet anyone like this after the Russo-Japan War. The man was almost not a Japanese, he felt.
'But still,' Sanshiro argued, 'Japan will start developing from now on at least.'

'Japan is going to perish,' the man replied coolly.
Anyone who dared say such a thing in Kumamoto would have been taken out and thrashed, perhaps even arrested for treason.[8]

It is not too much to say that virtually everything about the cultural geography of Japanese modernity is inscribed in this first sequence of *Sanshiro*. On Sanshiro's journey from the country to the city are layered such elements as past and present, Japan and the West, and Japan and its colonies. These elements are racialised and sexualised at the same time, as clearly seen in the figures of the Kyushu-coloured seducer and beautiful 'Westerners' at Hamamatsu. And above all, these elements are intertwined with 'culture' in all the senses I have described: *kyouyou*, which centres around the metropolis and by extension the West, *bunka* as denoting commercial and popular culture in Tokyo, the culture Sanshiro leaves behind in Kumamoto, and *shuuyou* which has further layered meanings in this case. It is sexual maturity on the one hand, and general personal development on the other. As I have said, Hirota is in the position to cancel and transcend all of these divisions, and precisely because he does so, he embodies *kyouyou* in the most liberal, enlightened – that is, paradoxically, the Western – sense.[9] And the power of Natsume Soseki is to make these elements converge into personal experience, in this case into the experience of Sanshiro. And I must confess that his experience, even after a century, still echoes with the experience of people like myself, who made the same journey as Sanshiro's, in my case from Yamaguchi (also in western Japan) to Tokyo. I venture to say that Sanshiro's experience, a city-migrant's experience, or the experience of being forced to be conscious of the multi-layered meanings of 'culture', is typical and paradigmatic of Japanese modernity.

Raymond Williams and the 'Problem' of Experience

Indeed, if we make a historical and geographical leap from Sanshiro's imaginary map, we could say that Sanshiro's map is also one which underlies Raymond Williams's works. I am tempted to say that Williams's criticism was formed and informed by his experience of going up to the city, and he shares the experience as a city-migrant with Sanshiro. In this regard, as Dai Smith's biography has shown, his criticism and his fiction can never be separated, and they have the same experience at the core.[10] Contrary to what is often said, Williams didn't only 'return' to Wales in his later years.[11] He was, throughout his career, always in the process of returning to his fundamental experience, and this process, and not the consummation of it, made up his writings. But here, a problem arises. The problem is about the word 'experience' itself. It may be worth returning to an early criticism mounted by Terry Eagleton in this connection. According to Eagleton, Williams's criticism is based on a Lukácsian belief that personal experience, when it is embedded deeply enough in society, can be described as 'typical'.[12] Hence his criticism of Williams as a Romantic humanist. Indeed, those who follow the tenets of poststructuralism may well be greatly perplexed by Williams's use of the word 'experience'. For example, in the interview with editors of *New Left Review*, Williams is asked, somewhat disapprovingly, about his use of the word 'community' in *Culture and Society* and about the lack of the problematics of imperialism and nationalism. He answers as follows:

> I think one of the reasons for this is that the particular experience which ought to have enabled me to think much more closely and critically about it was for various reasons at that time very much in abeyance: the Welsh experience. The way I used the term community actually rested on my memories of Wales, as I've said.[13]

In the interviewer's tone, we can detect some discomfort at Williams's affirmative use of the term community, but Williams wouldn't budge from his position. In a memorable passage from *Culture and Society* he noted that:

> If there is one thing certain about 'the organic community', it is that it has always gone. Its period, in the contemporary myth, is the rural eighteenth century; but for Goldsmith, in *The Deserted Village* (1770), it had gone; for Crabbe, in *The Village* (1783), it was hardly 'right and inevitable': for Cobbett, in 1820, it had gone since his boyhood (that is to say, it existed when Goldsmith and Crabbe were writing); for Sturt it was there until late in the nineteenth century; for myself (if I may be permitted to add this, for I was born into a village, and into a family of many generations of farm-labourers) it was there [...] in the 1930s.[14]

Does he simply mean that in his youth, in the community of the working class in Wales, there existed an organic community? Is he returning to his own experience to demonstrate that point? To answer these questions, we need to turn back to the 1930s, to the years that Williams refers to here, and consider who and what Williams was addressing.

Experiencing the Production of Modernity / Experiencing Distance

The 1930s, most of which Williams spent as a grammar school student in Abergavenny, was famously the founding decade of 'Cambridge English' represented by F.R. Leavis. The problematics and methods of his *Mass Civilisation and Minority Culture* and Q.D. Leavis's *Fiction and the Reading Public* (1932) were to have direct influence upon Williams and Richard Hoggart in the 1950s, which has given rise to a sometimes derogatory epithet 'Left Leavisism'. Left Leavisism, according to its detractors, is a simple reversal of the dichotomy of 'mass civilisation' and 'minority culture'. Where Leavis criticised the growing and alienated mass urban culture and tried to counter it with minority culture embedded in an ideal organic society – which amounts to the literary elite for Leavis – the invocation of popular culture or working-class culture as something unalienated or before alienation is based on the same logic: the logic of an organic community. This reversal is at the heart of the intellectual tradition leading to Cultural Studies.[15]

Raymond Williams doesn't fit such a schematisation. On the contrary, the passage I have quoted from *Culture and Society* cannot be understood without due consideration of his consciousness: the consciousness of his theoretical positioning against Leavis. Williams's use of the word 'experience' is perplexing. In the passage above, he does more than reverse the terms of Leavisism, and is saying more than that an organic society, like one's infancy, is 'always-already' lost, or that it is simply an ideology, or a false consciousness. Nor is he pitting a 'real' country against an imagined and idealised rural world. The reader of this passage is stranded between contradictory statements. On the one hand, the organic community 'has always gone', while, on the other, 'it was there'.

In *The Country and the City*, Williams states that in the late 1940s he was conscious of his separation from the village in which he had grown up,[16] and the effort to describe that experience took the shape of his novel, *Border Country*. In *Border Country*, Matthew's return leads to his recognition that the distance from his home has now been measured, resulting in a position where he can feel at one with his native place, without actually going home to live there. 'Not going back... but exile ending' as Matthew notes.[17] Compared with this, *Sanshiro* does not present transcendence through acceptance of exile, but only the beginning of exile. Sanshiro's last words are 'stray sheep' (in English) and it is a refrain from the words of Mineko, a liberated modern woman with whom Sanshiro falls in love but who marries her brother's friend. The phrase 'stray sheep' signals Sanshiro's loss of home and the beginning of his exile.

To return to *Border Country*, if we translate Matthew's words into Williams's theoretical terms, this novel can be said to be Williams's effort to 'measure the distance' from the organic community. In other words, the sense of 'experience' evoked in the above quotation from *Culture and Society* is not the experience of the real and substantial country, but the experience of the retrospective *construction* of it. And this is an experience that Williams shared with all the writers mentioned in the passage, and above all, with Leavis himself. It is precisely because this experience, the experience of the construction of an organic community, is a widely shared 'structure of feeling', that it is an idea worth examining. *Culture and Society* is this examination. It is the examination of the narrative, from the Romantics onwards, of the alienation from the organic community, and the overcoming of that crisis by moving beyond the binary opposition between a lost organic society and an alienated civilisation.

The project of *The Country and the City* can also be understood in these terms. It never celebrates rural culture as against urban culture, or working-class culture as against bourgeois culture. Its aim is to describe the forging of the opposition between country and city, past and future, the modern and the pre-modern, and the organic and the alienated, as a symptom and attempted resolution of the crisis of urban culture itself. In this sense, we can say that 'experience' for Williams is the experience of the production of modernity itself. Thus the last call in *The Country and the City* emerges as a real challenge for us:

> We can overcome division only by refusing to be divided. That is a personal decision but then a social action. I can only record what I have myself learned. Others will learn it quite differently. But I grew up, as I said, where the division was visible, in a land and then in a family. I moved from country to city, and now live and work in both.[18]

Here Williams emphasises the personal aspect of his argument, but from what I have traced so far, it should be seen as the general condition of modernity, as Williams himself states ten pages earlier:

> Most obviously since the Industrial Revolution, but in my view also since the beginning of the capitalist agrarian mode of production, our powerful images of country and city have been ways of responding to a whole social development. This is why, in the end, we must not limit ourselves to their contrast but go on to see their interrelations and through these the real shape of the underlying crisis.[19]

Thus, the division which Williams says was visible exclusively to him should be visible to us all, because it has been a response to 'a whole social development'. And finally, the 'experience' is also an experience of division and distance, division and distance that constitute modernity in a very deep sense.

'Double Vision' and the Question of Empirico-Transcendental Criticism

If so, how can we overcome divisions? How can we refuse to be divided? *Culture and Society* and *The Country and the City* were themselves, as we have seen, genealogies of various divisions that constitute modernity. I define 'genealogy' as a way of analysing how we have been historically contained by divisions, like country and city, so that we, at the present moment, can't see beyond those divisions. It is a paradoxical double move: *being* divided and at the very same time *seeing* that division. Here we touch upon the ultimate question of ideological criticism: It is a matter of being immanent and transcendent, empirical and transcendental at once. And it is one of the most important strands in Williams's criticism.[20]

This is especially the case in Williams's literary criticism, where we can see this strand most clearly by tracing the notion of 'double vision'. 'Double vision' is a phrase that Williams introduced in his book on Orwell.[21] It refers, in Orwell's case, to the position of being a colonial officer while criticising imperialism at the same time. *The English Novel from Dickens to Lawrence* is, surprisingly, a genealogy of double vision itself *as a structure of feeling*, without being named as such. About George Eliot, Williams writes: 'It is the emergence in the novel of that structure of feeling of the greatest Romantic poetry: at once a commitment to a personal vision and a passionate concern with the social experiences of ordinary life.'[22] Or about Hardy:

> He sees as a participant who is also an observer; this is the source of the strain. For the process which allows him to observe is very clearly in Hardy's time one which includes, in its attachment to class feelings and class separations, a decisive alienation.[23]

Daniel G. Williams, in his introduction to *Who Speaks for Wales*, quotes this passage as a prominent case of Williams's 'double vision'.[24] Here I want especially to emphasise that Raymond Williams saw double vision as a structure of feeling, and as it is a structure of feeling, it can be something forced and inevitable, 'the source of strain'. To make my point clear, we need to go on to the crux of the book: the chapter on Lawrence. This chapter is an account of how Lawrence went through the process of division and separation. In *Sons and Lovers*, William argues, there was no division between Lawrence as a participant and as an observer. But in *The Rainbow* and *Women in Love*, especially in the latter, separation sets in. Characteristically, Williams sees this shift in terms of language. We should see here again the geopolitics of 'culture' that we saw in *Sanshiro*. Separation for Lawrence – and for Williams – is the division between *bunka* and *kyouyou*. Double vision is, in this view, something *forced* on Lawrence to resolve the disparity between the language of his community and the educated language in which he narrates his stories. But we shouldn't see this as another Leavisite narrative of alienation. That is, Williams is not positing *Sons and Lovers* as an Eden before the fall. That is clearly foretold in the beginning of the chapter: 'We read the early works for signs of how the later ones came to be written. And this can leave out, obviously, other possible findings, such as failures to develop some particular early quality.'[25]

William was not looking for success in early works, but was rather trying to see how early promise failed. *The English Novel from Dickens to Lawrence* is not about how to overcome division, but about how the writers *failed* to do so. If Williams's book showed how double vision failed, or how double vision became a residual structure of feeling, this showing was *itself* a critical action. As the quotation above tells us, it was an attempt to rediscover the failures, those elements that were never developed. In other words, it was an attempt at identifying the 'residual' that had been hidden from our eyes by various divisions themselves. Indeed, Williams never dismissed double vision as a structure of feeling that had completely been lost. Rather, he tenaciously showed it at work in various – albeit in residual – forms; above all, in my view, in the form of his fiction. As the typescript quoted in Dai Smith's biography reveals, Williams's interest in the realist tradition in the novel was in 'the unique combination of that change in experience and in ideas which has been both [his] personal history and a general history of [his] generation.'[26] In this regard, *Border Country* can be, and must be, reread as a critical action just like his literary and cultural studies. In the same sense, *Border Country* can be regarded as a very *rearguard* novel, having to do with the residual form of double vision. But then, more specifically, what is the division which forced Williams to write *Border Country*? In Williams's own words, what is 'the real shape of the underlying crisis' in Williams's time? In the last section, I want to discuss, briefly, the problem of the genre and put *Border Country* in the context of a relatively new literary phenomenon in the 1950s; that is, the rise of the 'novels of initiation', which are to be clearly distinguished from the *Bildungsroman*.

Border Country as an Anti-Initiation Novel

Is *Sanshiro* a *Bildungsroman*? This question is germane to what I have been discussing so far, and my answer is no. Here, I won't go into the vast literature on *Bildungsroman* as a historical literary form, but will give a very simple definition of it, because I'm not trying to elaborate literary genres as such, or to evaluate *Border Country* by giving it some place in literary history, but to treat the emergence of a literary genre as a symptom of the vaster condition that both enabled and determined its form.[27] To do so, Williams's view of George Eliot will be of great help:

> George Eliot's novels are transitional between the form which had ended in a series of settlements, in which the social and economic solutions and the personal achievements were in a single dimension, and the form which, extending and complicating and then finally collapsing this dimension, ends with a single person going away on his own, having achieved his moral growth through distancing or extrication.[28]

As a form 'in which the social and economic solutions and the personal achievements were in a single dimension', Williams discusses briefly the so-called inheritance plot, the typical example of which is *Wuthering Heights*, which 'takes the crisis of inheritance at its full human value, without displacement to the external and representative attitudes of disembodied classes'.[29]

If *Bildungsroman* can be broadly defined as a narrative form which has to do with human development or growth, and if what Williams says is the case and there had been, before George Eliot, no individual human growth separated from its social and economic conditions, we can say that there was nothing in *Bildungsroman* that can be called inner personal or individual development in our modern sense. Rather, what we find is nothing more than upward class mobility. Compared with this, what I see as the rise of 'the novel of initiation' presents a complete break. The typical case I have in mind is Alan Sillitoe's first novel *Saturday Night and Sunday Morning* (1958).[30] An interesting thing about this work in the present context is that, much as it has been taken as a (working) class fiction, the protagonist's working-class life is nothing but a backdrop for his initiation into an adult life. That is, this novel is a complete reversal of *Bildungsroman* in the sense defined above. It knows no possibility of class mobility, but what is there is only the protagonist's inner growth through the course of the novel, for which his class-ridden life is a given, unchangeable 'environment', as Williams would have had it. But Sillitoe's novel is something quite different from what Williams had in mind when he saw in Eliot a transition to a new form. Rather, the words that Williams used to account for what *Wuthering Heights* is *not* might be a more appropriate description of this novel: 'displacement to the external and representative attitudes of disembodied classes'. This, I would contend, is one symptom of the 'division' in the 1950s. The proliferation of the novels of initiation signals the deepening of the process of individuation, so deep that one cannot even imagine a social change beyond what is given. And it is, at the very same time and at one stroke, the process of the severance of culture (in the sense of *shuuyou*, or personal cultivation) from society, or from classes as somehow changing and changeable knowable communities.

Broadly speaking, all this is applicable to the Angry Young Men in general, who established, in their own way, class politics as cultural politics, as distinct from social politics. In this respect, Peter J. Kalliney is right in defining class politics after the fifties less 'as a social and political reality' than 'as a symbolic condition'.[31] In his reading, Lessing's *The Golden Notebook*, for example, has no room for a social or economic solution to the protagonists' dilemma as a *Bildungsroman* would have done, but this is relegated to a cultural or psychological matter, with the result that class becomes only an anthropological marker; in this case that of 'things English'. (This 'anthropological turn', on which Esty and Kalliney construct their arguments, is precisely what Williams himself sensed in the shift of the meaning of the word 'culture', as the introduction to his *Keywords* shows.[32]) What Kalliney misses, however, in lumping together the Angry texts and the New Left texts into the broad historical field of imperial contraction and the redefinition of national boundaries, is the fact that the separation between the socio-political dimension and the cultural dimension of class politics has its partial origin in the 1950s, and still informs today's thinking about culture and society. And above all, what is missed is that Williams's 'cultural politics' was itself an action and intervention into the division of 'culture and society' specific to the fifties.[33] If the 1950s saw the division of class politics into the cultural and the socio-political elements, with the latter gradually obliterated from view, and if this crisis had a partial articulation in the form of the novel of initiation, the best way for us to read *Border Country* would be as an anti-initiation novel. This does not mean that it is against any form of initiation or human growth – on the contrary, *Border Country* does depict Matthew's initiation into a new mental condition. The novel may however be considered a generic intervention in that it offered an alternative model to the emerging novels of initiation in the fifties. Williams himself clearly states in *Politics and Letters*:

> The new forms of the fifties, to which many writers quickly turned, were usually versions of the novel of escape, which one part of Lawrence had prepared. Their theme was really escape from the working class – moving to the room at the top, or the experience of flight. They lacked any sense of the continuity of working-class life, which does not cease just because one individual moves out of it, but which also itself changed internally.[34]

Though in *Saturday Morning* Arthur never escapes from his working-class life, the emphasis here is not on the escape itself; but on the incapability to grasp internal changes in the working-class life itself, and to connect the experience of those changes to the changes in society in general. This explains why the counter-novel against this trend demands a protagonist who is in the position of at once forced and chosen double vision – like Matthew, a city migrant whose subject of study is demographic mobility. And above all, it is of great importance that Matthew is a scholarship boy like Williams himself, who embodies the ideal of liberal meritocracy under a welfare state.[35] In other words, he is someone who has experienced the liberating and at the same time uprooting effect of the welfare state. And, finally, as double vision, or the experience of 'distancing and extrication' was then already a residual structure of feeling, *Border Country* was a project to look for residual elements which constitutes the present-dominant – in other words, it was a genealogy of the present. (Hence its necessary structure of two plots, taking place in the past and the present.) Seen in this light, we can easily understand what came next after the genealogical investigations of *Border Country* and *Culture and Society*: *Second Generation* and *The Long Revolution*. It should be no surprise, from what I have been arguing, that in the unpublished conclusion of *The Long Revolution*, Williams displaces and extends the meaning of the word 'growth' and equates it with the process of the long revolution.[36] In this moving piece, Williams states that 'to make the long revolution active' is to see it 'as growth in every mind, as well as growth in the society.'[37] Williams sees the present as the result of the 'growth' through the preceding generations, and above all sees this process as incomplete, as still active. And *Border Country* is an investigation into this general 'growth', precisely by depicting the individual-social growth through generations. Matthew's individual growth is achieved by the very realisation that his growth is also 'growth in the society', because he feels that he has become stronger than his father by 'tak[ing] what is his'.[38] Furthermore, the death of Matthew himself is suggested at the very close of the novel, implying that this process is without an end. As he goes to his children's bedroom, his eyes look 'distant and clouded, as Harry's had been, standing in the living-room in Glynmawr'.[39]

In the light of the discussion so far, it should now be clear that *Sanshiro* is not a *Bildungsroman*. As the last phrase 'stray sheep' suggests, the novel is about modern individuation, and the solution provided in the novel can never be social nor economic, but cultural, in the sense of *kyouyou* and *shuuyou* in this case. In the course of the novel, Sanshiro is expected, in a certain limited way, to have transcended the metropolitan culture he has encountered, and this transcending act is precisely a form of *kyouyou*, as I have suggested. But that doesn't mean that *Sanshiro* properly belongs to the category of the novel of initiation. Sanshiro's experience marks a transitional moment after the Meiji Restoration, the beginning of Westernisation in Japan. So *Sanshiro* is a work that pursued a cultural solution to the material and general change in Japanese society.

My final question is whether the geographical-cognitive map of 'culture' in both works is applicable to our present situation. At first sight, it doesn't seem to be. Geographical mobility does not seem to be a matter of culture, but purely a matter of 'the mobility of labour force' under globalisation and neoliberalism.[40] Culture itself is under siege. Finance capitalism seems to have exacerbated and even completed the process of commodification and abstraction, to the extent that culture in all the senses discussed here seems to have nothing to offer to better our lives, let alone bringing about some change in our society.[41] Culture as education, or the meritocratic ideal which used to have a liberating impetus, seems to have been appropriated by the ideal of individual entrepreneurship.[42] But these merely *seem* to be so. The more the world seems dominated by some form of hegemonic power and ideology, the more we are in need of Williams's genealogical thinking to see 'the real shape of the underlying crisis', to see 'how the early promises failed', and to find in the residual the seeds of the future. My present essay itself has been such a genealogical endeavour, necessarily incomplete in itself, to see Raymond Williams as offering residual seeds for future growth.

Notes

1 Part of this essay has been published as 'Inaka mono no eibungaku: Raymond Williams to toshi bunka' ('English Literature for Rustics: Raymond Williams and Urban Culture') in *Eigo Seinen* (*The Rising Generation*) 151, no. 12 (March 2006), 10–13, and this essay is also based on a paper presented at the symposium 'Raymond Williams in Transit: From Wales to Japan' held at Swansea University on 16 October 2009, with substantial changes and additions. I am very grateful for the invitation to the conference and for the helpful comments provided.

2 Tomiyoshi Maeda (ed.), *Nihon gogen dai-jiten* (*The Dictionary of Japanese Etymology*) (Tokyo: Shogaku-kan, 2005).

3 Soseki Natsume, *Sanshiro: A Novel*, trans. Jay Rubin (Ann Arbor: Center for Japanese Studies, University of Michigan, 1977), 62–3.

4 Natsume, *Sanshiro*, 3.

5 Japan won the war thanks to Cardiff coal, and the territory that Japan acquired included a huge coalfield. See Yuuji Yamasaki, *Sekitan de sakae horonda daiei-teikoku* (*Coal and the Prosperity and the Decline of the British Empire*) (Kyoto: Minerva Shobo, 2008), 51–9.

6 Natsume, *Sanshiro*, 9.

7 Natsume, *Sanshiro*, 14.

8 Natsume, *Sanshiro*, 15.

9 It is a paradoxical feature of *kyouyou* or *kyouyou-shugi* (-*shugi* means -ism) that the denial of *kyouyou* itself is constitutive of *kyouyou-shugi*. In addition, Japanese *kyouyou-shugi* is also unique in that Marxist *kyouyou-shugi* has been (or had been) one of its leading vehicles. I

am not aware of any literature on this issue in English, but see Rieko Takada, *Gurotesukuna kyouyou (Culture: This Grotesque Thing)* (Tokyo: Chikuma Shobo, 2005).
10 Dai Smith, *Raymond Williams: A Warrior's Tale* (Cardigan: Parthian, 2008).
11 For example, the television documentary *Border Crossing: The Journey of Raymond Williams* (Dir. Colin Thomas, BBC, 2005), otherwise well made, concludes its narrative by arguing that Williams 'returned to Welshness'.
12 Terry Eagleton, *Criticism and Ideology: A Study in Marxist Literary Theory* (London: Verso, 1976), 22–3.
13 Raymond Williams, *Politics and Letters: Interviews with New Left Review* (London: New Left Books, 1979), 118.
14 Raymond Williams, *Culture and Society: 1780–1950* (New York: Columbia University Press, 1958), 259–60.
15 See, for example, Francis Mulhern, *Culture/Metaculture* (London: Routledge, 2000). It is to be noted that in recent studies on the relations between the New Left and 'Englishness', the same logic is at work. See for typical examples: Jed Esty, *A Shrinking Island: Modernism and National Culture in England* (Princeton: Princeton University Press, 2004) and Peter J. Kalliney, *Cities of Affluence and Anger: A Literary Geography of Modern Englishness* (Charlottesville: U of Virginia P, 2007).
16 Raymond Williams, *The Country and the City* (Oxford: Oxford University Press, 1973), 298.
17 Raymond Williams, *Border Country* (London: Chatto and Windus, 1960), 351.
18 Williams, *The Country and the City*, 306.
19 Williams, *The Country and the City*, 297.
20 Slavoj Žižek's notion of a 'parallax view', which is a view of antithetical and incompatible things – Kant's sensibility and understanding – at the same time, is quite close to double vision, but whereas Žižek sees the parallax view as a radical critical position to be achieved, Williams sees double vision as a structure of feeling – something that is already forced on us but hidden from sight. Slavoj Žižek, *The Parallax View* (Cambridge, Mass.: The MIT Press, 2006).
21 Raymond Williams, *George Orwell* (New York: Viking, 1971), 13.
22 Raymond Williams, *The English Novel from Dickens to Lawrence* (London: Chatto and Windus, 1970), 75.
23 Williams, *The English Novel*, 110.
24 Daniel Williams, 'Introduction', in Raymond Williams, *Who Speaks for Wales?: Nation, Culture, Identity*, ed. Daniel Williams (Cardiff: University of Wales Press, 2003).
25 Williams, *The English Novel*, 169.
26 Smith, *Raymond Williams: A Warrior's Tale*, 4.
27 Fredric Jameson, *The Political Unconscious: Narrative as a Socially Symbolic Act* (Ithaca: Cornell University Press, 1981). See also Fredric Jameson, 'Progress versus Utopia, or, Can We Imagine the Future?', *Archaeologies of the Future: The Desire Called Utopia and Other Science Fictions* (London: Verso, 2005), 281–95.
28 Williams, *The Country and the City*, 175.
29 Williams, *The Country and the City*, 176.
30 Apart from Sillitoe's novel, Doris Lessing's *Through the Tunnel* and, of course, William Golding's *Lord of the Flies* epitomise 1950s novels of initiation. The most important mediation between the nineteenth century novels and those of the 1950s is modernism and with it the general discourse concerning human interiority, including, above all, psychoanalysis. The key text in thinking about this mediation, in my view, is Williams's 'The Bloomsbury Fraction', *Culture and Materialism* (London: Verso, 2005), 148–69. This essay is sometimes seen as an example of Williams's aversion to high modernism (for

instance, by Patrick Brantlinger in '"The Bloomsbury Fraction" versus War and Empire', *Seeing Double: Revisioning Edwardian and Modernist Literature*, ed. Carola M. Kaplan and Anne B. Simpson [London: Macmillan, 1996], 149–67), but the emphasis in this essay is on how 'the notion of free individuals' became 'naturalized... in all later phases of English culture' (Williams, 'The Bloomsbury Fraction', 169). In other words, Williams saw modernism as avant-garde in terms of human individuation and dissociation from society, but something which had become naturalised (or became dominant) in the postwar culture of which Williams himself was a part. On the other hand, the most convincing explanation for the emergence of the novel of initiation in the U.S. in the 1940s and the 1950s would be the Cold War. On the liberalism of the Cold War era see Tobin Siebers, *Cold War Criticism and the Politics of Skepticism* (New York: Oxford University Press, 1993).

31 Kalliney, *Cities of Affluence and Anger*, 3.
32 Raymond Williams, *Keywords: A Vocabulary of Culture and Society*, rev. ed. (New York: Oxford University Press, 1983), 12.
33 The latest expression of this division of culture and society is what Nancy Fraser calls 'recognition-redistribution dilemma'. This impasse of left politics today is also epitomised by the Sokal affair, which Fraser mentions as a typical case representing the split between the social left and the cultural left (Nancy Fraser, *Justice Interruptus: Critical Reflections on the "Postsocialist" Condition* [New York: Routledge, 1997], 3). Of course, Sokal positions himself on the social left side, declaring himself as 'an unabashed Old Leftist' (Alan D. Sokal and Jean Bricmont, *The Fashionable Nonsense: Postmodern Intellectuals' Abuse of Science* [New York: Picador, 1998], 269). Interestingly, the direct predecessor of this affair is the 'Two Cultures' debate. For a detailed account of this debate, see Guy Ortolano, *The Two Cultures Controversy: Science, Literature and Cultural Politics in Postwar Britain* (Cambridge: Cambridge University Press, 2009).
34 Williams, *Politics and Letters*, 272.
35 It is to be noted that Leavis and Snow, both of whom were also scholarship boys, share the common ground of liberal meritocracy, despite their surface difference of position. See Ortolano and my 'Futatsu-no-bunka to han-kakumei, mataha, bungakuni "kiki" ha sonzai shinai (Two Cultures and the Counterrevolution, or, There Is No "Crisis" for Literature)', *Studies in English Literature* 2, The English Literary Society of Japan (2009): 307–16.
36 Raymond Williams, '"This actual growth"', quoted in Smith, *Raymond Williams: A Warrior's Tale*, 470–4.
37 Williams, '"This actual growth"', 473.
38 Williams, *Border Country*, 350.
39 Williams, *Border Country*, 351.
40 In this light, criticisms which take up the problem of mobility but do not take this into consideration require re-examination. For example, Paul Gilroy is very explicit that his emphasis is on culture, and not on material conditions which have sustained the alternative modernity (from a slave's point of view) which he delineates. Paul Gilroy, *The Black Atlantic: Modernity and Double Consciousness* (Cambridge, Mass.: Harvard University Press, 1993), 55.
41 For finance capital and its relation to postmodernism and the process of abstraction, see Fredric Jameson, *The Cultural Turn: Selected Writing on the Postmodern, 1983–1998* (London: Verso, 1998).
42 Kono, 'Futastu-no-bunka to han-kakumei'('Two Cultures and the Counterrevolution'): 314–5. See also David Harvey, *Brief History of Neoliberalism* (Oxford: Oxford University Press, 2005).

Translation and Interpretation: Raymond Williams and the Uses of Action

Takashi Onuki

Introduction: Action and Its Multi-Tiered Structure

This article is inspired by Raymond Williams's etymological method in volumes such as *Keywords*.[1] Informed by my attempts at translating Williams's work, the article aims to explore the plural meanings of the word 'action'. There is no inherent reason why Japanese should be the language used to explore the multiple uses of the word, other than that it happens to be my mother tongue. Raymond Williams, as his novel *Border Country* makes clear, was brought up in a context where there was an awareness of multilingualism (from the Welsh place names such as 'Glynmawr' to the Welsh poem that the main character has to recite), and it is my belief that a multilingual approach can open new avenues towards exploring and understanding Williams's work. 'Action' is probably one of the most perplexing words in Raymond Williams's writing, especially if you are translating it into Japanese. For, in Japanese, several words correspond to the English word 'action'. For clarity, a list of possible translations is included in Table 1, below. As will soon be obvious, each of the meanings of 'action' corresponds to a different word in Japanese. Needless to say, some of the translated words are correlated; nonetheless, others have distinct meanings. Meanings from *koudou* [1] to *koui* [4] are entangled; on the other hand, it is quite difficult for Japanese speakers to associate *koui* (a deed) with *sentou* (fighting) – both of which can be implied by the word 'action' in English. Above all, *suji* (a series of events) is very confusing here. The third column of the list represents a back translation of the translated words into English again. In translation *from* Japanese *to* English, *suji* [5] will be regarded as 'a plot'. Probably theatre scholars alone would associate 'action' with *suji*. This is also true of *sentou* [6]. The English word 'action' may signify behaviour, a plot, or fighting; Japanese speakers would find this very surprising.

Translating the word 'action' in Williams's writing forces us to think about its complexity, or its multi-tiered structure. This does not happen only when translating his articles or books. While preparing some essays in Japanese and quoting a phrase from Williams that, unfortunately, includes the word 'action', it is usually necessary to translate it. Interpretation and translation are closely connected with each other in Japanese writing – indeed in writing any language. I say 'unfortunately' because Williams's use of the word 'action' seems to be rather particular; indeed, I remember the experience of being actually at a

Table 1: Meanings of 'action' in English and Japanese

Meanings of 'action' in English	Corresponding words in Japanese	Translated into English again
1. the fact or process of doing or acting	*koudou* (行動)	an action, behaviour
2. forcefulness or energy as a characteristic	katsudou-ryoku (活動力)	Energy, the ability to take action
3. the exertion of energy or influence	*sayou* (作用)	operation, action
4. something done; a deed or act	*koui* (行為)	an act, a deed, an action
5. a series of events represented in a story, play, etc.	*suji* (筋)	a plot
6. armed conflict; fighting	*sentou* (戦闘)	fighting
7. (abbreviated)		
8. a legal process; a lawsuit	*soshou* (訴訟)	a lawsuit, an action
9. a word of command to begin, esp. used by a film director etc.	*akushyion* (アクション)	action

loss again and again while striving to interpret the following passage from the chapter on Brecht in *Modern Tragedy*:

Williams and the Uses of Action

CHAPLAIN: Mother Courage. I see how you got your name.

MOTHER COURAGE: The poor need courage. They're lost, that's why. That they even get up in the morning is something, in *their* plight. Or that they plough a field, in wartime. Even their bringing children into the world shows they have courage, for they have no prospects. They have to hang each other one by one and slaughter each other in the lump, so if they want to look each other in the face once in a while, well, it takes courage.

At the level of direct comment, this is, in summary, the dramatic action. But at the same time the naming of courage, and of Mother Courage, extends its scope. We need this woman if we are to look ourselves, and her, in the face. The drama, with this character at its centre, is a way of looking at a continual action.[2]

This quite complicated passage, which some might think obscure, includes a somewhat unconventional use of the word 'action'. Certainly, the first words I have underlined, 'the dramatic action', can be interpreted as representing a series of events on the stage (*suji* or an action as a plot). But what does Williams mean by the second phrase, 'a continual action'? What is it exactly that '[t]he drama [...] is [...] looking at'? Let us, first of all, seek a possible answer to this question. (I will discuss the adjective 'continual' later.)

Action, Double Vision, and Complex Seeing

Williams views Brecht's drama as an 'action' in itself, and as a way of seeing an action. Brechtian scholars might consider this distinction a variation on the German playwright's famous 'alienation effects'. Or, as Roland Barthes, who adapted the Brechtian inheritance for (post)structuralist criticism, mentions, Mother Courage is 'blind' to the forces impacting upon her life, but the audience is able to adopt a critical position because they see her blindness:

[...] Mother Courage [...] whose trade and life are wretched fruits of the war, is so much inside the war that she does not see it [...] she is blind, she submits without understanding; for her, the war is an indisputable fatality.

For her, but no longer for us: because we see Mother Courage blind, we see what she does not see.[3]

Barthes' argument is clear enough; indeed he is considerably clearer than Williams. However, Barthes here may be *too* clear. In other words, the renowned French critic who names Brecht's achievement 'a double vision'[4] may be reducing the problem of actions to that of ideologies; the character cannot see an ideology whereas the audience are able to look at it and critique it.

Would it be possible, then, for us to fully understand what Williams means in the quotation above by replacing the word 'action' with the term 'ideology'? The drama *Mother Courage and Her Children* could then be claimed to embody an ideology (is an ideology / action), and to offer 'a way of looking at a continual' ideology or action. This makes sense if we take it to mean that the play constructs its own ideology while demystifying the dominant ideology, thus allowing the audience to perceive its workings. The problem then lies in Williams's word 'continual', which raises a further question. The word 'continual' here would become almost worthless if the term 'ideology' were used as a substitute for the word 'action'. For what makes Mother Courage 'blind' to what she is doing – namely an ideology – is probably an oppressive, latent system, to which it matters little whether an ideology is 'continual' or not. If it did, the adjective would serve as rhetoric at best: a 'continual', that is, persistent and forceful, ideology or system.

Although this interpretation of Williams's 'action' as equivalent to 'ideology' seems possible, several things would be excluded if we were to adopt this definition. To think of 'actions' as equivalent to 'ideologies' is to exclude most of our common, ordinary usages of the word 'action'. Let us look again at Table 1. If pressed, an action as an ideology may be similar to an action as a plot – the plot as representing a series of events can be an ideology. Mother Courage is a part of such events but cannot see how they are developing; therefore, the action of *Mother Courage and Her Children* could be interpreted as an ideology, or at least some counterpart to it.

Nevertheless, all the other meanings of the word become residual; indeed, it is no longer possible to see the other senses such as behaviour, fighting, or even a deed. Thus, action might be viewed as a confusing term and should be used with some caution: define the word with quotation marks, or you will abuse it. Does it follow that Williams is using this word loosely or incorrectly? I think not, for Williams challenges us to turn our attention to those *residual* meanings that would be excluded by the 'correct' or commonplace usage.

The abstract usage of the word 'action' to denote ideology cannot be of any help for interpreting the following passage from the chapter on Brecht in *Drama from Ibsen to Brecht*: 'Complex seeing, in *Mother Courage* and *Galileo*, is not an attitude to the action, or a battery of separable techniques and effects; it *is* the action, in a profound way.'[5] Complex seeing is neither 'an attitude' to the plot, an abstract way of seeing 'what she [Mother Courage] does not see', nor 'a battery', some abstract theatrical method. 'It *is* the action', in the deepest sense of the word. Here we cannot translate it into any of the Japanese words listed. It is just possible to transcribe it as 'katakana', the square form of kana (which is a Japanese system of syllabic writing; 'kanji' is ideographic writing using Chinese characters – see Table 2). Let us, for a moment, interpret the phrase, 'it *is* the action, in a profound way', as follows: the word here is action – without quotation marks – whose clear semantic outline is difficult to discern because Williams strives *not* to exclude the term's residual and multiple meanings. Among the meanings that are probably present in this use of the term are action as behaviour, action as fighting – as in 'killed in action'. Indeed, there is also an echo of the sense in which Hannah Arendt used the word; we can find the residue of this Arendtian action in such a phrase as 'a man [person] of action' (see item 2 in Table 1, 'forcefulness or energy as a characteristic'). The Arendtian meaning of action (to be more precise, the experience that Arendt includes in the word) though surely residual now, still remains in our common, ordinary usage. I will return to the case of Arendt, but wish here merely to emphasise the multiple meanings of the term.

Table 2: Ideographic and syllabic representations of 'action'

	Kanji, ideographic writing	Katakana, syllabic writing
action	行動, 活動力, 作用, 行為, 筋, 戦闘, 訴訟, etc.	アクション [*akushyion*]

Williams usually seems to put his emphasis on the sense of a plot; on the other hand, when it comes to 'complex seeing', such an interpretation reaches a deadlock. The Barthes-Brechtian 'double vision' appears to be of assistance for breaking the deadlock, but this kind of reading, regrettably, excludes most of our common, ordinary usages of action. Above all, it throws away the Arendtian sense of action, a residue we need here and now, the residual meaning we need to negotiate with in the age of post-Fordism as Paolo Virno describes it.[6] However, before I turn to that residual meaning through an act of translation, it may prove useful to refer to a definition offered by Williams himself.

Drama can be further defined as *action* [...] *Action*, as a definition, can usefully indicate the method of the literary form, or the process of the theatrical performance. It must not be used, however, as if it were equivalent to a certain kind of performance, or a certain kind of dramatic substance.[7]

Though apparently easy to understand, these sentences are complex. First, action can be regarded as a form or process, but the accurate, clear definition is still conditioned by the auxiliary verb 'can' and the adverb 'usefully'. This sentence may be paraphrased like this: you can adopt this useful definition (action as a form or process), but it can serve, at best, for the time being and is not always of use. In addition, although I have just remarked that Williams's emphasis is basically on the sense of a plot, this is not the case here. A plot is just a variety of 'method[s] of [...] literary form'; it cannot be action itself, although it can be a subcategory of action. In the second sentence in the quotation, Williams is criticising the usage that identifies action with some particular genre of performance or with some particular behaviour, conduct, or gesture – namely a prescribed method of acting. Against prescribed meanings of the term, Williams offers the following 'as a definition': '*Action* refers to the nature of the literary conception; to the method of the literary work; and to the manner of its communication.'[8] What matters decisively here is the phrase 'the manner of its communication'. How is the literary work communicating? This is the central question in attempting to define Williams's use of action.

Complex Seeing as the Ideologically Impossible

If we shift our attention from the sense of 'action' as something occurring on the stage, to a sense of the word as designating the way in which the drama impacts on the audience, a different account of this article's opening quotation is possible. *Mother Courage and Her Children* is not just an action but 'a way of looking at' the action – what is happening between this literary work and its recipients. Such a perspective leads Williams to focus on a mistake made by critics in assessing Brecht's play:

> Criticism of the play has usually got off on the wrong track by starting with the question whether Mother Courage, as a person, is meant to be admired or despised. But the point is not what we feel about her lively opportunism; it is what we see, in the action, of its results.[9]

Mother Courage is *not* a character whom we should decide whether to praise as a stalwart woman or to loathe as a war collaborator. What matters here is not her collaboration but its outcome; to be more precise, 'it is what we see' of its consequences *in* 'the action'; the pivotal question Williams poses here is not what we feel about the action of the play. We see something not about but *in* the action, *in* all the things happening between *Mother Courage* and us. The audience in this sense is a part of the action of the play.

Williams's writing seems, to be sure, quite confusing, for *Mother Courage* is considered to be both 'a way of looking at' the action depicted, as well as a play which contains ways of looking within it. This might be seen as a common conflation in theatrical criticism, for to depict ways of seeing within the play is to encourage the audience to look self-critically at the actions depicted. The question then is whether there are times when you can be looking, simultaneously, at the action from outside, *and* seeing the action from within? Can you look at a process if you are in fact within it? If we follow the lesson of much ideological criticism, this kind of double vision is completely impossible. For Williams, however, Brechtian drama encouraged the kind of complex seeing from within and without the action of the play.

> When the play [*The Threepenny Opera*] was published, he [Brecht] wrote: It is a sort of summary of what the spectator wishes to see of life. Since, however, he sees at the same time certain things that he does not wish to see and thus sees his wishes not only fulfilled but criticised [...] he is, in theory, able to give the theatre a new function [...]. Complex seeing must be practised [...]. Thinking *above* the flow of the play is more important than thinking from *within* the flow of the play.[10]

'In theory' is right. Brecht had found his theory in the idea of complex seeing, but its practice was not yet realised in the actual play.

Brecht's complex seeing, for the present, appears almost the same as the Barthes-Brechtian double vision, which would enable us to look at 'the flow of the play.' But this is, for Williams, just '[i]n theory'. It must go through some test, 'the actual play', the actual communication between the literary work and us. The question which then arises is how complex seeing can be 'practised'. My earlier quotation from *Modern Tragedy* (1966) was revised by Williams two years later in *Drama from Ibsen to Brecht* as follows:

CHAPLAIN: Mother Courage. I see how you got your name.

MOTHER COURAGE: The poor need courage [...] They have to hang each other one by one and slaughter each other in the lump, so if they want to look each other in the face once in a while, well, it takes courage.

It certainly takes courage: not the isolable moral quality, but this character, this action. Past the justifications, the excuses, the 'bad luck,' the inevitabilities, it takes this action – of a mother destroying her family with the aim of preserving life – to see what is happening; to be able to bear to see it. If she were not so strong and persistent, there would be no life at all;

and at the same time, because she is strong and persistent, in a destructive society, she destroys the life that she has herself created. This deep and complex image, in a character and in an action, is Brecht's central structure of feeling, directly dramatized. <u>It is by looking this action, this character, in the face, that we see what we are doing</u>: the essential contradiction; the destructive acquiescence in the name of life; the persistent vitality in a continuing destruction.[11]

As the underlined sentence suggests, we are looking at this action 'in the face'. Mother Courage's plight is a real deadlock whose satisfactory solution we cannot bring about by any means. Instead of resolving her distressing predicament, we are forced to find ourselves 'torn' repeatedly and *continually* by her 'essential contradiction', which is indeed the same as ours; we as well as Mother Courage unwillingly agree to let the destructive society survive so that we can survive – 'the destructive acquiescence in the name of life'. In order to live longer, Mother Courage acquiesces in a society whose contradictions are so deep that she cannot escape from it. But *within* this action we, the audience, see who we are: we are Mother Courage.

This is the decisive shift of emphasis: it is we, rather than Mother Courage, who are behaving blindly. The play allows us to become aware of such blindness; first, we look at Mother Courage, whose deadlock then draws us into the place in which we have to look ourselves 'in the face'. We are *within* the (performance) process – we are blind – and also *above* such a process – we know the result of being blind. This happens simultaneously.

You could say that Williams here is going against the grain of (a Barthesian) Brecht, who prefers '[t]hinking *above* the flow of the play' to 'thinking from *within* the flow of the play'. For Williams, complex seeing is to see 'above' and 'within' the performance process at once, each of which can be called an action because they are inherent in the theatrical process. It is this ideologically impossible position – of being both above and within – which Williams regards as *being* 'the action, in a profound way'.

Action as the Arendtian Residual

We have just barely discerned the outline of the word 'action' in its deepest sense. However, a problem still remains; the answer mentioned above is only provisional. The purpose of this paper is to shed some light onto the word by translating it. In translation, we usually have to face its multi-tiered structure, or be aware of which meaning of the word 'action' is being discarded; those who translate become the more conscious of which meanings are excluded by a word's dominant usage. Williams's way of using action is 'profound', aiming at not excluding those things. So what kind of meanings or experiences is he striving not to repress or oppress? The sense of fighting, for instance, is surely not counted out. *Mother Courage and Her Children* is the drama, but it is also the action in the process of the long struggle or revolution against the alienation caused by the modern. The division between Mother Courage and us, the suffering of Mother Courage and ours, and Mother Courage's plight and ours. All these are the outcome of modern alienation, but, as in the first block quotation, we 'need this woman'. It takes Mother Courage for us to realise our own 'destructive acquiescence'. Then, as the extremely alienated, we may come to be associated with Mother Courage, and if the play achieves this, then its action is also a struggle in the process of the long revolution.

Indeed, this also signifies 'action' in Arendt's sense, which is surely residual now. But before entering this problem, let us briefly solve two quite pragmatic questions. Firstly, did Arendt have some influence on Williams? Williams lists Arendt in his acknowledgements to *Modern Tragedy* as one of his sources; as Pamela McCallum, the editor of a recent edition, points out, it may be Arendt's volume *On Revolution* that influenced *Modern Tragedy*; on the other hand, it may be Arendt's *The Human Condition*.[12] Williams reviewed *Between Past and Future* in 1961, and noted that the 'only general point that needs to be made about Hannah Arendt's new book [*Between Past and Future*] is that it is a worthy and natural successor to *The Human Condition*'.[13] We can therefore be confident that Williams had read *The Human Condition*, especially its discussion about action.

The second pragmatic question is the relation between Arendt's definition of action and our common usage of the word. As in item 2 in Table 1, action can refer to 'forcefulness or energy as a characteristic'. However, according to Arendt, the original form of action in ancient Greece has a quite different meaning. When you are free from all the 'necessities' of life, you can take action; it is labour (and often slave labour) that supplies such 'vital necessities'.[14] According to Arendt, an authentic form of action enables citizens in the ancient *polis* to take political action which is to be fundamentally distinguished from its modern counterpart. Nothing is farther from the ancient meaning of action than modern politics bound to private interests and economic necessities. Action must not be affected by such things. Nonetheless, this classical form of action did not exist for long because 'action' was 'also reckoned among the necessities of earthly life, so that contemplation [...] was left as the only truly free way of life'.[15]

As early as the Roman Empire, 'contemplation' replaced action as 'the only truly free way of life'; a dichotomy between contemplation and action became dominant. According to Arendt, the former (contemplation) is no more than what legitimates the inner freedom familiar to us, whereas the latter (action) paradoxically is no more than what satisfies our necessities. When we say 'a man [person] of action', its meaning comes from this reversed usage – he or she is so energetic as to avoid introspection replacing it with an active need to supply the necessities for others. The Arendtian action thus remains only as a residue – now no one is more restricted by the condition of life than 'a man [person] of action'.

Finally, I will try to answer the question of whether or not it is this residue – the ancient Greek 'action' – with which Williams is striving to negotiate. For Arendtian contemplative action reminds us of the very action that we have experienced in *Mother Courage*:

> The *polis*, properly speaking, is not the city-state in its physical location; it is the organization of the people as it arises out of acting and speaking together, and its true space lies between people living together for this purpose, no matter where they happen to be. 'Wherever you go, you will be a *polis*': these famous words became not merely the watchword of Greek colonization, they expressed the conviction that action and speech create a space between the participants which can find its proper location almost anytime and anywhere. It is the space of appearance in the widest sense of the word, namely, the space where I appear to others as others appear to me, where men exist not merely like other living or inanimate things but make their appearance explicitly.[16]

Living in the dark areas of modern alienation, we are suddenly, forcedly drawn into the space in which we make our 'appearance explicitly' to *ourselves*, finally realising what we are doing, though we are 'merely like other living or inanimate things' and we have been suffering from the same extreme alienation as Mother Courage.

We come to see what we are doing, that is, an act of giving a tacit consent to the destructive society. But, for we know not what we do, we implicitly agree so as to survive, to fulfil our necessities of life; then, to realise it within the action of a play is, at least, an attempt to get out of such a kingdom of necessities and determinations. In the modern age, action becomes possible, against the received idea, not because we are not affected by any necessities, but because we are exposed to such limitations so thoroughly that we are compelled to negotiate with, not to do away with, those human conditions restricting us. Therefore, what happens between Mother Courage and us is also action, to be more precise, a new pre-emergent form of (Arendtian) action, which Williams finds by negotiating, possibly unconsciously, with the Arendtian residual in our common, ordinary usage of action.

But as Williams in *Modern Tragedy* says, 'the question remains, inevitably, whether this is really as far as we can go'.[17] We cannot but wonder whether this structure of feeling – we are forced to associate with each other as the extremely alienated – is being appropriated by the dominant. Williams's complex seeing seeks a way out of the ideological dominant. Through the vehicle of theatrical action we come to realise our own predicament. We move to a position both within and without the ideological simultaneously. The resulting 'double vision' allows for the emergence of new forms of active consciousness and is therefore a significant resource of hope.

Notes

1. An earlier version of this paper was presented at a symposium 'Raymond Williams in Transit From Wales to Japan', which was organised by The Centre for Research into the English Literature and Language of Wales, Swansea University on 16 October, 2009. I wish to express my deep gratitude for helpful comments from the floor.
2. Raymond Williams, *Modern Tragedy*, ed. Pamela McCallum ([1966] Peterborough, ON: Broadview, 2006), p. 236. Underlining is mine; italics in the original.
3. Roland Barthes, 'Mother Courage Blind', *Critical Essays*, trans. Richard Howard (Evanston: Northwestern UP, 1972), 34. Italics are in the original.
4. Barthes, 'Mother Courage Blind', 33. It should be pointed out that we have to distinguish 'a double vision' by the Barthesian Brecht from 'double vision' in Williams's writing. As for the latter, please refer to Williams's *Orwell* (London: Wm. Collins, 1971), 18; and Daniel Williams, 'The Return of the Native', introduction to Raymond Williams, *Who Speaks for Wales?: Nation, Culture, Identity*, ed. Daniel Williams (Cardiff: University of Wales Press, 2003), xv–liii.
5. Raymond Williams, *Drama from Ibsen to Brecht* ([1968] New York: Oxford University Press, 1969), 285.
6. See Paolo Virno, *A Grammar of the Multitude: For an Analysis of Contemporary Forms of Life*, trans. Isabella Bertoletti, James Cascaito, Andrea Casson (Los Angeles: Semiotext(e), 2004), and *Post-Fordism no Shihon-Shugi: Shakai-Kagaku to Human Nature (Capitalism in Post-Fordism: Social Sciences and Human Nature)*, trans. Hashiramoto Motohiko (Kyoto: Jinbun-Shoin, 2008).
7. Raymond Williams, *Drama in Performance*, rev. ed. (London: Watts, 1968), 173. The italics are in the original.
8. Williams, *Drama in Performance*, 173.
9. Williams, *Modern Tragedy*, 235.
10. Williams, *Modern Tragedy*, 230; Williams's italics.
11. Williams, *Drama from Ibsen to Brecht*, 286. The underlining is mine, and the word 'torn' is taken from *Modern Tragedy*, 236.
12. Pamela McCallum, 'Reading *Modern Tragedy* in the Twenty-First Century', introduction to Williams, 13–14.
13. Raymond Williams, 'Thoughts on a Masked Stranger', review of *Between Past and Future* by Hannah Arendt, *Kenyon Review* 23 (1961): 698.
14. Hannah Arendt, *The Human Condition*, 2nd ed. (Chicago: University of Chicago Press, 1998), 7.

15   Arendt, *The Human Condition*, 14.
16   Arendt, *The Human Condition*, 198–9.
17   Williams, *Modern Tragedy*, 225.

'To Feel the Connections': Collectivity and Dialectic in Raymond Williams's *Loyalties*

Yasuhiro Kondo

Raymond Williams's *Loyalties* (1985) was the last novel that he published in his lifetime. This novel has much in common with his first published novel *Border Country* (1960), and, as if to inclusively cover significant events in the author's lifetime, dramatises a history which takes us from the Spanish Civil War to the miners' strike in 1984. Those historically important events are lived by three generations of characters. The novel comprises five main parts, and a prologue and epilogue entitled 'first' and 'last'. The main parts deal with the period from 1936–1984, while the 'first' and 'last' function as the frame in which a young man named Jon Merritt talks with a television director about a series of programmes on espionage. The relationship between Jon and the characters of this novel are revealed in the course of the narrative, and the theme of 'loyalties' is foregrounded in connection with those events which have to do with espionage. This ethical word 'loyalties' seems to be the keyword for interpreting the novel. The story indeed converges on the term, but what this novel embodies cannot be completely reduced to the word. In this article, I will explore what this novel attempts to embody through depicting the commitments of its characters to the significant historical events in the twentieth century. In so doing, I should like to accentuate the theme of 'connections', which literally and dialectically connects every part and every character of the novel to the attempt at finding 'a way of learning our future'.[1] My focus is on the intermeshing of the personal and the social, the public and the private, and what the inter-connections between the social and public spheres mean in *Loyalties*.

I

Two characters named Gwyn and Norman play central roles in *Loyalties*. Gwyn Lewis, who grows up in a Welsh village called Danycapel, graduates from Cambridge and now lives in London as a scientist; Norman Braose, a son of a British diplomat, spends his university years at Cambridge in the 1930s, works for the British government and now lives in a huge estate near the Cotswolds after his early retirement. In *Border Country*, 'the father-son relationship', to use Williams's own words, 'comes through as a movement of generations';[2] likewise in *Loyalties* the relation between the two characters –

Gwyn is a natural son of Norman – is the hinge on which the story is unfolded. Though this novel can be regarded as a variation on Williams's first published novel, the former complicates 'the father-son relationship' and relativises the relationship by the protagonists' connections with other characters in terms of filiation, affiliation and other social relationships.

Those complex relationships begin in 1936 in a small Welsh village; at a barn in the village, young men from Wales and Cambridge give speeches on anti-fascism, on communism and socialism. Then Norman makes acquaintance with a Welsh girl named Nesta; her future husband, Bert, a local working-class man devoted to communism, delivers 'a strong, moving, impromptu speech' and relates 'the struggle of the Spanish people to their own experiences of struggle' in the Welsh valleys.[3] While the solidarity between the working-class people in the Welsh valleys in the days of the General Strike in 1926 is the focus of the narrative of *Border Country*, at the beginning of *Loyalties* the solidarity of the people in South Wales is connected to that of those who rise in unity against fascism in Spain. This kind of unity or solidarity beyond social and national identities not only shows the possibility of collective movements in a much wider perspective, but, ironically enough, causes the excruciating relation between Gwyn and his father Norman. This is because Norman never commits to Nesta, but has ephemeral relations with her before abandoning both her and their son, Gwyn.

In the latter half of the novel, from the 1960s onwards, the story converges on Gwyn's attempts to know the truth of 'the father-son relationship'. After the speeches in the Welsh village, Bert goes to the frontline of the Spanish Civil War; Norman is said to go to France to engage himself in some activity supporting the anti-fascist war. Nesta gives birth to Gwyn in 1937, and Bert raises the child virtually as his own. As the narrative proceeds Gwyn's sense of belonging to a social class, and his loyalties to a class, become complicated. As a result of being raised by Nesta and Bert in the Welsh village, he is a member of the working-class family. Though Gwyn is notified of the fact that Norman is his real father, he prefers to think of Bert as his real father. Gwyn regards Norman's abandonment of him and his mother as a class-based rejection of a working-class girl; he takes Norman to be disloyal to his mother and to be a member of 'a class of betrayers'.[4] The tortuous relationship between classes within British society, as embodied in the relationship between father and son, renders the meaning of 'loyalties' ambiguous.

In that sense, the problem of filiation described in *Border Country* becomes deepened in Williams's last published novel. In *Border Country*, the father figure is divided into two characters: Harry as 'a loved physical father' and Morgan Rosser as 'a quite different "social father"'.[5] In *Loyalties*, the figure is far more bitterly divided into the two polarised personae: Bert and Norman.

Polarised as they are in terms of their social and national belonging, both of them commit themselves to the fight against fascism. In *Border Country*, Matthew, a scholarship boy, leaves his working-class family to go to Cambridge, returns home to his father's deathbed, and understands the social connections through his relationship with his father. As Daniel Williams notes, drawing on Williams's own analysis of Thomas Hardy's *The Return of the Native*, Matthew's understanding is made possible by 'seeing the matter in [his] own living conditions from both inside and outside' as 'a participant who is also an observer'.[6] In other words, Matthew understands his experience in terms of 'a kind of conscious double vision', which Raymond Williams detected in George Orwell's writings.[7] Such a 'conscious double vision' is also required of Gwyn, but this is more difficult in *Loyalties* than it was for Matthew in *Border Country*.

It can be said that in *Border Country*, the suffering of its protagonist is somehow palliated by 'seeing the matter in his own living conditions from both inside and outside' of his own social belonging or loyalties. Paying attention to the 'feeling male body', Susan Brook argues that the ending of *Border Country* describes 'a corporeal identification between Matthew, his father, and the community, as the individual bodies merge into one', regarding the 'process of reconnection and reconciliation' in *Border Country* as 'a fantasy that Williams the theorist would probably have baulked at, bluntly identifying the feeling male body with reconciliation, wholeness, and community'; she points out that 'a markedly nostalgic element' can be found in the process in which 'the metropolitan intellectual comes to embody in a very literal manner the energy and feeling associated with his father, the worker and union activist from an earlier generation'.[8] However, these 'reconnections' and 'reconciliations' are not simple resolutions of Matthew's difficulties, for they result in the acquisition of the 'double vision' that enables him 'as a participant who is also an observer' to grasp the binary oppositional conditions of a modernity rooted, as Williams would go on to theorise, in the relationship between the country and the city, and the working class and the bourgeoisie.

Meanwhile, Gwyn is faced with such binary oppositions from birth, which makes his loyalties to only one of those oppositions impossible; he cannot obtain the 'corporeal identification' between himself, Bert, and his native Wales. The impossibility of identification is bitterly epitomised by the facial injury which Bert received in a Second World War battle. The face plays a significant role in the bond between child and parent, and thus Bert's seriously injured and disfigured face may be seen to represent symbolically the problematic nature of Gwyn's affective identification with his adopted father. Furthermore, the pictures of Norman and Bert painted by Nesta play a crucial role concerning Gwyn's identification with his father(s). Towards the end of the novel, Gwyn returns to his hometown and is faced with these two paintings. The picture of Norman is characterised by a 'sharp yellow and a surprising light blue' which seem to 'be reduced to startling blue eyes and loose yellow hair', but also seem to express 'a great burst of sunlight and sky'.[9] The brightness of the colours reflects Nesta's passionate feelings during her period of ephemeral relations with Norman. On the other hand, the picture of Bert is quite shocking to see:

> The oils were streaked and jabbed to the domination of the damaged eye: hard pitted lines of grey and silver and purple pulling down the staring dark socket. The whole face, under the cropped hair, was distorted around these lines which pulled from the dark hollow. Angry streaks of crimson and purple pulled beyond the hard shoulder.[10]

The stark materiality of this painting contrasts strikingly with the brightness of Norman's picture. Gwyn's description of Bert's damaged face as 'intensely beautiful' makes Nesta scream suddenly. His aestheticised view of the painting and his implicit, underlying, romanticised identification with his adopted father violently upsets her. What this devastating confrontation of Gwyn with the paintings emphasises is the tension between identification and representation, and between different conceptions of selves and others. Being loyal to something presupposes a kind of identification. But Gwyn's aestheticised, possibly child-like, response to Bert's painting represents a form of identification that is unacceptable to Nesta for whom the painting represents pain, suffering and disfigurement. Gwyn cannot help but be confronted with the difficulties posed by the question of loyalties.

II

Loyalties, then, is neither the story of its protagonist's reconciliation with the working class like *Border Country*, nor the palliative narrative which facilitates his identification with his father(s). Yet, as its title indicates, it is certain that the theme of loyalties drives the narrative onwards. In one of the few studies of *Loyalties*, Bruce Robbins conceives of Norman's vocation as a spy as a manifestation of Raymond Williams's own guilt about being an intellectual. Robbins says that 'Williams establishes a hidden equation between intellectual work and treason' and argues that his Welsh novels 'are all about the choice and the politics of vocation': those novels show that 'intellectual work is what makes the protagonist leave Wales and what keeps him from coming back to it, and is thus a betrayal of his most fundamental loyalty'.[11] Although Gwyn is also an intellectual who lives away from Wales, his return to his native country does not bring him any consolation or reconciliation. Gwyn's desire to identify himself with the working-class people living in the Welsh valleys is hampered by Nesta's denial of such a romanticisation of the country and the working class. When Gwyn returns to Danycapel to see his dying father, he says to his mother, 'I live in the wrong place, Mam'. Nesta replies, 'Well, that's where you're wrong, Gwyn'.[12] In this novel, it can be said that the pain of 'betrayal' and 'treason' is more allotted to Norman than to Gwyn. Nevertheless, the truth of Norman's vocation is never fully revealed; neither does he expect to be released from the pangs of guilt caused by his profession by means of a confession of his secret activities.

If there is no redemption in *Loyalties*, neither is there an escape from the past. Despite Gwyn's attempts at distancing himself from Norman, the likeness between them is insistently brought to the fore. On Bert's deathbed, Bert says that Gwyn belongs to Cambridge.[13] Just as Norman's occupation is relentlessly conditioned by the post-war political situation, so what Gwyn is engaged in has to do with 'the science' that is 'a matter of policy' against the background of the Cold War.[14] Thus this novel foregrounds the background of their occupations and problematises post-war British society itself. In 1945, Norman and his friends talk about 'a reformist Labour government' and about communism which now loses its *raison d'être* after the anti-fascist war has ended and which carries the risk of becoming 'anti-liberal, anti-democratic, and then in practical terms subversive, even treasonable'.[15] In the years when the meanings of loyalties to political ideals are drastically changing, those who devote themselves to such ideals should be faced with the existentialist problem of 'making choices'.[16] Those crucial years in post-war history are emphasised in relation to the protagonists' occupations and political stances. The violent suppression of the 'attempted coup in Hungary' and the 'faked intervention in Suez' are mentioned as a 'counter-revolution' and 'imperialist manoeuvre'.[17] A man named Monkey, who has the experience of being engaged in espionage with Norman, says: 'It was 1956. We were all being changed'.[18] The year 1956 is one of the most crucial years for leftist movements in Europe, and in this respect, Norman is also at the mercy of the post-war political situations which corrode the ideals of the left. Attempting to link radical movements in 1968 to those in the 1930s, Gwyn maintains that 'Vietnam is our Spain' and emphasises the connections not only between his generation and Bert's generation but also between 'the struggle in the pits and the struggle for Spain'.[19] In addition, he points out that those radical movements have a 'common cause' which is held by 'people who are basically different from each other'.[20] Yet, ironically, it is such a 'common cause' that makes both Gwyn's need to distance himself from Norman, and his desire to identify with Bert, impossible.

That is the very situation that Bruce Robbins discusses in relation to tragedy. He points out:

> Williams takes Spain and its anti-fascist alliance as the war's central meaning: a moment of 'temporary fusion' drawing together otherwise irreconcilable social classes and groups in a common struggle, sending Welsh miners and Cambridge undergraduates off together to fight a distant enemy.[21]

This is a kind of Utopian moment in which an alternative form of collectivity may manifest itself beyond the divisions of classes and nationalities; at the same time, however, the meaning of loyalties is likely to be ambiguous and the relations of people united under some common cause can later become all the more bitter following the temporary nature of the previous 'fusion'.

The complexity and ambiguity of loyalties caused by the 'temporary fusion' of classes in the wars, followed by the change of the political situation during the Cold War, brings about 'the opprobrium' which Norman realises 'would result from the sudden and arbitrary criminalizing of what had been the war's international solidarity'.[22] Faced with such a change, and facing the 'opprobrium' caused by the ruse of history where past loyalties are now questioned, Norman makes the choice which Bruce Robbins considers to be essentially tragic. Referring to Williams's *Drama from Ibsen to Eliot*, Robbins argues that '[t]he tragedy is, in particular, how vocation comes to be redefined "not as social reform, but as the realization of the actual self"–how "social reform" is diminished to "self-fulfilment"'.[23] It seems that even if a character remains true to his loyalties, being loyal to his own belief turns out to be a 'self-fulfilment' that consequently contradicts the ideal of 'social reform'. Monkey says to Gwyn that Norman 'was a most dedicated communist' but 'the political complications were beyond him'.[24] In addition, Monkey explains the reason why Bert and Norman, who are both devoted to anti-fascist and communist causes, pursue such different paths: 'Because they had chosen a different activity. They were known and active communists. Thus they had a different loyalty.'[25] Thus, individual choices are foregrounded, and it seems that the rhetoric is inevitably 'diminished' to the problem of 'self-fulfilment'.

Gwyn condemns Norman as 'unfit to relate to others' and says, 'What you once thought about communism [...] is no more than a projection of what suited you at the time'. To this censure Norman replies that this is 'the shout of the barbarian [...] announcing the triumph of public language, public record, public power, over each and every personal reality'. Gwyn retorts that 'the personal and the political come in the same breath. We have no space to separate them.'[26] Here, it can be said that the tragedy of conflict between the son and his father is caused by the separation between the personal and the public. Although the son accuses his father of his yielding to the separation, Gwyn himself wants to regard his resentment against Norman as 'personal'; Gwyn's wife points out that the problem is at once 'personal and social [...] in one seamless cloth'.[27] This is what Williams calls 'the deepest and most characteristic form of tragedy in our century':

> [W]hen we arrive at that final division, between society and individual, we must know that an assertion of belief in either is irrelevant. What has actually happened is a loss of belief in both, and this is our way of saying a loss of belief in the whole experience of life.[28]

Since loyalties presuppose both being individual and being social (for even if being loyal is an individual or personal choice, the relation constructed is social whether the relation is that between two individuals or that between an individual and a group), the 'loss of belief in both' the individual and the social, or both the personal and the collective, logically leads to the impossibility of loyalties.

Does the novel's narrative then paradoxically suggest that loyalties are ultimately impossible? Is this novel an exploration of 'a loss of belief in the whole experience of life' as lived by the characters in the difficult times of political and social change? If we try to answer these questions by reading the doomed relationship between Norman and Gwyn only, we can hardly expect encouraging answers. By describing the difficulties of the dominant way of life from the perspectives of both Norman and Gwyn, Williams attempts to 'look beyond' those protagonists' deadlock 'into the genuine complexity: the connections and contradictions between individual goodness and social action'. This is the method of the 'conscious double vision', or what Williams here terms 'complex seeing'. Through depicting both individuals' experience of difficulties and aporias, 'the experience is generalised within an individual. It is not the good person against the bad, but goodness and badness as alternative expressions of a single being [...] No resolution is imposed'.[29] This novel is, therefore, aimed at looking 'beyond' the alternatives of 'goodness and badness' into the conditions of 'modern tragedy' itself by the method of 'double vision' or 'complex seeing'.

III

The questions Williams raises in *Loyalties* reverberate with the concerns of other post-war thinkers. Williams's dialectic method may be described by adapting Fredric Jameson's words, for example as he aims at 'the transcendence of this opposition toward some collective logic "beyond good and evil" [...] [W]e take dialectical thought to be the anticipation of the logic of a collectivity which has not yet to come into being'.[30] In *Loyalties*, unanswered questions about the truth of Norman's espionage and insoluble problems of loyalties are to be the very bases of the dialectical method towards 'some collective logic "beyond good and evil"'. What stands 'beyond good and evil', and seemingly beyond the thematic issues of the story, is history. 'History is [...] the experience of Necessity', Jameson formulates, and the Necessity is 'a narrative category'. And he adds that 'History is what hurts, it is what refuses desire and sets inexorable limits to individual as well as collective praxis, which its "ruses" turn into grisly and ironic reversals of their overt intention.'[31] Being 'a narrative category', history is read and, through that reading, constructed or (re)textualised dialectically. As we have seen, this novel weaves significant historical events into its story and describes both individual and collective praxis against the background of those historical events. Then, history in the novel is, as Jameson formulates it, the reading of the dialectical intercourse between such individual and collective praxis and what the Necessity imposes on the praxis. Those difficulties and aporias with which Norman and Gwyn are confronted in the novel are, therefore, the manifestations of history as what 'sets inexorable limits' on them. History construed and constructed in this way entails 'tension' which, as Williams puts it, 'we are formally invited to consider'.[32]

Here we need to pay attention to the textual characteristics of *Loyalties*. What informs this novel is unanswerability, of which the unanswered question as to the exact nature of Norman's espionage activities is an example. Norman thinks of 'interrogating the past' as an 'unknown country', and says that 'what happens when it begins to be interrogated [...] is always genuinely unknown.'[33] 'What happens' when the past 'begins to be interrogated' is this novel itself: Gwyn's attempt to know the truth of the relationship between his mother and his real father, and, above all, Jon's project to make television programmes about spies, are the very act of 'interrogating the past'. The result of such an interrogation is not revelation, however, for things remain 'unknown': Gwyn cannot reach the truth of his parents' relationship, and Jon's project remains, even in the final chapter of the novel, an unfinished project. Likewise, Monkey remarks to Norman that 'it is the end of the story that makes its telling impossible'.[34] It seems that what matters in reading the story of Norman is not the 'secret' that needs to be 'revealed', but rather the apprehension of his function in the novel, and in history; this is true of other major characters.

The lack of 'solutions' or 'revelations' characteristic of a spy story relates to the novel's critique of representation, which is essentially concerned with the theme of loyalties, belonging, and identity. Loyalties to a social class – for example, Gwyn's self-consciously committed attitude towards the working-class – typify the problem of representation. When Gwyn says to Norman, 'I am trying to speak for him [Bert]', the latter relentlessly refutes Gwyn's claim: 'You can't. [...] It's a morass of illusion and rhetoric'.[35] Gwyn's belief that he can 'speak for' his adopted father and Welsh working-class people is thus undercut; in addition to the problems of filiation and social classes, those of nationality and other affiliations complicate the issue of loyalties. Monkey says to Gwyn that '[t]here are traitors within a class to a nation, and within a nation to a class'. And, interestingly, he adds that '[t]his is a narrative [...]'.[36] As we have seen above referring to Jameson's formulation, the experience of such a 'narrative' imposes 'inexorable limits' upon the characters. The limits are encapsulated in the impossibility of representation (evoked in the novel by television, by painting and by the binoculars), and in the paradoxical difficulty of making lasting loyalties.

IV

Loyalties, then, persistently presents a critique of representation and identity. The 'connection(s)' (a key word in the novel) between representation and identity is embodied most suggestively in the pair of binoculars which were given to Bert in Spain in memory of a Cambridge student who was killed there. On his deathbed, Bert passes the binoculars on to Gwyn. Although, as we have seen, Gwyn is discomforted by Bert's suggestion that his adopted son now belongs to Cambridge, the binoculars bridge the gap between Gwyn and Cambridge. But it should be noted that this does not mean that the binoculars fill the gap, but rather that they help Gwyn measure the distance between himself and the man who brought him up. In a moving scene in which the binoculars and its original owner are described, the Cambridge student talks about the significance of volunteers fighting on the frontlines. Some of the volunteers smile to hear his lofty but hyperbolic words; yet, Bert takes them seriously and feels connections:

> He could hear the same words in his own mind [...] still deeply and closely connected. The words were at a great distance. [...] But that was the distance they had set out to close: from the rhetoric to the practice; from the party to the army. It was the language he had used himself, on that day at the barn, above Danycapel.[37]

In the 1930s, Cambridge students and Welsh miners cooperated to fight against fascism; this has a potential to become a radical form of collectivity, though the goal of achieving the collectivity is 'at a great distance'. The student's binoculars symbolically help them to close the distance 'from the rhetoric to the practice' and 'from the party to the army' by way of measuring the distance between the things that frequently seem to be antagonistic or oppositional.

Yet, there can be no complete bridging of the gaps of history and experience, for where there is no distance, binoculars are of no use. What is at stake here is, to use the terms of semantics, the distance between the sign and the referent; both measuring the distance and keeping it are necessary to keep 'a phantom of reference alive'.[38] Since the referent is to be compared to 'the residual', this figuration naturally links to Williams's well-known argument about the dominant, the residual and the emergent. The residual has 'an alternative or even oppositional relation to the dominant' and should be distinguished from what 'has been wholly or largely incorporated into the dominant'.[39] In the novel, Norman is characterised as someone who was once a radical, who was actually 'at the barn above Danycapel', but is now 'incorporated into the dominant' and has 'achieved comfortable integration into the new international capitalism'.[40] He, with his natural son, personifies the predicament of the left in post-war Britain. On the other hand, the residual is embodied in what Eagleton calls 'the greatest, most protracted piece of industrial militancy in the annals of British labour history' – the miners' strike of 1984.

When Gwyn returns to Danycapel in 1984, he trains the binoculars upon a hill where 'a high column of smoke' rises, and says to his wife, 'Bert gave them to me because he wanted me to know the connections. To feel the connections'.[41] That rising smoke may be associated with a beacon fire which signals that 'the emergent' is now ignited. What ignites 'the emergent' is the strike; it allows 'the residual' possibility of collective action embodied in the General Strike of 1926, the anti-fascist collaborative movement of the 1930s and other collective actions which have intermittently erupted through post-war history to live again. By using the binoculars, Gwyn examines the distance between the present and the past, between the dominant and the residual.

The emergent becomes possible only when the dominant is connected to the residual that carries 'an alternative or even oppositional relation to the dominant'. That is why the protagonist has to have two fathers: Norman as the dominant and Bert as the residual. Though the fact that Gwyn has two fathers initially causes tragedy that does never release him from the difficulties, it is only by confronting both Norman and Bert, and by measuring the distance between himself and his two fathers that he gets over both the tragedy and his romanticised view of the working-class collectivity. In *Border Country*, Matthew says, 'By measuring the distance, we come home'.[42] As has been argued, Gwyn's return home is far from an end or goal. While Matthew may feel reconciliation, Gwyn is not allowed to feel consolation but 'to feel the connections'. It is through the binoculars that he sees 'a modern *future* in which community may be imagined again'.[43] *Loyalties* aims to create the historical and experiential groundwork for this act of imagination.

Notes

1. Raymond Williams, *Loyalties* (London: Hogarth Press, 1989), 365.
2. Raymond Williams, 'The Tenses of Imagination' in *Writing in Society* (London: Verso, 1991), 264.
3. Williams, *Loyalties*, 22.
4. Williams, *Loyalties*, 359.
5. Williams, 'The Tenses of Imagination', 264.
6. These phrases are quoted by Daniel Williams from Raymond Williams's essays 'The Practice of Possibility' and 'Community', respectively. Daniel Williams, 'Introduction: The Return of the Native', in Raymond Williams, *Who Speaks for Wales?: Nation, Culture, Identity*, ed. Daniel Williams (Cardiff: University of Wales Press, 2003), xviii.
7. This phrase originally appears in Raymond Williams's *Orwell* (London: Wm. Collins, 1971), and is quoted by Daniel Williams, 'Introduction', xxi.
8. Susan Brook, *Literature and Cultural Criticism in the 1950s: The Feeling Male Body* (Houndmills: Palgrave Macmillan, 2007), 36–7.
9. Williams, *Loyalties*, 344–5.
10. Williams, *Loyalties*, 346.
11. Bruce Robbins, 'Espionage as Vocation: Raymond Williams's *Loyalties*', in Bruce Robbins (ed.), *Intellectuals: Aesthetics, Politics, Academics* (Minneapolis: University of Minnesota Press, 1990), 277.
12. Williams, *Loyalties*, 247.
13. Williams, *Loyalties*, 256.
14. Williams, *Loyalties*, 274.
15. Williams, *Loyalties*, 108.
16. Williams, *Loyalties*, 109.
17. Williams, *Loyalties*, 183.
18. Williams, *Loyalties*, 320.
19. Williams, *Loyalties*, 220.
20. Williams, *Loyalties*, 323.
21. Robbins, 'Espionage as Vocation', 286.
22. Robbins, 'Espionage as Vocation', 286.
23. Robbins, 'Espionage as Vocation', 281.
24. Williams, *Loyalties*, 242, 315.
25. Williams, *Loyalties*, 318.
26. Williams, *Loyalties*, 364.
27. Williams, *Loyalties*, 293.
28. Raymond Williams, *Modern Tragedy* (London: Chatto and Windus, 1969), 138.
29. Williams, *Modern Tragedy*, 196–7.
30. Fredric Jameson, *The Political Unconscious: Narrative as a Socially Symbolic Act* ([1981]; London: Routledge, 2007), 277.
31. Jameson, *The Political Unconscious*, 87–8.
32. Williams, *Modern Tragedy*, 197.
33. Williams, *Loyalties*, 265.
34. Williams, *Loyalties*, 313.

35 Williams, *Loyalties*, 360.
36 Williams, *Loyalties*, 317.
37 Williams, *Loyalties*, 55.
38 Jameson, *The Political Unconscious*, 503.
39 Raymond Williams, *Marxism and Literature* (Oxford: Oxford University Press, 1977), 122.
40 Williams, 'When Was Modernism?' in *Politics of Modernism: Against New Conformists* ([1989]; London: Verso, 2007), 35.
41 Williams, *Loyalties*, pp. 326–7.
42 Williams, *Border Country*, 436.
43 Williams, 'When Was Modernism?', 35. Italics in the original.

The 'Far West' after Industrialisation: Gwyn Thomas, Ishimure Michiko and Raymond Williams
Yuzo Yamada

I

Since my university is located in Osaka, I often have to take a trip between two commercial areas called Kansai and Kanto.[1] The literal meanings of 'Kansai' and 'Kanto' are 'west' and 'east' of the 'Hakone border' that divides the west of Japan from the east, with Mt. Fuji as a gigantic gate. However, as I was born in Kyushu (the most southwestern of Japan's main four islands), I have always thought that these terms are misleading because both of these regions, Kansai and Kanto, are geographically located in the central belt area of our bow-like country. 'Kanto', often identified with the Greater Tokyo area, is the east end of this belt whereas Kansai, including the old capital cities such as Kyoto and Osaka, is its west end. Both regions are so close to each other (the distance is around 500 kilometres that bullet trains traverse only in two and a half hours) that I may perhaps use the verb 'commute' for a journey between the two capital markets of central Japan. In this paper, I will turn my eyes far out of this centre, far west of it, towards Minamata. Minamata is remembered around the world as the site of Minamata Disease, which was caused by the release of mercury poison in the waste from the Chisso chemical factory. In fact, Minamata has been closely linked with Kansai and Kanto, for the sufferers of the Disease repeatedly 'sat in' and demonstrated in front of Chisso's two main branch buildings, located in Osaka and Tokyo, when they started the sustained (and still ongoing) struggle for compensation in the 1960s.

Why, then Wales? In an essay titled 'Between Country and City' (1984), Raymond Williams points out that to lump together under the descriptor 'sub-product' miners who have lost their jobs due to redundancy and industrial waste is nothing but pure ideology at work. It is, in his words, 'an attempt to separate out the often unwanted but usually predictable and even necessary results of a whole productive process, keeping only the favourable outputs as real "products"'.[2] Criticising the Thatcherite use of the word 'efficiency', he insists that we should take into account 'the full social costs, including the costs of maintaining growing numbers of the displaced and unemployed and the usually overlooked costs of the crisis of the cities to which so many of them gravitate'.[3] He wrote this in 1984 and said that this was a worldwide phenomenon, which is still recognisable here in the more globalised world. If the nexus of Tokyo–Osaka–Minamata can be compared in structural terms with that of London–Manchester–South Wales, powerful responses to ruthless industrialisation can be found in two writers based in the western regions of Britain and Japan: Gwyn Thomas (1913–1981) in the Rhondda, and Ishimure Michiko (1927–) in Minamata.

Gwyn Thomas is little known in Japan. I first came to know his name through the writings of Dai Smith and Raymond Williams, because I had no chance of knowing him through translation, nor was I likely to learn about him as a part of the canon of English literature. My discovery of Thomas has led me back to the work of Ishimure Michiko, with which I was familiar. In looking back at the incipient New Left movement of the late 1950s, Stuart Hall once said, 'As a colonial, I certainly felt instinctively more at home in the more socially anonymous metropolitan culture, though I regretted *ULR*'s [*University and Left Review*'s] lack of organic connections to non-metropolitan working-class life'.[4] Neither Thomas nor Ishimure, we can safely suppose, shared Hall's sense of regret, because both of them were based in their own non-metropolitan 'wests' for most of their lives. However, their experiences of living temporarily in metropolitan centres – Thomas in Oxford and Madrid, and Ishimure in Tokyo – cast a long shadow over their activities. In this sense, to follow a Williamsian formulation, they came home by measuring the distance. With reference to Raymond Williams's analysis of the Welsh industrial novels, my intention here is to compare the two novelists and to focus on how they both teased a resistant narrative out of their respective languages or dialects within the context of the modern capitalist system.

II

It is not sheer coincidence but necessity that quite a few of the novels staged in the 'far west' regions on which this article focuses, feature the first-person narrative voice. Both Thomas's *All Things Betray Thee* (1949) and Ishimure's *Kukai Jodo* (1969) adopt a first-person narration. Even Williams's novel *Border Country* (1960) has been read autobiographically, though its story is told by an omniscient narrator. However, it is, as Dai Smith says, 'a deceptive novel' in that it urges us not only to trace one man's personal trajectory but also to think deeply about the general trajectory of society.[5] No less deceptive is Gwyn Thomas's *All Things Betray Thee*. In the very beginning of the story, the first-person narrator introduces himself this way: 'They called me The Harpist. For years I had roamed the land, a small harp attached to my shoulders with cutting thongs of leather when I was on the move. On that harp I played at evening to any group of people who wanted to listen'.[6] This beginning, along with the descriptions of the Welsh landscape and iron towns, lets us anticipate that the narrator/traveller will describe several groups of Welsh people at the time of the Industrial Revolution. Yet, when we continue to read a few pages more, this anticipation is betrayed, for there are neither local Welsh references nor any exact descriptions of local places, and the story turns out to be totally different from any orthodox English (or it seems, Welsh) 'novel'.

The narrator's opening claim that 'They called me The Harpist', is somewhat deceptive for it is immediately followed by this remark: 'Now my harp was gone. My shoulders, as I moved, were itchily light and alien'. Then, we are informed of an incident that took place at an inn he visited two days previously. The harpist had irritated a prosperous yeoman by talking about the deprivation and poverty of the peasants. Drunk and angry, the yeoman kicked the narrator's harp into splinters. So, from the beginning, the harpist/narrator is deprived of his harp, and it seems that even if the narrator should be a detached observer of the Merthyr Rising (1831), he is not inherently possessed with any privileged tool with which to make himself heard. This is effective because Thomas prevents the reader from clinging to the old stereotypes about the Welsh Bard. The harpist's shoulders are 'itchily light and alien'. This is a marvellous start in that it clearly makes the narrator's position advantageous and precarious at the same time. Throughout the story his position is elusive and precarious to such an extent that he can give a humorous answer when later, in the middle of the uprising, he is spotted by a county sheriff and asked what his occupation is. He curtly answers, 'I'm a harpist, without a harp'.[7]

All Things Betray Thee is formed through the combination of tales of the harpist's travels while searching for his best friend, the events of the uprising and its suppression, as well as the people's engagement and betrayal in the process. At first glance, it reads like a documentary that lacks any of the clear plots employed in novels, but it turns out to be a self-conscious representation of historical processes from the observer's point of view. This fiction is replete with examples of black humour and self-deprecation. Raymond Williams's interpretation of a passage in the novel is helpful in understanding this. A character named Connor, a radical lawyer, talks to the harpist in this manner:

> You are wiser than the rest. You could have done quite well if your minds had opened out on the piggery. But some of you are *cursed* with the urge to be making assertions that are either too big or too deep to fit into the box of current relations. So we have to broaden the box or whittle down our assertions.[8]

Williams focuses on the use of the word 'cursed' to explain the potential ambiguity of a subordinated people, whose visions are 'larger also than is tolerable, when you are that far down and still seeing that far up'.[9] This remark is not an assertion that they – the harpist and men like Connor – are different but a straightforward interrogation of the harpist (and of the reader as well), an interrogation that asks, 'Are you wiser or cursed?'

The voice of the first-person narrator gives way to a chorus of competing voices in the process of the people's uprising and defeat. While hesitating about which side he should support, and whether he should stay or leave, the harpist is exposed to harsh criticism regarding his position. As Longridge, the most militant rebel leader, tells him:

> The whole instrument of your passion is being retuned. We all have a set of special pities which we work off in different ways. Harping is the simple way of doing it. But to look for and find the strings of significance that to-day hang loosely between men and which must be drawn tighter before any real sweetness of melody will be heard in living, that's the job, harpist. Do that and you will see the very face of the joy whose mere anus you have been fiddling with to date.[10]

Once there was a time when he was contented with giving consolation by his harping to the subordinated people under deplorable conditions, but here he has come to know that there are always other places and other joys that exist. This recognition results in his final attempt to understand the cowardly shopkeeper, Lemuel, who betrayed him and nearly put him to death. In spite of one character's remark that 'I wouldn't let him live [if I were you]', the harpist responds: 'We're both learning, Lemuel and I. Bigger or littler, we're all growing'.[11] And with this ambivalent hope of growing in his mind, he finally leaves the iron town at the conclusion of the novel. In the end, the harpist, gazing toward the town he has left, utters:

> On its summit I looked down. There below me was the house of Penbury, big, smiling and living with light. I turned, walking away from Moonlea, yet eternally towards Moonlea, full of a strong, ripening, unanswerable bitterness, feeling in my fingers the promise of a new enormous music.[12]

As Williams pointed out, '*All Things Betray Thee* is a moment of transition in Gwyn Thomas's writing'.[13] In Thomas's previous novels such as *The Dark Philosophers* (1946) and *The Alone to the Alone* (1947), the first-person narrators are merged with groups of their jobless friends, and keep a collective record of the events that befall their communities. But here in *All Things Betray Thee*, a shift of convention takes place in which, as Williams notes, the trajectory of 'a struggle' is mapped out as Gwyn Thomas finds 'the voice of the history, beyond either the flattened representations or the applied ideological phrases'.[14] Along this rough trajectory, the harpist/narrator pulls together voices from all of the periods leading to industrialisation, including elements of class prejudice, religion, domesticity and even aspiration and desire. As many have pointed out, this narrative is a choral composition of an alternative history of the process of modernisation, and therefore is appealing beyond his time. It urges those of us who find ourselves in the twenty-first century to retrace this process of modernisation and to listen in to 'the slow music of its renewal'.[15]

III

In turning to Minamata we're moving to the 'far West' of Japan – which is internationally referred to of course as the 'far east'. Ishimure Michiko was born on Amakusa, the most westerly small island in Kyushu, in 1927. Before she committed herself to the sustained struggle of the Minamata Disease victims for compensation, she was a poet of folklore and nature with an imagistic style, and was known in a small literary circle in Kyushu District. In the late 1950s when she joined this literary circle, 'culture' was a new word for the people's struggle in Kyushu. In this district, as in south Wales, the coal and iron industries were drastically waning, and the miners and colliers were under severe pressure. This resulted in the 1959 Miike miners' strike, one of the most historical events in modern Kyushu history. Against this background, Tanigawa Gan, ex-communist and activist, regularly published a journal titled *The Village of the Circle* and its members – including Ishimure – supported the miners' causes culturally with their pens. Although most of the members were based in the Miike and Chikuho coalfield area (in northern Kyushu), they were, from the beginning, destined to be involved with Minamata Disease. Both Tanigawa and Ishimure – Minamata was Tanigawa's birthplace and was a residential area for Ishimure – must have known not only that quite a few miners who lost jobs at Miike came down to Minamata to find work at the gigantic chemical company Chisso, but also that an obscure and devastating disease had been spreading in the coastal area since 1956.

Her detailed account of Minamata Disease first appeared in *The Village of the Circle* in January 1960. To this issue she contributed a piece of reportage titled 'An Obscure Disease'. Here she recorded the victims' physical dysfunctions – including general paralysis, deformities of the limbs, mental retardation and speech disorder – from the viewpoint of a sympathetic but detached observer. While recording what Yuki, an elderly woman, says of her condition, the narrator seems to assume the role of an invisible interviewer. This is the voice of the patient who was no longer able to eat by herself due to general paralysis:

> Well, the other day I tried to drink soup from a bowl without the help of the attendant. As she left my room, giving up putting a spoonful of soup into my mouth, I came up with an idea. After making sure that I wasn't being watched by anyone, I placed my hands on the floor this way, crawled on elbows and knees toward the bowl, and then put my mouth to the edge of the bowl and tried to drink soup. I managed to drink a little without using my hands. Then I thought I'd rather eat in this manner thereafter, if this didn't trouble anyone and if they allowed me to close the door at supper.[16]

However vivid this kind of testimony might be, it is still an arranged testimony. Ishimure seeks to hide her own presence by speaking in the voice of the elderly woman. While this confers agency on the speaker, we are aware that this is a voice being performed by Ishimure. We might say that this narrator has not yet become a distinguishable individual, and has not set herself apart from the people of Minamata for whom she speaks.

Throughout the 1960s, Ishimure contributed several other reports about Minamata Disease to such local periodicals as *The Modern Record* and *Kumamoto Topology*. These early sketches of Minamata Disease culminated in the epochal writing of *Kukai Jodo: My Minamata*, a compendium of the sufferers' voices that is deeply infused with the vocabulary and accents of the Minamata dialect. This title has been translated by an American scholar as 'Paradise in the Sea of Sorrow'.[17] In addition to the Buddhist nuance of the main title, we need to pay attention to its subtitle: *My Minamata*. As this clearly says, it is *her* (Ishimure's) Minamata. Yet the impression given is that this vision is not limited to Ishimure herself, which perhaps explains why the American translator consciously mistranslated the subtitle as 'Our Minamata Disease'. This time Ishimure is quite conscious of the narrator's position in her writing, and introduces the first-person narrator ('watakushi', that is 'I') from the very beginning. Here the narrator is gazing at an old fisherman who can no longer fish in the poisoned sea and says: 'This old fisherman looked just like the old peasants in my own village'.[18] In this way, the narrator starts telling the story by inserting her own voice in the text. Rather than assuming the voice of others, she begins to present herself as a participator in, and observer of, the collective circle of the working-class people in Minamata. Ishimure now views her subjects less as victims deserving the reader's pity, and more as agents who can resist and respond to their environments. Evidence for this shift can be gleaned from Ishimure's revised version of Yuki's confession that was quoted above. Let us compare those two passages:

> Ha, ha, it's funny, that reminds me of something very funny. The other day I made a big discovery [hatsumei]. Do you wanna know what it was like? I discovered that humans, too, can eat on all fours. Well, the other day I tried to drink soup by myself. As the soup kept running out of my mouth as usual, the attendant gave up and left my room. Suddenly I came up with an idea. I looked around to make sure that I wasn't being watched by anyone, because I was ashamed of my plan. Then I placed my hands on the floor this way, pushed my bottom up in the air, crawled on elbows and knees toward the bowl, and then put my mouth to the edge of the bowl and tried to drink soup. I managed to drink a little that way without using my hands. I felt amused and happy. But how base I was! From now on I will ask the attendant to leave me alone to eat on all fours. Ah, ha, ha, ha! How funny it is! The human mind is amazing, because we can find a way to get ourselves out of a fix.[19]

What was a pitiable complaint, is now a big discovery (hatsumei) with which 'to get herself out of a fix'. In other words, the Disease sufferers are no longer miserable victims with retarded minds but warriors against the strife who fight with the tools of improvisational humour and self-deprecation. Ishimure transposed the original tone of lamentation into a resource of hope and struggle, and along this line, attempted to give a cultural form to the struggles and protests of the sufferers of the Disease.

What is, then, the main reason for *Kukai Jodo*'s success in drawing attention to ruthless exploitation? The novel's language is one of the answers. At first glance, all of the testimonies provided by the sufferers seem to be what Ishimure heard from them on the spot, and therefore a genuine representation of their voices, as has been believed since the work was first published. But we can see that this actually isn't the case if we compare the testimony that first appeared in *The Village of the Circle* with the corresponding testimony from *Kukai Jodo*. Japanese readers may have found the former version to be more readable, because there was less use of the raw Minamata dialect than in the latter version. For example, a standard Japanese adjective 'itoshii' (lovable) is replaced by the Minamata counterpart 'mozoka', and 'kawaiso' (feel sorry) is replaced by 'gurashika'. So, in light of these changes, we can safely say that the language of the testimonies is a result of Ishimure's own aesthetic choices. But what is more remarkable is Ishimure's creation of the first-person narrator who is herself a participant in the campaign for compensation. There are quite a few passages where we can sense the flow of the narrator's consciousness:

> This was what Pathological Professor Takeuchi stated and has stuck in my mind ever since: 'Pathology begins from death'.

Pathology begins from death.

YONEMORI Hisao. Date of Birth: 7 October 1952. Patient No. 18. Date of onset of the disease: 19 July 1955. Date of Death: 24 July 1959.[20]

With this technique of pseudo-stream of consciousness, the narrator successfully impersonates an investigator of the cause of the Disease and uncovers the facts of it, saying, 'To me, the autopsy I witnessed took on some characteristics of a ritual, and urged me to engage in a tacit conversation with the dead victims of Minamata Disease, and thus I entered their realm'.

The shift of style from observation to participation in *Kukai Jodo* demands a recognition from the reader that the whole issue is neither an easy case of defeat vs. victory nor the identification of a 'them' and an 'us'. As a matter of historical fact, the litigation group of the Disease patients resisted using the word 'victory' when the 1973 verdict in court went in their favour. This is not only because they thought their agony would never end, even if a good sum of money were paid for them as compensation, but also because they resented the fact that people in central Japan were not interested enough in this issue, but regarded it as if the event had happened far abroad. In those days, the performative campaign with banners by the litigation group was criticised as too showy, but it was, we may suppose now, a performance to make central Japan understand that there are other places and people that still exist.

The second part of *Kukai Jodo* records a statement from the leader of the demonstration:

> We can't do it properly whenever we talk to the CEO chaps. Because we speak the fishermen's tongue, whereas they are all graduates from Todai (Tokyo University) and speak modernized Japanese. We're awfully daunted in front of them. Above all, if we went and asked them to meet us in these fishermen's work-clothes, they wouldn't meet us, they would think of us as yakuza who came to extort them. We'd better learn from the past failure, that too rough uprising of our union. It was daft. This time we're gonna dress up properly, so that they won't be too much alarmed by how we look. So, we've just decided we're gonna dangle down 'konbu' [kelp or seaweed in English] from our necks.[21]

'Konbu' stands for a black tie in the fishermen's jargon, and it has a derogatory nuance. After explaining this in the following passage, the narrator adds that this word is 'uttered inarticulately as if it had a shameful sound to it'. Notice the 'konbu' (kelp) dangling down from their necks. This ambiguous gesture is

IV

Finally, I would like to consider Thomas and Ishimure in our contemporary context. Two years ago, there was much debate about the 'myth' of 1968 in the mass media in Japan. The publishing market was filled with heated discussions about what really happened in 1968. The answer varies: student power in Paris and Tokyo, the Vietnam War, Maoism, and so on. It probably was an epochal year. In reading what Perry Anderson said in 1968, his fervent criticism of the attitude of the 'old culturists', especially Raymond Williams, is noticeable. Anderson curtly branded their idea that culture is a whole way of life as anthropological nonsense, because its totalising idea is 'incapable of dealing with structural antagonisms'.[22] But 'structural antagonisms' is a tricky abstraction, because we cannot escape from being arbitrary when we decide on which antagonism is structural and which is not. And in opposition to Williams's early stance, issues that are either too local or too residual are likely to be bypassed. Therefore, I was not surprised to notice that those critics of the myth of 1968 did not mention Minamata at all. 1968 was the very year when the government for the first time adopted an official stance about Minamata Disease (a decision that came far too late, since the capitalist government had long sided with the company on the issue), and it concluded that the Disease was definitely caused by the Chisso Company.

Ishimure completed *Kukai Jodo: My Minamata* in December of 1968, whereas on the other side of the world, Williams presented his *May Day Manifesto* to the British public. In this small book, he emphasised that modernisation is 'the "theology" of a new capitalism', because it 'opens up a perspective of change, but at the same time it mystifies the process, and sets limits to it'.[23] No doubt, the Chisso chemical factory, which was built in a small fishing village in 1908, was a symbol of modernisation, and it created employment and tripled the village population (to 42,000) in half a century. Yet, the modernisation mystified its process and continued to leave its 'by-product', or mercury-poisoned wastewater, hidden from the eyes of the people. As a result, it brought about a schism between the factory workers and the patients, though in fact they overlapped with each other. Since the late nineteenth century, modernisation has contributed to the development of Japan as an imagined community that saw itself as the most westernised nation-state in Asia. But we may say that the Japanese 'national community' created by that process of modernisation has not made enough effort to listen to the voices and address the problems of its diverse and locally actual communities. As Raymond Williams said, when commenting on Welsh communities within a British context, 'to destroy actual communities in the name of "community" or "the public" is then evil as well as false'.[24]

In the far west of both these industrialised nation-states, south Wales and Minamata, the languages differ but the voice is, at times, strikingly similar.

Notes

1. An earlier version of this paper was presented at the international symposium hosted by The Society for Raymond Williams Studies in Japan at Japan Women's University in Tokyo on 25 September 2010.
2. Raymond Williams, 'Between Country and City', in *Resources of Hope* (London: Verso, 1989), 229.
3. Williams, 'Between Country and City', 232–3.
4. Stuart Hall, 'The "First" New Left: Life and Times', in *Out of Apathy: Voices of the New Left Thirty Years On*, ed. Robin Archer et al. (London: Verso, 1989), 23.
5. Dai Smith, 'Forward' to Raymond Williams, *Border Country* (Cardigan: Parthian, 2005), x.
6. Gwyn Thomas, *All Things Betray Thee* (London: Lawrence & Wishart, 1986), 7.
7. Thomas, *All Things Betray Thee*, 258.
8. Thomas, *All Things Betray Thee*, 205 (my italics).
9. Raymond Williams, 'The Welsh Industrial Novel', in *Problems in Materialism and Culture* (London: Verso, 1980), 228.
10. Thomas, *All Things Betray Thee*, 206.
11. Thomas, *All Things Betray Thee*, 315.
12. Thomas, *All Things Betray Thee*, 318.
13. Thomas, *All Things Betray Thee*, 'Introduction' by Raymond Williams, vi.
14. Raymond Williams, 'Working-Class, Proletarian, Socialist: Problems in Some Welsh Novels', in *Who Speaks for Wales?: Nation, Culture, Identity*, ed. Daniel Williams (Cardiff: University of Wales Press, 2003), 155.
15. Thomas, *All Things Betray Thee*, 'Introduction' by Raymond Williams, x.
16. Ishimure Michiko, 'An Obscure Disease: Reportage', *The Circle Village* 3, no. 1 (January 1960), 36 (my translation).
17. Ishimure Michiko, *Paradise in the Sea of Sorrow: Our Minamata Disease*, trans. Livia Monnet (Ann Arbor: University of Michigan Press, 2003).
18. Ishimure Michiko, *Ishimure Michiko Zenshu (Complete Works)*, vol. 2 (Tokyo: Fujiwara Shoten, 2004), 11.
19. Ishimure, *Ishimure Michiko Zenshu*, 114 (my translation).
20. Ishimure, *Ishimure Michiko Zenshu*, 132 (my translation).
21. Ishimure, *Ishimure Michiko Zenshu*, 543 (my translation).
22. Perry Anderson, 'Components of the National Culture', *New Left Review*, I/50 (July–August 1968): 49.
23. Raymond Williams (ed.), *May Day Manifesto 1968* (Harmondsworth: Penguin, 1968), 45.
24. Raymond Williams, 'Mining the Meaning: Key Words in the Miners' Strike', *Resources of Hope*, 124.

'A Narrative of Unsolved Cases':
A Reading of *The Fight for Manod*
Yasuo Kawabata

The Narrative of Unsolved Cases

At the beginning of chapter VIII of *The Fight for Manod*, the last volume in Raymond Williams's Welsh trilogy, published in 1979, Matthew Price hears a rumour from the postman and farmer Ivor Morris that a burglary has been committed overnight in a cottage at Parc-y-Meirch where an old lady lives alone. The postman tells Matthew that someone has taken her saved pension money, more than sixty pounds. He continues:

> 'Only we have to expect it a bit in the summer, with the visitors around. But now, this time of year, I don't understand it.'
> 'She didn't hear anything?'
> 'No, she doesn't even hardly hear me, and I bring her milk and bread.'[1]

The narrative then shifts its focus to a letter that Matthew has received. That letter, sent initially by his first research student, has been forwarded from Matthew's old home in London to the cottage in Manod, the small, depopulated town in the Welsh border country where Matthew has moved with his wife Susan. The letter offers Matthew the post of Director of a new Institute and Library of Industrial Wales, the details of which are given to the reader through the dialogue between Matthew and Susan. Strangely enough, the burglary at the beginning of the chapter is never mentioned again in the novel.

What makes this 'strange' is our assumption as readers that the episode of the burglary should provide a preliminary allusion, or a clue, to the actions that follow. It is hinted that the burglar is most likely a local person, who has certain information allowing him or her to commit the crime, specifically that the old lady is hard of hearing. Moreover, the sum stolen in the burglary is not huge. One might assume that the burglar must have been in desperate need, to have deprived an aged widow of her meagre savings, despite being in full knowledge of her impoverished circumstances.

The individuals who might have had reason to commit this burglary have appeared in chapter V: Trevor Jenkins and his wife, Modlen. Trevor works for a farm owned by his much older brother, Gethin Jenkins, but his actual conditions of employment are ambiguous. Trevor and Gethin are brothers, and this allows the parsimonious Gethin to exploit Trevor's labour for his own profit. Trevor finally receives his wage after repeated reminders to his brother, but his wife soon notices that the cost of her clothing has been intentionally deducted from it. Feeling humiliated and furious, she heads to her brother-in-law's the next day, only to be mollified by him with fair words. We may surmise that the earlier burglary episode is included to indicate the pressing circumstances of the Jenkins family. But it remains curious that it is never mentioned again. It is left untouched as an unresolved issue, and even at the end of the story the reader remains tantalised by the lack of a clear resolution.

An experience of Matthew Price's in his childhood, recorded in *Border Country* (1960), may provide some clues as to Williams's intentions here. In his native village of Glynmawr, Matthew is called 'Will'. One spring day in 1926, he appears to have lost money on an errand. 1926 was the year of the General Strike, and in *Border Country* Matthew's father Harry, who has worked as a signalman since 1920, participates in the strike with other colleagues. Income is slim during the strike, with Harry only getting the 'strike pay' of 24 shillings a week. Will, who has just begun his first year of elementary school, is asked by a neighbour, Mrs Lewis, to go to the shops for her. Since she does not have any change, he is entrusted with a one-pound note in a purse, a fairly large amount at the time for a small boy to carry on an errand. When he comes to the shop, however, the shopkeeper tells Will that the purse is empty. One pound is equivalent to the Price family's rent, and Harry searches for it desperately and in vain. Finally, he decides to take one pound from behind the caddy in the back-kitchen of the house, money which has been kept aside for the month's rent. But as soon as Harry has given it to Mrs Lewis, his wife Ellen informs him that the money has been found. Mrs Lewis has, so it is told, simply forgotten to put the money in the purse.[2] While this episode may seem simply one of the many little misunderstandings of daily life, it should not be read merely as such. In fact, an inexplicable feeling of suspicion and uncertainty pervades the episode, because all those involved are poor and therefore under suspicion. Before the matter is resolved, the idea that Will has lost the money is one of several possibilities. Will's mother Ellen regards Elwin, the boy her son has been with, as a dubious character, while Harry seems to have suspected Mrs Preece, the shopkeeper, of taking the money. In the midst of such tension, the news that the money has been found fails to produce resolution or closure. The narrator does not intervene to expose the 'truth' of the scene, but allows the alternative possibilities to stand. The novel depicts the feelings and actions of each figure, objectively, with extensive dialogue. Their conversation reveals how these characters are feeling and associating with each other in this particular time and place. But the multiple perspectives articulated in the dialogue leave things open and unresolved. This is a characteristic method of Williams the novelist.

The Mysteries of Manod

Williams had used suspense as a structuring technique in *The Volunteers* (1978), a story which proceeds as a mystery narrated by a political journalist, who has observed a sniper attack on a politician in Wales. *The Fight for Manod*, published the following year, while employing the same realist form as the previous two works in the trilogy, adopts a fictive framework which allows for the intensification of the role of mystery in the text.

Manod is a fictional location in the Welsh border country, where, because of the stagnation of the local economy, the population is shrinking. The plot proceeds with a description of the project to construct a new city based in the area. Matthew Price, now aged 58, is a professor of economic history at London University, when he is offered a government consultant job for 'the Manod development' by Robert Lane, of the Department of the Environment. He moves to Manod with his wife Susan to undertake further research, taking a year's leave from university. The project is treated as a government secret, and certain details are concealed from Matthew. According to the initial information provided by Lane, the governmental project, which had been suspended shortly after its launch in the early 1960s, is now being revived for reasons that are not completely clear. Lane talks about the vision of the new city consisting of a collection of small towns, each populated with between 100,000 and 120,000 people in total, and argues that

> If it ever gets built, and who knows about that, it will be one of the first human settlements, anywhere in the world, to have been conceived, from the beginning, in post-industrial terms and with a post-electronic technology. And then just think of it Matthew: a working city, an advanced working city, in that kind of country. With the river, the mountains, it would be a marvellous place.' (*Manod*, 13)

Sensing something dubious about this new project, Matthew begins researching the place. He gradually realises that the planned sites have already been purchased and houses are under construction. It seems that investments by property developers are already in progress, in spite of the fact that the project should have been kept strictly confidential.

Peter Owen, who has also been invited to be a consultant by Robert Lane, is more sceptical about the project than Matthew is, for he has accepted this job in order to discover the secret intentions behind the project. As Peter has confided to Matthew in the early stage of their work, the plans are 'the deception', feigning 'Urban arcadia, on paper. In fact a slum of the mind' (*Manod*, 74). Peter had been a leading figure in *Second Generation* (1964), the second volume of Williams's trilogy.[3] Another member of the second generation of emigrants from Wales to England, Peter was a graduate student studying sociology at Oxford, who had given up pursuing his degree because of a conflict with Lane, who was his supervisor at the time. He had been gaoled for six months because of his anti-Vietnam War activities, which disqualified him from securing a university academic post, although his publication of *Industrial Estate* had received a high degree of praise and recognition. Lane, while remembering the ideological split as well as personal discord with his former student, offered this job to him with full confidence in his capabilities.

If *The Fight for Manod* is to be regarded as mystery fiction, Matthew and Peter can be categorised as detectives, solving the mysteries of the Manod project by cooperating with each other. Peter takes the lead role in revealing the truth. While Matthew remains in the village, Peter goes off to the continent, leaving behind his wife Beth and their new-born baby. His travels bring Peter to the truth of the matter, when he discovers that the real power behind the project is the international conglomerate ABCD (Anglo-Belgian Community Developments). As he sees, the Manod project 'runs back to ABCD, which provides all the capital. [...] And their capital, in turn, is as to sixty-forty a split between an oil company subsidiary and a London merchant bank' (*Manod*, 157). As he unravels the mysteries of the project, Peter discloses that Manod has in fact been chosen to be a practical, working model of a city based on alternative modes of energy consumption:

> What was once just their ploy to supply the demand, to get the city built to consume their oil, is now more than that, though it still of course includes it. It's now a radically different energy design, and for that, they believe, they must start somewhere clear, build it in from the beginning. In the whole of Western Europe there were eight of these plans that they put on their short list. But what they need, fairly quickly, is at least one working mode: a new city built to a different energy pattern. [...] Manod attracted them because of the original design, which was actually very close to their own. What they call the cluster city: with minimal internal transport; district power and heating obviously; and then of course the communications technology, which is actually the major energy saving. (*Manod*, 157)

On hearing Peter's explanation, Matthew agrees with him about the inner, concealed workings of the destructive business, saying 'this whole land deal's probably criminal: at least in the sense that it's a speculation based on access to what's supposed to be secret' (*Manod*, 159). That does not mean, however, that Matthew disengages himself from the project once and for all. At this point Matthew and Peter are shown to be essentially different, with totally contrasting personalities and ideological attitudes. Peter makes up his mind to go public with the results of his investigations, exposing its ulterior intentions. In the ante-penultimate chapter, Peter walks out of the room in the middle of a committee meeting which is also attended by Matthew, asserting in front of the Environment Minister that the project is 'an organized rip-off for an oil company subsidiary and merchant bank' and amounts to little more than 'technical bullshit' (*Manod*, 192). Peter's final announcement is that 'I'm resigning', and 'I shall take all this where it ought to be taken: to the public who'll be expected to finance it' (*Manod*, 193).

If the hero of this novel were the strong-minded Peter, in the prime of life, who sees everything in black and white, the story would recognisably belong to the 'mystery' genre, which would follow a central character whose persistence reveals the truth behind the mystery of Manod, leading to the identification of the culprits. However, it is rather Matthew Price, elderly and seemingly indecisive, who plays the leading part in the novel, with Peter as a supporting figure. After Peter leaves the meeting, Matthew stays on and continues posing his questions persistently to the Minister:

> 'I don't necessarily share Dr Owen's opinions. There were several good things in the original scheme. And on balance there are more in the scheme as now revised. But the crucial factor – you must really appreciate this – is who the people are to be. For this is a country bled dry by prolonged depopulation. Not far away, in the valleys, there is a ravaged and depressed old industrial area. If it can be clearly seen that in these new ways, bringing the two needs together, a different future becomes possible, a future that settles people, that gives them work and brings them home, then through all the dislocation, through all the understandable losses and pains of change, there could still be approval, significant approval: not just the design of a city but the will of its citizens.' (*Manod*, 193)

Upon hearing Matthew's surprising intervention, the Minister expresses his formal gratitude, saying 'Well thank you, Dr Price. [...] You've reminded us all of the most basic considerations. In fact more than reminded. You've lifted our eyes. You've given us perspective. We are all most grateful' (*Manod*, 194). However, in spite of the appreciative comments, whether Matthew's opinions have been genuinely accepted remains dubious. As a result of the excessive stress of the occasion Matthew collapses from a heart attack shortly afterward.

Yasuo Kawabata

The Hero Remains Unrequited

Throughout this novel, in fact, the voice of Matthew Price is rarely paid attention to by others. Instead, his opinions are often rebuked, especially by Peter Owen. Both Peter and Matthew are left-wing intellectuals, but Peter cannot understand Matthew's tenacious, less spectacular, fight for Manod, as the older man expresses his will to continue his investigations, even after it is revealed that the Manod project is 'bullshit': 'But that's an entirely false position', Peter reproaches Matthew, 'You'll still have months of working for a fraudulent scheme'. Matthew replies by noting that he's working 'For a possibility inside it', and is willing to continue 'Until the possibility ends' (*Manod*, 185).

Peter requires a decisive 'black or white' stance almost for everything, whereas Matthew works in shades of grey. Local people, including Gwen Vaughan, for instance, also reproach Matthew. When her brother Ivor sells the farm to the estate agent, John Dance, Gwen can no longer live with him, and she throws the responsibility back on Matthew: 'What rights do any of you have, Mr Price, to come in here, breaking us up?' (*Manod*, 141). Matthew tries to persuade her, explaining his position, but it proves impossible to calm her fury. John Dance also blames Matthew for his troubles. When Matthew refuses to allow the redevelopment project which is to be built next to his current residence, the estate agent accuses him of being an outsider with little interest in the area's viable development: 'Yes indeed, Dr Price, you must go. Walk away, like the rest of them. Back to England, back to your caste' (*Manod*, 170). The reader knows Matthew's beliefs. He is a person who would never accept being conned by a developer, and it seems appropriate here that he should defend his position rationally, adducing reasons for his refusal. Strangely enough, however, Matthew never does so in the novel; it seems he does not even intend to explain his motives.

Matthew's attitudes and behaviour here remind us of his father, Harry Price, in *Border Country*, who turns down Morgan Rosser's proposal that they launch a promising new business together. Morgan is also shocked by Harry's refusal, for he believes that the new business will be much more lucrative than working as a signalman. Harry never tries to explain his reasons in detail, and Morgan (like the estate agent Dance) remains somewhat offended by the rejection of his plans. His early exposure to such frictions can be seen to inform Matthew's attempts at developing relationships with the local people, and the importance he places on the need to engage with the community. The 'people' that Matthew tries to protect in his statement to the authorities and to the Minister in the meeting referred to above, are not conceived as an anonymous crowd or a 'mass'. These people are a vivid reality to him: individuals with minds of their own, who can shock him by expressing their personal emotions, and cannot be unproblematically 'known' or patronised. This world view contrasts with that of Peter Owen, who simply devotes himself to the mission of exposing the secret plot behind the Manod project. Owen does not become closely involved with the locals, and neither does his companion, Tom Meurig. It might be too much to say that they would consider a closer relationship with the locals as meaningless, but at least it is not a priority for them. Their cause stands as an abstract one for that reason:

> 'The thing is', [Peter] said, over his shoulder to Matthew, 'never confuse the mountain with the goats'.
> 'If it were as simple as that', Matthew muttered. (*Manod*, 178)

Matthew does not like Peter think of everything simply in terms of a decisive dichotomy, as black and white.

The Locals

The limits of such simplistic binaries are indicated in Williams's own novelistic practice, where (at least for a Japanese reader) the descriptions of the locals are amongst the particular strengths of his novels. The sister and brother Gwen and Ivor Vaughan appear in the novel as representatives of the farming community. Still single, Gwen dotes on her brother Ivor (who is 17 years younger than her). She has brought him up, and opposes his engagement to Megan Parry. There is, of course, a practical reason for her opposition, in that she'd be unable to live with the couple together in the same house. The description of Gwen in chapter III, as, for example, in her horse-riding, her face disfigured by a dermatological disease, her rescuing of Ivor after the accident during his work, and her devoted care of his injury, obviously deviate from ordinary realism, and, as Tony Pinkney aptly observes, this feature belongs to the realms of horror fiction and the Gothic novel:

> Alienated from adult heterosexuality […] incestuously fixated on her dead father who […] seems constantly on the point of rematerialising […] acting as a savagely possessive and perhaps sexually jealous mother to her much younger brother Ivor […] the spectacularly disfigured Gwen is one of the most extraordinary creations in all of Williams's fiction.[4]

Juliet, the wife of John Dance, is also an extraordinary figure. She is as pretty as a doll, catching people's eye, but her face is 'ice-cold': 'Strangers said that she was lovely; or beautiful; but no one who knew her well ever used these words without prompting, and then only reluctantly' (*Manod*, 111). She suffers from an eating disorder, and is usually very quiet. Once someone starts talking about food, however, she suddenly becomes talkative and bursts out with paranoid delusions, which makes people fall silent.

These figures verge on the grotesque. Despite their strong sense of self-interest, direct social conflict is largely avoided, for they somehow manage to cooperate with each other in order to sustain the community. This is conveyed powerfully in chapter X, which describes the wedding party of Ivor and Megan. All the locals gather in one place at the same time. By this chapter, each character has been established in the reader's mind and has a tangible impression and image. Williams's emphasis here on individual difference within a communal event reflects his well known affirmation in *Culture and Society*, that 'There are in fact no masses; there are only ways of seeing people as masses.'[5]

Remembrance of the Past, Dreams of the Future

Peter Owen recalls that, when Matthew lectures 'about the past you can hear his voice break' (*Manod*, 66). This remark sounds sarcastic, but at the same time it identifies precisely the moment of Matthew's remembering of the past as it breaks emotionally into his present. Living again in a place close to his native village, Matthew frequently experiences such moments of remembering his past, his childhood. In *Border Country*, relative poverty did not result in destitution. Indeed, the life of the Price family in *Border Country* is characterised by a happy atmosphere. The details of Harry's supplementary activities, such as beekeeping or growing crops, contribute to the sense of self-sufficiency and communal richness. Images relating to agriculture are vital, with the frequent references to honey-bees seeming to symbolise the communal life and vitality that Harry and his family have enjoyed. That is the milieu Harry Price never wants to abandon, even if Morgan proposes a new, more profitable job, because the signalman heartily believes that it is a lifestyle of irreplaceable value. This is the sense of nostalgia for plenitude Matthew holds on to in his mind in *The Fight for Manod*. The village of Glynmawr has much changed, the railway station his father was working at has been pulled down, leaving no traces, but Matthew still continues to project memories deep in his mind on to the future. 'Come on, Matt, you want it to happen. You want that city to be built', a friend suggests. Matthew replies:

'Well, I want that country replenished.'
'That country? You mean Wales, or that valley?'
'Well, I could even say Britain, if you pushed me. I want the pattern to break, to some new possibility.' (*Manod*, 187)

Oscillating between the memory of the past and a possible future, Matthew often hesitates and mutters in the present. As John and Lizzie Eldridge observe, Williams's characters express their struggle to 'find the words', and this acknowledgement of 'the continual difficulty of expressing the inexpressible is in itself its articulation'.[6] For Williams, the novel was an effective medium for addressing such an aporia. And it is this that explains the teasing recurrence of unsolved mysteries in his work. Human motivation, caught between the influences of the past, the motivations of the present and the consequences in the future, is as unfathomable as history itself. *The Fight for Manod* asks us to consider whether people are being robbed of their inheritance by the development project, or are witnessing a feasible future for what was previously an impoverished and economically exhausted environment. Is the Manod project the promise of a utopia, or a desecration of the sacred grounds of historical and communal memory? The challenge is comparable to that of 'Utopia no hatsugo kunren' ('Utopian exercises of articulation') advocated by the Japanese critic Jiro Ono.[7] Making full use of past, present and future, as the tenses of imagination, *The Fight for Manod* could be regarded as a text that urges its readers to engage in acts of articulation and interpretation. Is the 'fight for Manod' a fight to resist the project in the name of a past community which, after all, these 'bourgeois intellectuals' have already departed from, or is there a sense in which the real fight is to bring about the Manod project, but in a form that is closer to the needs of the local people rather than what the state planners, property developers and international capitalists want? How should local concerns be articulated in a globalised world? How can the possibility of Utopia (even a tainted Utopia) be sustained? *The Fight for Manod* asks us to consider these questions. It is indeed a narrative of unsolved cases.

Notes

1. Raymond Williams, *The Fight for Manod* (London: Hogarth Press, 1988), 131. Hereafter page numbers for the novel are parenthetically supplied in the text.
2. Raymond Williams, *Border Country* (Cardigan: Parthian, 2006), 136.
3. Raymond Williams, *Second Generation* (London: Hogarth Press, 1988).
4. Tony Pinkney, *Raymond Williams* (Bridgend, Mid Glamorgan: Seren, 1991), 79–80.
5. Raymond Williams, *Culture and Society 1780–1950* (New York: Columbia University Press, 1983), 300.

6 John Eldridge and Lizzie Eldridge, *Raymond Williams: Making Connections* (London and New York: Routledge, 1994), 158–9.

7 Jiro Ono, *Utopia no Hatsugo Kunren [Utopian Practice of Articulation]* (Tokyo: Shobun-Sha, 1981). Jiro Ono (1929–82) was a Japanese literary critic and scholar. Arguably his most important contribution was to the study of William Morris, synthesising the products of recent Morris scholarship to make the writer, artist and socialist relevant to contemporary Japan. His writings, mostly in Japanese, have something in common with those of Raymond Williams. As a director of a radical publishing firm, Shobun-sha, in Tokyo, he was also responsible for publishing Japanese editions of Williams's *Keywords* and *The Country and the City*, as well as of Richard Hoggart's *The Uses of Literacy*. His books include *Utopia no Ronri [The Logic of Utopia]* (Tokyo: Shobun-sha, 1969), *Undo to-shite-no Utopia [Utopia as a Movement]* (Tokyo: Shobun-sha, 1973), *William Morris: Radical Design no Shiso [William Morris: His Idea of Radical Design]* (Tokyo: Chuokoron-sha, 1973), *Soshoku Geijutsu: William Morris to sono shuhen [Decorative Art: William Morris and His Circle]* (Tokyo: Seido-sha, 1979).

Afterword: Found in Translation
Dai Smith

Sometimes, it seems, you have to go half-way around the world to gain a fresh perspective on familiar things. Certainly that was the experience – invigorating, reassuring, eye-opening – that Daniel Williams, Tony Pinkney and myself had at the two days of seminars and conference on the work of Raymond Williams held in Tokyo in September 2010. Invigorating because our Japanese colleagues were so rigorous in their presentations as to Williams's precise meaning and overall intent, alert to the fertility and the flaws within the wider framework of critical and cultural studies. Reassuring because our own previously published work on Williams – Pinkney as an early and eloquent champion of the subtleties of the too-readily dismissed fiction, Daniel Williams as a determined defender of the importance of Williams's stance on both Wales in his reality and the concept of realism in his fiction, and myself as a biographer insistent on the complex interactions between the life and the processes of the work – had clearly intrigued our hosts as they, in recent years had moved away from the previous, imported and imitative, marginalisation of Williams as a (critical) thinker and (creative) writer with relevance to our ongoing and contemporary situation. And, finally, eye-opening because the comparative perspectives Japanese scholars explored with us – societal in terms of impact outside academe, fictive in terms of similar, or at least comparable, odysseys that had been both corporeal and intellectual – acted to re-focus Williams within the context of his own bold assertion that the 'local' was inevitably the best focus for and starting-point of the 'global', and that then, in different ways, the return journey had to be made if we were to change, as generation by generation we must, to make a meaningful future in common.

So, Takashi Onuki shows us how by unpacking via multiple translation the strictly untranslatable singularity of words – namely 'action'– we can plot a pathway through the thickets of Williams's work on drama. For Onuki, that work validates 'double vision' as a 'complex seeing' which dispels the fog of ideology in which all can see only the self-directing hand in front of their own face, whereas 'double vision' allows for 'the emergence of new forms of active consciousness'. Onuki, echoing Williams, calls this 'a significant resource of hope'. Shintaro Kono explicates *Sanshiro*, a 'Condition of Japan novel' from 1909 by Soseki, as the transmigration of its eponymous hero from rural to urban life, to Tokyo and university, as an encounter with 'multi-layered meanings of "culture" [which is] typical and paradigmatic of Japanese modernity'. Kono suggests that such a mapping of Sanshiro's experience and consciousness also 'underlies Raymond Williams's work'.

Key Words 9 (2011), pp. 144–147

It seemed to me, hearing and reading these and other papers last autumn, how lilliputian some of Williams's detractors have been in their facile assumption that it is the transferable and abstract nature of critical thinking, not the differentially rooted but universally shared specificity of a lived experience, which attracts and signifies. Not in Japan. Not today. And not, for Williams's avid readers outside academically entrenched circles, even in his own lifetime. He brought the experience of his life, simply felt and profoundly considered, to what otherwise remains merely an abstraction, one not vivified by any actual human existence. This, of course, condemns him for many as being wretchedly confused by the interaction of being and seeing. He knew the accusation, and its source, and put it this way, typically in his fiction, in *Loyalties* (1985) where Gwyn, illegitimate son of Norman Braose and legitimate heir to Bert Lewis oscillates (infuriatingly?) in the manner that Williams, over and over, chose to underline as both his learned outcome of analysis and his stubbornly nurtured localism of spirit:

> It was not that he was now renouncing his new ways of seeing and arguing. It was that bursting out under them was this long repressed class anger which he knew would seem absurd anywhere beyond its own sites and communities [...] it was coming through against the Braoses: that is even against people in that other and hated class who in terms of belief and positions were already on his side: 'our' side, as he had, without thinking put it. Yet the Braoses were often quicker than his own people to talk the hard general language of class. Where Bert would say 'our people' or 'our community' the Braoses would say with a broader lucidity, 'the organised working class', even still 'the proletariat' and 'the masses' [and] he had been told [...] that the shift to generality was necessary. What could otherwise happen was an arrest or a relapse to merely tribal feeling. And he had wanted even then to object: 'But I am of my tribe'; except that he had seen, with examples, and from the lessons of repeated political failures [...] the general solidity of the argument.[1]

'Except that' is a disclaimer Williams could have worn as a personal identifier. It is what Yasuhiro Kondo depicts so well in his essay on the 'connections' between each and every character and event in *Loyalties* – that intermeshing of the personal and the social, the public and the private – as to the transference between past and future which Gwyn must discover in the present by confronting the legacy of both of his 'fathers'. Or as Yasuo Kawabata puts it in his reading of *The Fight for Manod*, the last of Williams's 'Welsh Trilogy', on which he speculates as a mystery and Utopia combined: 'Instantly oscillating between the memory of a past and the possibility of a future Matthew [Price] often hesitates and mutters in the present.' The balance, constantly in danger of tipping over, between (past) articulation and (future) inexpressibility is what, for Kawabata, made the form of the novel genre, for Williams, such 'an effective medium to deal with such an aporia'. And once again a Japanese scholar is able to see Williams reflected in the parallel career of a near contemporary, Jiro Ono (1929–82), writer, critic and scholar, radical publisher and editor, whose quest for imbuing his work with effect and relevance made him instrumental in introducing two such mavericks as William Morris and Raymond Williams to Japan.

For me personally, as I listened and waited to give my paper in the final session of the Colloquium, the conviction grew that in Japan the 'late' and growing discovery of Williams as a figure who spoke to shared dilemmas had come unaccompanied by the baggage of cultural and theoretical positioning that placed him differently in Britain. Particularly, in conversation outside the formal sessions in Tokyo, the connection between his fiction writing and his other modes of work was readily understood and indeed appreciated. One Japanese colleague asked me why Williams had said so sharply, in *Politics and Letters* in 1979, that 'literally none of my English official colleagues has seen a chance of making sense of [...] the whole range of my work.'[2] I told him because, with a few significant and 'unofficial' exceptions, it was, and is, true. This had been brought home to me again when the pieces by John Lucas and Sean Matthews appeared in *Key Words 6* in 2008.[3] To have then, as one of the papers in the Tokyo Conference held in his name, a fascinating comparative coupling of 'two writers based in the western regions of Britain and Japan', would have given Williams an accord of satisfaction rarely found by him in the eastern regions of London or Cambridge. For that he would have needed to go much further east. Yuzo Yamada looks, separately and conjunctively, at Rhondda's Gwyn Thomas (1913–81) and Minimata's Ishimure Michiko (1927–) to explore the social residuum of hugely exploitative industrialisation and at the culturally 'resistant narrative' they 'teased out of their respective languages or dialects [...] within the context of the modern capitalist system'. Yamada delivers the key insight that it is by the extreme distinctiveness of their language, savagely bilious and grotesquely comic in turns, that they found a style capable of representing the extreme distortions, of body and mind, visited upon the people in the places which serve as their exceptional subject matter. 'Both cultural and material' you might say, in echo of Williams.

I returned from Japan convinced that there is still a great deal to do in the 'measuring' of Raymond Williams if we are to elucidate the 'meanings' he strove to explore. My own work on him came, through the irresistible pull of the evidence I uncovered, to centre on his 'making' as a contribution to that wider endeavour of restoring the 'whole range of his work' for our possession

Dai Smith

and use. And that is what we will try to further at a future Conference on 'Translating Raymond Williams' at Swansea University in the near future. Meanwhile there is this rich and thoughtful present offering from Japanese writers and scholars to spur us on.

Notes

1 Raymond Williams, *Loyalties* ([1985]; London: Hogarth Press, 1989), 292–3.
2 Raymond Williams, *Politics and Letters* (London: Verso, 1979), 296.
3 Editors' note: Dai Smith's response to this Debate is published separately in this issue.

Debate
A Response to John Lucas and Sean Matthews
Dai Smith

Both John Lucas and Sean Matthews said extremely complimentary and welcome things about my biographical study *Raymond Williams: A Warrior's Tale* (2008),[1] the ostensible cause of their articles in *Key Words* 6, and both had correctly and helpfully questioned issues of fact and interpretation therein.[2] I am grateful to Lucas for spotting my inadvertent copying of a mistaken account of Edgell Rickword's relationship to *Scrutiny*, and I corrected it in the paperback edition of *A Warrior's Tale* (116).

However, and for Lucas particularly, it was still Williams the would-be novelist, published and unpublished, more than the would-be biographer, who was mostly in the firing-line here. It turned squarely on Lucas's amazement, almost indignant and righteous in tone, that Williams could ever, ever, have thought he might possess any of the gifts of a novelist. My detailed evidence to the contrary was accepted reluctantly, sadly almost, in terms of Williams's life-long aspiration but decidedly not for any outcome on the page, printed or otherwise. For Lucas, the problem lies in Williams's alleged lack of all the common attributes: 'an interest in words, in rhythm, cadence'. Whether that, in its turn, is any kind of adequate descriptor, of both fiction in general and of Williams's own variegated writing in the genre, I'll leave to others, though it's certainly more of a subjective cultural assumption than it is, on my reading of the evidence, any kind of objective material witness. Crucially, Lucas concedes his personal judgement does not address the 'larger question as to the kind of novels [Williams] wanted to write'.

I could, perhaps, have made plainer the implicit points about Williams's fiction, and notably the formal reasons for the long gestation of *Border Country*, which lie beneath a biographer's explicit, and I hope scrupulous, decision to set before the reader evidence from the life. And what is clear from that, beyond the surprised disbelief of more speculative biographers, is that the 'issue' of his Welshness was centrally, but differently, present in both the life and the work. In his life, over time, this was actual, hidden, distorted, discovered, revealed and scrutinised. In his fiction, never without disclaimers concerning its complexity, it is absolutely out in the open from the start as an individual given, and as a social marker whose desired dual representation forces to the fore the question of appropriate form through writing. The pivot of my book is the proof that if *Culture and Society* was born (published 1958) before *Border Country* (published 1960), it was thinking and writing endlessly since the late

1940s about form and fiction that was the immaculate conception of both his early signature books. To put it another way, if Wales was by happenstance the personal crucible, for Williams, from which the alchemists of *Culture and Society*, none of them Welsh, are taken and tested, then, in all of the versions of *Border Country*, from 1948 to 1960, his serial attempts at writing a generational novel of working-class life, Wales as a disputed culture and evolving society is alone, and by inescapable choice, the crucible in which he has to find the value of his own base metal of origin.

On the relative merits of *Border Country* we will have to continue to disagree. However, and though I might indeed have said more about 1930s discussions of Marxism and Literature in Cambridge in 1939–41, I still feel I said enough on that topic to both indicate Williams's knowledge of, say, Ralph Fox and yet not of Christopher Caudwell – as elsewhere I pointed to his relative lack of 'consciousness' of pre-war Leavis, a fact that continued to surprise Eric Hobsbawm when he chaired the launch of my book in Birkbeck – as I stressed the 'double life' he felt he was leading at the time, and over which a deal of his unpublished, and yes mostly unpublishable but profoundly revealing, fiction later mused. A biography should never dwell on what should or might have been at the expense of what did happen and why. Nor is there any doubt, from the evidence, that Williams's personal and political relationships with those Public Schoolboys, his Cambridge contemporaries, who were in the Communist Party before him pre-war and stayed in post-war, was prickly and sometimes hostile.

Lucas chides me for my alleged lack of knowledge of some names and texts which were not name-checked by me, as they were not in any significant sense by Williams, and draws attention to Andy Croft's fine account of such volumes and associated ideas in his 1990 *Red Letter Days: British Fiction in the 1930s*.[3] If he had checked himself, he would have found therein relevant work of mine from 1982 cited and footnoted. Croft not surprisingly thanks Arnold Rattenbury, who was indeed a student acquaintance and literary 'co-worker' of Williams, as footnote 68 on page 488 of my biography documents, in his Acknowledgement, text and notes for all his help and encouragement. He was an intellectual figure much attuned to the issues Croft discusses and to the pitch of the debate in the Cambridge circles he and Williams shared. But there were parallel lines in that Cambridge, too, and Williams did not cross them as much as Lucas feels he must, or should, have done. As Lucas tells us, Rattenbury, in the 'Communist youth league' at school in Bath with Edward Thompson, before Cambridge, followed the 1930s debate and its fortunes in that seminal journal of the Communist left, *Left Review*, even before he went up to university. Before Cambridge, at a further geographical and social distance, in Abergavenny, Williams was, as a schoolboy, reading *The Daily*

Herald. He first read any Marx, *The Communist Manifesto*, after a trip to Paris in 1937, and despite, from around the age of seventeen, being a member of the local Left Book Club, had to tell his astonished *New Left Review* interlocutors in 1979 that not only was the Club run solely by Labour Party members but that locally 'there was no awareness of a British Communist Party'. Purblind? Or replete with the contradictory knowledge and impulses, the 'Double Vision', that vivified the life and mind of Raymond Williams? Either way, unlike the informed and informative Rattenbury, there is no mention in any shape or form whatsoever in Croft's scrupulously researched literary history of Williams. Conclusions may, I think, be appropriately drawn.

Raymond Williams went up to Cambridge on a diet of Wells and Shaw and Huxley, and if I had been writing a close study of influences I should have spent more time there, or on the 'moderns' he rapidly discovered, along with film and performing arts: 'by the second year [1940/1] Joyce was without question the most important author for us [...] *Ulysses* and *Finnegans Wake* [...] the texts we most admired and counterposed to socialist realism. Joyce was much more attractive than Lawrence, for example, who was generally thought – although I doubted it – to be virtually a fascist.'[4] I agree with Sean Matthews that, in the later 1940s and certainly the 1950s, Williams becomes much more directly engaged with and by Lawrence, and that's why, on page 3 of *A Warrior's Tale*, I actually refer to 'the novel of generations, notably of *Sons and Fathers*, which *Border Country* had, at long last, become.' And that is why too, though Matthews says Lawrence is 'not mentioned' in my book, he is indeed variously referred to on pages 10, 218, 244, 245, 258, 280, 382, 400, 424 and 455. Admittedly, because these were passing references, he escaped the index, perhaps an indication that it is for someone else to write a different kind of book than my particular biographical one. In the same vein, Lucas says he knows of no mention by Williams of Grassic Gibbon's *A Scots Quair*, so I am happy to direct him to the chapter, 'The Border Again', in *The Country and the City* (1973) where Williams discusses it over three pages.

It is the difference from, and of course intimate connections with, England, as a society and polity to be perceived hegemonically even as it is experienced pluralistically, which required Williams, in his 'plain' and 'anxious' fashion, as Lucas would have it, to worry away at his fictional bone within an adjunct but significantly differentiated tradition of fiction-writing in English, one that did not, any more than distinct modes in Scottish or Irish writing did, emanate from that perceived and dominant England. This tradition, as we can indeed call it by 2011, at least in Wales where university Centres for its research now exist and where the Welsh Assembly Government has supported the (re)publication of *Border Country* since 2005 in the Library of Wales series, is still relatively unknown or misconceived in England (despite Cunningham,

Eagleton, Kermode and some others). It is not simply the 'proletarian writing' of the thirties or variations of 'grand guignol' Celtic mistiness from Caradoc Evans to Richard Llewellyn and beyond. It has, through a number of writers, its own felt rhythms and driven purposes.

This is a large claim, I know, and one I have no space here to substantiate, but there are now scholars, such as my colleague Daniel Williams, who have been engaged elsewhere with adding subtleties of theory and critique to my bare assertions, and I believe wider knowledge of what has been worked on in Wales, in the last decade or so, would go some way, at least, to undoing the incomprehension with which Williams's stubborn insistence on the 'whole range of his work' has been met.[5] I have made the case in more detail, for Williams's own writing and the wider tradition, in my latest book, so here I will only quote his 1986 Introduction to Gwyn Thomas's 1949 novel *All Things Betray Thee*, to show his consciousness of all this:[6]

> Many forces worked to make Welsh writers of this period [from the 1930s] adopt different perspectives from most contemporary English writers whose language they now both shared and used for themselves. [...] [I]n both their received tradition and their local contemporary stance, they were not persuaded by that dominant English pressure, now crude, now subtle, to leave the pain and anger of this crisis to politicians, economists, sociologists, historians, keeping literature to what was said to be its true deep concern with private lives and private feelings. In every year since the stance was gained, Welsh writers emboldened by what their colleagues were doing have encountered the indifference or the anxious correction of the English literary establishment. [...] [I]n this tradition, Welsh writers cannot accept the English pressure towards a fiction of private lives: not because they do not know privacy, or fail to value the flow of life at those levels that are called individual, but because they know these individuals at what is always the real level: a matter of inevitable human involvement, often disconcerting, which is at once the mode and the release of the deepest humanity of the self. This is a lesson painfully administered by the history of their own people.[7]

There is a photograph from 1976 of Raymond Williams presenting Gwyn Thomas with Arts Council Wales's Lifetime Achievement Award. For me it is a signal of rather more than the ceremonial or honorific kind. Raymond Williams, it seems, knew in the anxious and matter-of-fact plain manner of an imaginative writer confronted by the deep and intimately known nature of his own true subject matter which particular seam of English-language fictional writing was his to work. And as I have indeed stressed in *A Warrior's Tale*, he did so unremittingly, and in the way available to him even if, for some, his subsequent rhythm and cadence will require translation. In such a tradition, it may well be that juxtaposition is the key to comprehension.

Notes

1. Dai Smith, *Raymond Williams: A Warrior's Tale* (Cardigan: Parthian, 2008).
2. John Lucas, 'Raymond Williams Novelist?', *Key Words* 6 (2008): 16–22; Sean Matthews, '"Other Possible Findings": Raymond Williams, Writer', *Key Words* 6 (2008): 23–30.
3. Andy Croft, *Red Letter Days: British Fiction in the 1930s* (London: Lawrence and Wishart, 1990)
4. Raymond Williams, *Politics and Letters: Interviews with New Left Review* (London: New Left Books, 1979), 45.
5. See, for a recent example, Katie Gramich (ed.), *Mapping the Territory: Critical Approaches to Welsh Fiction in English* (Cardigan: Parthian, 2010), where twelve essays, including Daniel Williams on the 'Realism' of *Border Country*, deal with volumes in the Library of Wales series, in which there are in 2011 some 30 texts, under my general editorship.
6. The chapter 'Crossing Borders' in my *In the Frame: Memory and Society, 1910 to 2010* (Cardigan: Parthian, 2011) does precisely that.
7. Raymond Williams, 'Introduction' (1986), to Gwyn Thomas, *All Things Betray Thee* (1949); repr. in Raymond Williams, *Who Speaks for Wales: Nation, Culture, Identity*, ed. Daniel Williams (Cardiff: University of Wales Press, 2003), 160–1. *All Things Betray Thee*, with Williams's original foreword, is to be republished by Parthian in the Library of Wales series in October 2011.

Reviews

Layla Al Maleh (ed.), *Arab Voices in Diaspora: Critical Perspectives on Anglophone Arab Literature.* Cross/Cultures Series in Post/Colonial Literatures in English 115. Amsterdam and New York: Rodopi, 2009. xii + 491 pp. €100 hb. ISBN 978-90-420-2718-3.

Of all the shockwaves sent by September 11 2001, perhaps one of the most surprising was its effect on Anglophone Arab literature. After a century of neglect, the sudden (if problematic) visibility of the Arab 'other' in the American and British cultural imagination saw the sales rocket of English-language novels by authors of Arab descent, and universities begin to place these 'timely' texts on their curricula, as frameworks for discussing the unstable climate of East–West relations. Although a certain Orientalism may have underpinned this new interest, its effect on academic and cultural consciousness has been unexpectedly enlightening. Rather than affirming the 'otherness' of the 'Arab mindset', Arab Anglophone literature has instead drawn attention to the hybrid nature of its authors' experiences and identities, and the vibrant contributions they continue to make to English literature in the United States, the UK, Canada and Australia. The significance of Anglophone Arab literature has finally begun to be recognised beyond the realms of Middle Eastern studies. It is at this crucial moment that Layla Al Maleh's edited collection of critical perspectives intervenes, presenting a range of interdisciplinary, transhistorical analyses designed to make these texts accessible and engaging to scholars of English, postcolonial, world and 'ethnic' literatures, as well as to gender, postcolonial and cultural theorists.

Although this collection is the first of its kind, its editor acknowledges that Anglophone Arab literature is nothing new. English-language works written by diasporic Arab authors have been around since the start of the twentieth century. What *is* new today about Anglophone Arab literature is its classification as such. Many of the texts and authors discussed in this collection have received critical attention elsewhere: in regionally or nationally focused accounts of Arab writing or, on occasion, in studies of postcolonial or multicultural British literature.[1] For Al Maleh, though, the diasporic nature of these authors' experiences, and their use of the English language, warrant

---

1   See, for example, Yasir Suleiman and Ibrahim Muhawi (eds), *Literature and Nation in the Middle East* (Edinburgh: Edinburgh University Press, 2006) for work on Lebanese diasporic writing; Susana Onega and Christian Gutleben (eds), *Refracting the Canon in Contemporary British Literature and Film* (Amsterdam/New York: Rodopi, 2004) for work on Leila Aboulela.

consideration within a separate canon. In the thorough 'Overview' with which the volume begins, she makes a compelling case for considering Anglophone Arab literature as a distinctive literary trajectory in its own right, mapped out in three stages, beginning with the emergence of the '*Mahjar* (early-twentieth-century émigrés in the USA)', followed by 'the Europeanized aspirants of the mid-1950s', and subsequent, present-day 'hybrids' (11), who occupy an array of global and ideological positions. Al Maleh provides authoritative surveys of each stage, supplementing her work with a wealth of explanatory and contextual footnotes that guide those unfamiliar with key concepts in Middle Eastern studies through this fascinating terrain. Particularly useful is Al Maleh's overview of relevant journals, magazines, festivals and organisations in the field, which correctly portray Anglophone Arab literature as a thriving force on the contemporary literary scene. What emerges from the 'Overview' is a strong sense of diaspora as a space of intellectual freedom, but also as a politically charged arena in which international and regional politics collide. These are tensions which are explored further in the essays collected here.

After the clear and logical structure of Al Maleh's 'Overview', it comes as something of a surprise to find that the seventeen essays that follow are not grouped in any obvious way; nor are they linked by any kind of editorial 'gloss', as they might have been if arranged in subsections with short introductions – a common enough format for edited collections. This makes it somewhat difficult to discern the essays' relationship to the categories that Al Maleh maps out in her overview; and indeed, the volume feels rather difficult to navigate, not least because of the absence of an index, or of any cross-referencing between the essays themselves. While this renders the text's value as a reference work somewhat problematic, the essays themselves nevertheless stand as authoritative studies in their own right, and fruitful, if implicit, dialogues emerge between them. The first two essays, for example, both explore the work of one of the earliest Anglophone Arab authors: Kahlil Gibran, a figure considered to be the 'founder of Arab-American literature', but also, as Waïl S. Hassan argues, a problematic author for his internalisation of Orientalist stereotypes. Hassan is a prominent figure in postcolonial studies, where he has argued for the necessity of increased attention to Arab literatures within the current climate of 'East–West' relations,[2] and in the present essay, 'Gibran and Orientalism', he reveals the importance of learning lessons from Gibran's 'failure of cultural translation' (90) in the present day, when a certain Orientalist pressure is still being inflicted on Arab-American subjects to stand as representatives for a culture towards which they may bear a much more nuanced relation. Richard E. Hishmeh's 'Strategic

---

[2] See Waïl S. Hassan, 'Postcolonial Theory and Modern Arabic Literature: Horizons of Application', *Journal of Arabic Literature* 33, no. 1 (2002): 45–64.

Genius, Disidentification and the Burden of *The Prophet* in Arab-American Poetry', offers a compelling counterpoint to Hassan's study by exploring the ways in which Gibran's prophetic tone can be related just as much to models of Western visionary Romanticism as to Orientalist literature. It is commendable that Al Maleh remains unafraid to place two such different readings of Gibran alongside one another; but what is striking about both Hassan's and Hishmeh's essays is the way in which Gibran's status as a 'cultural mediator' invites the use of equally cross-cultural, interdisciplinary sources – from those of classic 'English literary studies' to the postcolonial perspectives of theorists such as Gayatri Spivak and Gloria Anzaldúa. Indeed, the relevance of postcolonial tropes of liminality, 'third-space' and hybridity resonate throughout the volume, and essays by Cristina Garrigós, Marta Cariello, Samaa Abdurraqib, Fadia Suyoufie and Lamia Hammad all turn to work by canonical postcolonial figures such as Bhabha and Rushdie. These somewhat celebratory visions of interstitial identities and 'glocal' communities are however counterbalanced by a number of essays which address the regional and international conflicts that haunt the imaginations of many displaced or exiled authors. Both Carol Fadda-Conrey's and Dawn Mirapuri's essays draw attention to the traumatic legacies of the Lebanese civil war, while Yasmeen Hanoosh offers a fascinating account of the fraught 'ethnic discourses' occupied by Chaldean-Americans – a migrant population with origins in the disenfranchised Catholic minority of Iraq. Works such as these act as an important reminder to postcolonialists that global flows of people should not always be glorified as signs of a 'borderless world', but are also indicative of material hardships and personal pain induced by imbalances in global power.

One of the most striking features of the book, however, is the rally of essays that emerge on contemporary Arab women writers half-way through. In one sense, this is unsurprising; for as Al Maleh indicates in her 'Overview', writing by diasporic Arab women has flourished in the late twentieth and twenty-first centuries, engendering a wealth of transcultural feminist critical work by scholars such as Miriam Cooke, Fadia Faqir and Anastasia Valassopoulos.[3] One of these critics, Fadia Faqir, is herself a novelist, and her extraordinary novel *Pillars of Salt* receives attention in one of the stand-out essays in this volume. In 'How to be a Successful Double-Agent: (Dis)Placement as Strategy in Fadia Faqir's *Pillars of Salt*', Diya M. Abdo explores the intricate mesh of ideological and cultural subject-positions that Arab women writers

3   See, for example, Miriam Cooke, *War's Other Voices: Women Writers on the Lebanese Civil War* (London: Cambridge University Press, 1988); Fadia Faqir (ed.), *In the House of Silence: Autobiographical Essays by Arab Women Writers* (London: Garnet, 1998); Anastasia Valassopoulos, *Contemporary Arab Women Writers: Cultural Expression in Context* (London: Routledge, 2007).

such as Faqir must negotiate. With deft critical insight, Abdo outlines the way in which, for example, Faqir's 'Arabized' use of English serves as both resistance to the 'masculinism' of Arabic, and as a 'counter-colonization' of the English language; while her characters manage simultaneously to attack Islamic discourses on gender, and to resist the 'Westernized cooptation of her struggle as a Muslim and Arab woman' (242). A similar fusion of postcolonial and feminist discourses also proves highly productive in Marta Cariello's essay, 'Bodies Across', in which her lyrical comparative analysis of writing by Ahdaf Soueif, Fadia Faqir and Diana Abu Jaber explores the ways in which female bodies come to act as sites of both 'translation and trauma', the politics of the Arab world and Britain played out through their personal relationships. In the current European climate of obsessive and often dictatorial debate over religion, ethnicity and cross-cultural women's rights, these essays offer an important reminder that the construction of 'selfhood' is a complex matter for those caught between cultures and histories; but they also reveal women themselves as capable of producing imaginative and subversive negotiations of these discourses, sometimes through the most unlikely of mediums, as Brindha J. Mehta reveals here in her rhapsodic study of 'The Semiosis of Food' in Diana Abu Jaber's novel *Crescent*.

The quality of scholarship in this volume is undeniable. From the eminent scholar Geoffrey P. Nash's authoritative account of Leila Ahmed's distinguished career to the refreshingly autobiographical musings of emergent scholars such as Victoria M. Abboud, it is clear that there is a wealth of academic activity on Anglophone Arabic literature in a variety of academic and regional contexts. It is essential for these voices to be raised in unison; yet this essay collection leaves the reader with the frustrating sense that Al Maleh's project would have benefited from a more strategic commissioning of essays in order to provide a greater scope and structure to the volume. Several essays on the same authors are included, and while it is interesting to see the opposing critical perspectives assumed on their work, an introductory volume such as this requires breadth as well as depth. With this in mind, it is a shame to see that many of the authors mentioned in the 'Overview', such as Ismail Mahjoub or Ghada Karmi, remain undiscussed in the subsequent essays, while some of the most exciting emergent authors currently making an impact on the field, such as Suheir Hammad, get no more than a fleeting mention. Indeed, as a whole, the collection focuses much more on fiction than on memoir or poetry – genres of equal significance, if of less immediate interest to teachers. While it is in one sense commendable that the editor resists reducing each essay to 'single-issue politics', as locating them within subsections might have done, this decision also means that the volume ends up skirting around rather than confronting directly some of the most politically potent but also timely issues for a Western readership, such as

Reviews

Islam and, indeed, Islamophobia, or the attitudes of Arab diasporic authors such as Naomi Shihab Nye, Suheir Hammad and Ahdaf Soueif towards the Israeli–Palestinian conflict. While works by diasporic authors should not be reduced to ethnographic artefacts, neither should the political commitments of their work be underplayed. At a technical level, it must be said that a number of typographical errors, notably inconsistencies in the spelling of authors' names, need ironing out in the first print run of this volume, an important consideration given the book's potential value as a pedagogic tool.

Ultimately, though, such technical issues fail to detract from the significance of this essay collection. In her own essay on the construction of hyphenated 'Arab-American' identities post-9/11, 'From Romantic Mystics to Hyphenated Ethics: Arab-American Writers Negotiating / Shifting Identity', Al Maleh invokes the words of the American-Palestinian poet Naomi Shihab Nye in a way that seems to speak for all diasporic Arab authors, and to sum up the ethos of this volume as a whole:

> Then speak beauty if we can – the beauty of culture, poetry, tradition, memory, family, daily life. Because men with hard faces do violent things, because fanaticism seizes and shrinks minds, is no reason for the rest of us to abandon our songs. Maybe we need to sing louder (445).

Al Maleh's essay collection goes a long way towards proving that Anglophone Arab literature has things that are both urgent and beautiful to say, not only about the ever-evolving nature of 'East–West' cultural encounters or about diasporic Arab cultures, but also about the experiences of loss, belonging, survival and creativity which are integral to diasporic communities all over the world, as to human experience in general. As an introduction to the variety of critical perspectives from which Anglophone Arab literature can be approached, this volume will undoubtedly make it easier for students and scholars of postcolonial, cultural, gender and literary studies to integrate these voices into their courses and their research. Indeed, in the quality and energy of the debates opened up by this work, Al Maleh's edited collection acts as a vital catalyst for what must now become a more strategic and sustained enquiry into the conversations that Anglophone Arab writing might engender across disciplinary, cultural and geographical boundaries.

Anna Ball
Nottingham Trent University

George Parfitt, *Being Anglo-Caribbean*. London: Lulu, 2009. 145 pp. £9.95 pb. ISBN 978-1-4092-5484-3.

George Parfitt's *Being Anglo-Caribbean* is a touchingly personal account of the author's attempt to come to terms with the complexity of his diasporan identity; firstly as a white (or 'Anglo-Caribbean') child born, and residing, in Trinidad, then later as a white Trinidadian living in the UK. In grappling with his identity, he 'tries on' different alignments; some quite specific, such as a national identity as a Trinidadian, and others more general, as he explains: 'I wondered increasingly about what it might mean to be West Indian. What was a West Indian? What did other West Indians think was their identity? Is there a peculiar West Indian identity – and do I /can I share it?'(7). The indeterminacy about whether or not he can claim a West Indian identity resides in his whiteness, a condition of uncertainty famously portrayed by the 'white cockroach' Antoinette in Jean Rhys's *Wide Sargasso Sea* (1966).

While Trinidad was – and remains – a country with a deeply ingrained class system based on, in Parfitt's words, '[i]deas of the superiority of whiteness', he also refers to 'the category of the unspeakable: "poor whites" who had dropped to the bottom of society' (31). It is fascinating to find mention of this group of people. Following the demise of the British slave trade, there was a growing number of poor white people living on Caribbean islands. Whilst wealthier whites in the Caribbean may be found in history books (as plantation owners, overseers, colonial administrators, etc.), poor whites have been a largely neglected group, so it is refreshing to find them acknowledged here.

Despite the reference to this mainly ignored sector of Caribbean society, however, in Parfitt's Trinidadian world, race and class are fairly comfortably aligned. The book, as a memoir, provides an adult's perspective on his childhood and the racial hierarchy of Trinidad at this time, and the adult Parfitt questions much of what he took for granted as a child. He recalls visiting the estate house 'most weeks' and writes: 'No memory of the black staff she must have had. Perhaps, in some half-conscious way, we were conditioned to not "see" blacks? Perhaps (which might be the same thing) we took them for granted, as part of the landscape' (11). Similarly, while Parfitt explores with some enthusiasm the linguistic creativity and hybridity in Trinidad, capturing the vibrancy of the island's culturally and racially mixed community, his Trinidad was largely unaffected by racial tension and unease. As Parfitt notes: 'My memories of Trinidad include few instances of racial tension. There were accepted differences and exotic elements, but these were simply natural' (107). His comments are interesting, given the very different picture of mid-twentieth-century Trinidad presented by Indian-Trinidadian writers like Ismith Khan and Ramabai Espinet – theirs is a Trinidad marked by racial conflict and violence. Trinidad's most famous writer, V.S. Naipaul, claimed in his book *The Middle Passage: Impressions of Five Societies – British, French and Dutch – in the West Indies and South America* (1962) to find the island's racial tensions 'at first sight, puzzling'. More recently, however, the recurring problems between Indian-Caribbean and African-Caribbean people, in particular, have been traced back to the earliest days of Indian indenture by such critics as David Dabydeen and Brinsley Samaroo in *Across the Dark Waters: Ethnicity and Indian Identity in the Caribbean* (1996) and Shalini Puri in *The Caribbean Postcolonial: Social Equality, Post-Nationalism and Cultural Hybridity* (2004).

Yet, this book, as a deeply personal account, should not be criticised for what it excludes; Parfitt reminds us that memories are partial and incomplete, and brings to life his Trinidad of the mid-twentieth century, and his later attempts to wrestle with this absent homeland. In the second part of the book, he tries to find answers to questions concerning identity and belonging in Caribbean literature, but the writing he looks at both includes, and excludes, him. As he records, Jamaica Kincaid's *A Small Place* (1988) made him feel 'upset and displaced. […] [In] sharing the guilt of the English, I was in effect being expelled from the West Indies by Kincaid – even though I am West Indian – since I happen to be white' (96). Whilst his is not a comprehensive attempt to survey Caribbean – or even Trinidadian – literature, literature is at the heart of this book and Parfitt's attempt to understand his identity.

Towards the end of the study, he reflects at length on his diasporan position. Caught between the UK of his current habitation and ancestral origin, and the Trinidad of his birth and childhood, he experiences a sense of unbelonging: 'I can truly say that I feel at home in mixed-race Sparkhill, but I also feel at times that, in the broad sense, I am homeless, or at least of divided home, domestically at home here, "spiritually" at home in Trinidad' (133). By the book's close Parfitt is unable to resolve the larger questions concerning his own identity and sense of belonging.

This book is a clear departure from Parfitt's previous works on seventeenth-century writing and literature of the First World War. As a memoir, necessarily, it presents a subjective, partial view of life in Trinidad. It is candid; at times, confessional, and extraordinarily honest. This is a welcome addition to the field of diasporan studies, and a most charming memoir.

Abigail Ward
Nottingham Trent University

Alun Lewis, *In the Green Tree: The Letters and Short Stories of Alun Lewis*. Cardigan: Parthian Library of Wales, 2006. xv + 189 pp. £7.99 pb. ISBN 1-90263-887-5.

Alun Lewis died, almost certainly by his own hand, while serving as a captain in the 6th Battalion, South Wales Borderers in Burma in 1944. Prone to bipolar disorder, he had been entangled in a complicated extramarital affair, and his anomalous situation, as a committed socialist, obliged by his commission to keep his working-class squaddies and the native population in order, could not have helped mental stability. It's clear from the letters home excerpted here, as from these eloquently understated stories, that he found his relationship with the Indian Raj stressful and distressing. In his foreword to Lewis's posthumous second collection of poetry, *Ha! Ha! Among the Trumpets* (1945), Robert Graves wrote that

> It is only when death releases the true poet from the embarrassing condition of being at once immortal and alive in the flesh that the people are prepared to honour him; and his spirit as it passes is saluted by a spontaneous display of public emotion. This explains the heavy black headlines in the Press of March 1944: ALUN LEWIS THE POET IS DEAD. Search the back-files and you will find no preparatory announcement: ALUN LEWIS WRITES GREAT POETRY.

Graves went on to quote a letter from Lewis which sums up the manic-depressive condition from which much of his best writing emerged:

> I live in a certain rhythm which I'm becoming able to recognize. Periods of spiritual death, periods of neutrality, periods of sickening normality and insane indifference to the real implications of the present, and then for a brief wonderful space, maybe every six weeks, a nervous and powerful ability moves upward in me. India and the army both tend to fortify and protract the negative and passive phase, and if I am suddenly excited and moved by something I have seen or felt, the excitement merely bounces on the hard unchanging surface like a rubber ball on asphalt. I think I'm most completely normal when I'm roaring across the country on a motor-bike, aware of the flow and the tradition of peasant life, passing gay funerals with beautifully attired corpses propped up on canopied platforms, or when I'm peeping at Victorian-Gothic princely palaces in corrupt Native State towns, or eating a coconut in a jungle village in communion with the dancing and chanting youths before the pot-bellied elephant-god of luck.

Lewis inevitably and haplessly sympathised with the nationalists' struggle for independence, even though this on occasions assumed violent proportions. The short story 'The Raid' recounts with some subtlety the mixed feelings of the young conscript officer in charge of a night raid on an Indian village to arrest 'the man' (he is only ever called this) wanted for planting a bomb in a cinema, killing 'three other ranks.' '"Of course we want the man alive, sir, if it's at all possible [...] with public opinion in India what it is"', the D.A.P.M. advises as the party sets out. Challenged about what 'the man' has done by one of the privates, 'always [...] a bit of a Bolshie' who has 'had his knife into me for two and a half years because I was a bank clerk in Civvy Street and played golf on Sundays', the officer thinks he has 'scored pretty heavy over his Red stuff this time' with the information that the bomb had killed three British troops: '"Is that good enough?"', he asks sharply. Arrested unharmed, the culprit is asked by another soldier why he did it, and 'After a long silence the chap said very quietly. "For my country"', to which the squaddy responds simply, '"Everybody says that. Beats me."'

An admirer of Edward Thomas, whose poetry influenced his early work and to whom he dedicated one of his best-known poems, Lewis here recollects the response of that equally reluctant soldier-poet who told Eleanor Farjeon that, hating no German, he had enlisted 'Literally, for this', crumbling a clod of English earth between his fingers. Like his fictional private, Lewis recognised that one man's terrorist is another's freedom fighter, and these stories are salutary reading for anyone alert to the ironies of post-imperial states still caught up in the murky business of imposing allegedly 'democratic values' on the remoter reaches of the Indian subcontinent. In their deft deployment of multiple voices and displaced perspectives, unexpectedly reminiscent of Katherine Mansfield's short stories, the vignettes collected here offer a shrewd insight into the fraught consciousness of a socialist and Welsh patriot aware of the conflicting claims of other peoples and nations.

Lewis was fascinated by India, its difference and its parallels. 'It really is an amazing, spectacular land', he wrote from Karachi in September 1943, 'but something seems to have gone wrong at the root of it. I sense a perpetual undercurrent of mockery and hostility towards us among the people.' He feared there would be 'no peace with the Indians until we've fought them', and felt 'very sad about it all, for my heart is in the right place and I don't agree with the Britisher School nor the Churchill School', wishing that he'd come there as a doctor, teacher or social worker, 'anything but a soldier. It's not nice being a soldier in India.' But, taking a 300-mile excursion by motorbike, he was 'glad to find' a different India amidst the jungle hamlets, whose peasants 'neither cringe nor beg nor sneer', evincing instead 'a humanity that imperialism and snobbery haven't spoiled'. This trip was, he wrote, 'a unique experience. You enter a separate world, remote, unperturbed, indifferent, serene, and it makes your own troubles and fears fall away and remain outside in the world of roads and spaces.' These stories and letters alike are caustic in their contempt for the 'demoralising' influences of Empire and modernity on India's 'flat and featureless philosophical voids', 'like influenza, this tinpot civilization that is so easy to export by radio and gramophone and film', 'devalu[ing] everything, from true music to true love [...] mak[ing] everything cheap and easy and immediate'.

Long out of print, this collection, first published in 1948 by Lewis's widow Gweno, is here newly edited for Parthian's Library of Wales by the writer's biographer, John Pikoulis, who charts in an afterword the circumstances of the book's genesis and the changes he has made to restore the original form of the letters, which had been over-edited by Gweno. A Foreword by Owen Sheers offers a brief appreciation of Lewis's work and life. The present edition reproduces the engravings by John Petts which illustrated the original, including a striking frontispiece portrait of the poet. It is prefaced by Vernon Watkins's sonnet on Lewis's death, which provided the original, if not very illuminating title for the collection. *In the Green Tree* is a valuable addition to the Library of Wales's reprints of neglected and marginalised Welsh writers, a project commendably supported by the Welsh Assembly Government. The series' general editor, Dai Smith, Raymond Williams's biographer and occupant of the Raymond Williams Chair in the Cultural History of Wales at Swansea University, describes its aim as 'to open up the borders that have denied some of our best writers a presence in a future Wales. [It] has been created with that Wales in mind: a young country not afraid to remember what it might yet become.' It would be good if Parthian were now to publish the long overdue definitive edition of Lewis's *Collected Poems*, first mooted more than a decade ago.

Stan Smith
Nottingham Trent University

Michael Higgins, Clarissa Smith and John Storey (eds), *The Cambridge Companion to Modern British Culture.* Cambridge: Cambridge University Press, 2010. xvi + 323 pp. £18.99 pb. ISBN 978-0-52-168346-3.

Cultural studies has always been riven between, on the one hand, the drive to construct a totalising meta-discourse, and, on the other, the desire to find methodologies rigorous and flexible enough to address its multifarious objects of enquiry, without converting them into mere metonymies of its own hegemonic practice, in the process stripping them of their uniqueness and specificity.

The first of several invocations of Raymond Williams in the present volume indicates the dilemmas of a project that seeks to uncover a highly-wrought framework of signification in the practices of the everyday. John Storey, in 'Becoming British', quotes Williams's famous definition of culture as 'a particular way of life, which expresses certain meanings and values not only in art and learning but also in institutions and ordinary behaviour [...] the characteristic forms through which members of the society communicate' (16). One can see here both the potential of the kind of cross-disciplinary cultural analysis Williams helped articulate, but also, given the looseness of the definition, the possible pitfalls. In less adept hands than Williams's it is a definition that has at times been stretched wide enough to accommodate almost anything, and consequently to lose coherence in a kind of imperial overreach.

This expansionist ambition can be read as both success and failure: success in that 50 years on, cultural studies is now firmly established as a discipline; failure, since its focus at times remains imprecise, its rationale unclear and the multiple fields it combines harvested uncritically, as if eroding their differences rather than eliciting that which makes them singular. That said, it is important not to downplay the struggle involved in elevating the everyday to a status worthy of study. Ken Jones, in his illuminating chapter on ideological convulsions within the English education system, quotes a speaker at the National Union of Teachers conference in 1961 (the same year as Williams's observation) who argued that 'There exists not merely this sort of elite culture [...] but some different kind of culture which it is necessary to seek out by going into other people's experience' (46). Jones deploys this as part of a wider discussion of education's own culture wars. But it is also possible to read in the speaker's imprecise phrasing the novelty and perceived difficulty of advocating this kind of imaginative connection with other lived worlds. And it is this type of connection, a kind of intellectual outreach over five decades, that has prompted valuable incursions into the ostensibly obvious or mundane. Whether studying soap operas, sport, comic books or alternative comedy, cultural studies has undeniably enriched our understanding; an achievement not diminished by the fact that a kind of lowest-common-denominator critical theory has also been responsible for many a frothy or solipsistic commentary. Happily this collection is not one of them. Despite its wide-ranging ambition to cover the waterfront of British culture, it largely succeeds in being a useful primer while also (with occasional exceptions) conveying some genuine depth of engagement.

Any survey of 'British' culture is in danger of chasing its tail: niggling away at the constructed nature of national identity while still searching for its essence. Discussing this dynamic, John Storey cites Tony Blair's rhetorical heavy breathing about Britain and Britishness: 'This country is a blessed nation. The British are special, the world knows it, in our innermost thoughts, we know it. This is the greatest nation on earth' (22). Such claims of exceptionalism may raise an easy sneer: it would be a brave politician indeed who delivered a speech declaring their proud nation to be deeply ordinary. But Blair's tub-thumping does prompt an absorbing question: precisely where do we draw the line between crude appeals to national character and a critically nuanced attempt to calibrate with a proper historical specificity the construction of Britishness in its many forms? As Storey argues, 'nations are never only ever invented once: invention is always followed by reinvention' (13). Indeed, much that is most fertile in contemporary British culture comes from the continuing fission and fusion of the global and the local, as Storey emphasises: 'We should not really speak of British culture at all but of British cultures' (23). This is not to imply that trying to define the 'Britishness' of British culture is fruitless, even if seeking to distil such an essence can have something of the quality of nailing jelly to a wall. Instead it is to acknowledge that carried within any such project is an awareness of its own limitations. It is shaped, in part at least, by a Beckettian sense that ultimately it will fail, and that the task itself requires redefining.

But if the task at hand is to fail better, then this collection succeeds more than most, despite perhaps the unfortunate timing of its publication: it inevitably feels a little behind the cultural curve now that the decade of easy money, cheap credit and asset inflation has imploded and a genuine convulsion in the British body politic appears to be taking place. Consequently, while *Modern British Culture* is frequently lucid in its analysis, some contributions have a slightly weathered feel, as if the days of Britpop, the bubble economy and 'Cool Britannia' are already so far behind us that they are ready to be collated and filed in a dusty archive. While offering a nod to recent calamities, Valerie Reardon's perceptive introduction to contemporary British art, for instance, still feels a little too bound by the gravitational pull of the era of the art market boom, museum mania and the (rapidly ageing) Young British Artists.

Nevertheless *Modern British Culture* provides a substantial overview of cultural studies at the time of its writing. Its seventeen essays survey everything from fashion (Caroline Evans referencing the Italian designer Giorgio Armani and his identification of a British 'cult of cool scruffiness' (217)) to theatre, film, poetry, newspapers, political communications and the 'banalisation' of politics. Several, including Ellis Cashmore's 'Sport in contemporary Britain', are exemplary, combining a sense of introductory verve whilst drilling down to specifics in search of depth and rigour. Cashmore contrasts the amateur ideal in sport with the monetised marketing/ entertainment nexus that helps define organisations such as the English Premier League. He charts with precision the decline of the Corinthian ideal and the commodification of sports that can be seen to have turned modern football, for instance, into a metaphor for global capitalism, with players becoming assets and teams brands. We have come a long way from *Roy of the Rovers*.

Similarly, the frequently excellent David Crystal presents a considered introduction to the current ebbs and flows of English. The 500 words a decade that enter and remain in the language, roughly one a week, demonstrate its vitality and international reach. How much of this is 'British' is a moot point: as English spreads and absorbs international influences it demonstrates how a language can contain traces of intense locality whilst simultaneously becoming a lingua franca of sorts. The internet plays no small part in this increasingly frequent collision between the global and the local, and it is a surprise that Crystal's chapter is one of the few to invoke its growing influence. He argues that after little more than a decade of widespread use this radically decentred form is already transforming both us and our language: 'It is now possible to see blogs in which utterances run on with little or no punctuation, in much the same way as James Joyce ends *Ulysses*' (39).

Along with Crystal's, the best of these essays are scrupulous and incisive, interrogating their subject with rewardingly granular detail. To avoid producing a superficial pick-and-mix, contributors adopt a variety of tactics. Some, such as Sarah Street in her chapter on film, engage with individual case studies to permit a deeper analysis of specific works alongside an overview. It is a tactic that on one level works well but which also inevitably raises questions of selection. It is perhaps a bit out of kilter, for example, to award Mike Leigh's *Vera Drake* significant attention in a short chapter on British cinema. Equally Jane Arthurs' astringent survey of British television is knocked a little off balance by allocating space to an analysis of Jamie Oliver's television career. At other times a different selective pressure results in a somewhat *ad hoc* approach to the parameters of intellectual enquiry. Patricia Waugh's survey of fiction seems to define the subject as purely *literary* fiction, a telling contrast with Michael Mangan, whose piece on theatre stretches the elastic to incorporate flash mobs, musicals, amateur dramatics, community theatre and re-enactments of the English Civil War. While inconsistently applied and in principal no more valid than any narrower engagement, this expansionist tendency pays dividends both here and in other incursions into less familiar territory, including Clarissa Smith's chapter on British sexual cultures and Tariq Modood on the cultural positioning of the Muslim community in Britain. Thankfully there is throughout little of the kind of critical narcosis that periodically gives cultural studies a bad name. There is the odd lapse, however: few, even of those familiar with the stir it provoked, would agree that the *Shamen*'s controversial hit *Ebeneezer Goode (E's are Good)* 'had shaken the walls of the establishment in 1992' (264), as Sheila Whiteley would have us believe in a hipster skim through the recent history of British popular music.

There are some inevitable omissions, in particular, any extensive account of the impact of the internet and social media in the British context. Some contributions begin to develop intriguing lines of argument only to be cut short, constrained by pressures of space and the need to demarcate a boundary between the included and the excluded. Ken Jones's compelling contribution on schooling, for example, is one such essay rich in ideas worth developing further. His dissection of a concept of education designed neither to imbue wisdom nor encourage creative thinking, but instead to generate what was described at a European Union council meeting as a 'competitive and dynamic knowledge economy' (43), unpicks the way this orthodoxy frequently turns 'choice' into a cover for marketisation. Jones argues that, in this new reality, changes in education, and the devolution of financial powers to school level, have 'laid a basis for the emergence of powerful new management cultures' (49). He suggests that this has led to a situation in which 'England is the educational spectre haunting Europe – the homeland of a "neo-liberal" model in which schooling is subordinated to an economic agenda, opposing voices marginalised and egalitarian ambitions abandoned' (44). Worthy of a chapter in itself, this trend can be read as representative of a more dramatic reshaping of British culture: the promotion of managerialism and business-speak along with an often crudely applied consumerist ideology throughout the public sphere. While this displacement of alternative value systems may not be unique to Britain, it has gained peculiar traction here. Perhaps Tony Blair was right after all: Britain is 'special'.

Philip Smith

Robert J. Balfour (ed.), ***Culture, Capital and Representation.*** Palgrave Macmillan, in association with the Institute of Commonwealth Studies and the Institute of English Studies, 2010. xiv + 256 pp. £50 hb. ISBN 978-0-230-24645-4.

In the wake of the global credit crisis of 2007, Bernard Madoff, and Niall Ferguson, it seems as though it's not just dusty and timeworn Marxists who are talking about capitalism as an historically emergent and unstable system of exchange, one that can no longer provide a convincing reification of social relations or cultural value. Along with the remarkably widespread feeling that national and international financial systems are critically flawed, there is increasing incredulity towards the notion that capitalism can be progressively refined in the pursuit of morality, justice, and fairness. Any readers hoping to find in Robert J. Balfour's volume an in-depth exploration of this new cultural condition will probably be disappointed, as will anyone looking for a trenchant return to the Marxisms of the mid- or late-twentieth century or a sense of Marxism's reinvigoration by figures such as Badiou, Hardt and Negri, Rancière, Therborn, or Žižek. But, as a cultural history of capital that is concerned not with confirming perceptions of capitalism's corruption by the avaricious few but with exploring the long-established structures by which social and personal worth is abstracted as monetary value, this is not a disappointing collection. The history that emerges from these essays is an extensive one, beginning with reflections on political economy in the seventeenth century and ending with market deregulation and the transnational movement of capital at the close of the twentieth century; refusing the constraints of disciplinary knowledge, this collection works across literary studies, economic history and theory, social history, cultural studies, the visual arts, and philosophy.

While Marxism – recent or otherwise – does not provide many of Balfour's contributors with an optic that brings capital's symbolic connections into focus, it does receive substantial attention in Leigh Claire La Berge's 'Reading Finance Capital' and Ben Roberts' 'The Gold Standard and Literature: Money and Language in the Work of Jean-Joseph Goux'. Both of these essays are complex and nuanced in their treatment of the symbolic value of money, and they are among the most notable contributions to Balfour's volume. La Berge takes as her point of departure Marx's argument in *Capital* that the surplus value elicited from commodity production is to be found not in the object produced, but in the time that is attached to production. Looking to Dreiser's 1912 novel *The Financier* for evidence of the conjunction between narrative time and financial value, La Berge argues that 'The narrative trajectory of *The Financier* is essentially accumulative. Socio-symbolic meaning accrues over time by representing capital, which accrues over time' (126). Roberts' essay takes on Derrida's reading of Goux's reading of Gide's *Les Faux-Monnayeurs*, arguing that Derrida focuses too narrowly on *The Coiners of Language* when claiming that the monetary value of gold becomes 'de-fictionalized' in Goux's distinction between literary historical moments. In a more comprehensive reading of Goux's work, Roberts carefully and meticulously considers how he 'maintains a consistent critique of the general or universal equivalent in all its forms' (144), establishing all monetary value – including that of gold – as a conventional virtuality that never transcends the cultural or historical.

Ruth Livesey, in another outstanding contribution to Balfour's collection, obliquely questions such perceptions of money's simulacrous and immaterial state. Extending familiar responses on the place of money in Dickens' *Our Mutual Friend*, Livesey highlights the centrality of financial credit to this novel and traces the reconfiguration of citizenship, domesticity, and capital after Disraeli's proposals to reform the franchise. 'It is not that money is a fiction in this novel', Livesey writes, 'but rather that its pervasiveness threatens to denude established narratives of character, origin, family and identity of any significance' (85)[1]. Literary textuality, as a site of meaning which variously works to confirm and contest the commodification of cultural value, remains focal to much of the work gathered together by Balfour; for György Fogarasi, epitaphic writing by Wordsworth and Gray figuratively establishes vitality as a speculative investment in the eternal; Rekha Rosha finds in Benjamin Franklin's 1793 autobiography an 'entanglement of memoir and money' that moves between documentary accounting and personal accountability; and Christopher J. Fauske explores Swift's objections not to financial acquisition as such, but to the decadent and indulgent flaunting of wealth. However, while many essays in this collection consider the place of capital in literary texts, other contributions extend the notion of representation to different forms of cultural production. Guillaume Evrard thus discovers, in the Paris Exposition of 1937, grain elevators symbolically celebrated as an architecture that promotes both national agricultural wealth and international modernity; Elton G. McGuon identifies Gordon Gekko, Oliver Stone's principal character in the 1987 film *Wall Street*, as the kind of maverick law-breaker who is structurally integral to the mythopoeic re-imagining of America.

Culture, Capital and Representation is circumscribed by an introduction and a conclusion, both authored by Balfour. Helpfully setting out and summarising the volume's motivation and trajectory, these chapters also thematically draw together and extend the issues addressed in each essay. These framing chapters are mostly subtle, sensitive, and insightful in their response to the often very complex material that is considered in the volume: the introduction, for example, describes the production and maintenance of symbolic systems as immanent to the 'profitable fantasy' which 'threatens to eclipse the real altogether by making it discursively invisible by means of language, media and ideology which collude in a colonial-global fantasy until the particular sufferings – displacement, deprivation and disenfranchisement – of individuals become invisible' (4). On occasions, however, the conceptual register slides

---

1   Editors' note: this essay is a revised version of the article by Ruth Livesey which first appeared in *Key Words* 5 (10–25), 'The Representation of the People and *Our Mutual Friend*'. © The Raymond Williams Society 2007.

into a less delicate treatment of debates about cultural production and the real. Thus, again in the introduction, we read: 'For postmodernists there is no distinction between "fact" and "fiction". "Fact", as a category, is exploded. It is just as likely to be culturally produced and mediated as an airport novel. Both factual and fictional texts are referential to a reality that no longer exists and both are subject only to the constraints of language' (4). Such moments are rare, however, and this provocative collection has been assembled with scrupulous editorial care.

Philip Leonard
Nottingham Trent University

Notes on Contributors

Anna Ball is a Lecturer in Postcolonial Studies at Nottingham Trent University. Her research explores the pertinence of postcolonial feminist enquiry to cultural expression within the Middle East, and is focused particularly on the work of female authors and filmmakers. Her book, *Palestinian Literature and Film in Postcolonial Feminist Perspective*, is forthcoming with Routledge in August 2012.

Tony Crowley held the Chair of Language, Literature and Cultural Theory at the University of Manchester and is currently the Hartley Burr Alexander Chair in the Humanities at Scripps College, California. He is the author of a number of monographs on the politics of language, including the prize-winning *Wars of Words: The Politics of Language in Ireland 1537–2004* (2005). He is presently completing two studies: 'Joyce and the language questions' and 'Language in Liverpool: History, Narrative and Cultural Identities'.

Simon Dentith is a Professor of English at Reading University. He has published widely on nineteenth- and twentieth-century writing, and his most recent book is *Epic and Empire in Nineteenth-Century Britain* (2006). He has a long-standing interest in the work of Raymond Williams, and is currently on the editorial board of *Key Words*.

Yasuo Kawabata is Professor of English at Japan Women's University, Tokyo. He has published widely on William Morris and George Orwell, including *Orwell no Mother Goose* (1998) and Japanese translations of Morris's *News from Nowhere* (2005) and Orwell's *Animal Farm* (2009). His latest publication is *George Best ga ita* [There once was George Best] (2010) which is the first Japanese biography of the legendary footballer of Manchester United. He is a member of Raymond Williams Kenkyukai, or the Society of Raymond Williams in Japan, and organised and chaired the one-day symposium 'Fiction as Criticism / Criticism as a Whole Way of Life: Raymond Williams in Transit II' held in Tokyo on 25 September 2010.

Yasuhiro Kondo is Lecturer in English at Tokyo University. His research interests are in twentieth-century English literature. He has published essays on D.H. Lawrence, Raymond Williams, Doris Lessing, and John Fowles, including 'Doris Lessing's Strategies: Reading, Writing, and Feeling in *The Golden Notebook*' in *Studies in English Literature: Regional Branches Combined Issue* (1: 2009).

Notes on Contributors

Shintaro Kono is Assistant Professor at the Graduate School of Commerce and Management, Hitotsubashi University, Tokyo. His field of research has been British modernist fiction and Marxist literary theory, including Raymond Williams. He is the author of 'Tenses of Experience: An Archaeology of Future in The Volunteers', published in the Japanese journal *Eigo Seinen* [The Rising Generation] (2009). He has translated Fredric Jameson's *Cultural Turn* and Edward Said's *Culture and Resistance* and other critical writings into Japanese, and is now working on Raymond Williams's *Culture and Society* and *The English Novel from Dickens to Lawrence*. His current projects include the genealogy of liberalism (and its relation to statism and communitarianism) in Britain and Welsh writing in English.

Edward Larrissy is Professor of Poetry and Head of School in the School of English at Queen's University, Belfast. He is a Member of the Royal Irish Academy, and a Fellow of the English Association. His authored books include *Yeats the Poet: The Measures of Difference* (1994), *Blake and Modern Literature* (2006) and *The Blind and Blindness in Literature of the Romantic Period* (2007). He is also the editor of, among others, *Romanticism and Postmodernism* (1999), *W.B. Yeats: The Major Works* (2000) and *The First Yeats: Poems by W.B. Yeats 1889–1899* (2010).

Philip Leonard is Reader in Literary Studies and Critical Theory at Nottingham Trent University. He is the author of *Nationality between Poststructuralism and Postcolonial Theory: A New Cosmopolitanism* (2005), and co-editor of the journal *Writing Technologies*. He is currently writing *Literature after Globalization: Text, Technology, and the Nation-State*, which is due to be published by Continuum in 2013.

Takashi Onuki is Associate Professor at the School of Business Administration, Kwansei Gakuin University. He has published articles on David Hare, David Edgar, and Arnold Wesker, as well as Raymond Williams. In collaboration with Shintaro Kono, he has written articles for the serial project, *Keywords for Life in the 21st Century*, on the online journal *Web Eigo-Seinen*. The works that he has co-translated include *New Keywords: A Revised Vocabulary of Culture and Society* (Tony Bennett et al. eds), and Edward Said's *Reflections on Exile and Other Essays* and *Culture and Resistance*.

Dai Smith is the Raymond Williams Chair in Cultural History at Swansea University. He is also Chair of the Arts Council of Wales and Series Editor of the Welsh Assembly Government's Library of Wales for classic works written in English from or about Wales. He has written widely on literature and society – *Aneurin Bevan and The World of South Wales* (1993) and *Wales: A Question for History* (1988) – books in which artificial discipline boundaries are deliberately broken down. For television he has presented and scripted a number of award-winning documentaries and, as a broadcaster, sought to deepen popular appreciation of Welsh culture and history.

Philip Smith is a documentary filmmaker. His extensive work for British, European and American networks includes films in the BAFTA and RTS award-winning Channel 4 series *This is Modern Art; Superfly*, which won the 2002 RTS award for best science programme; and the opening film in the Digital Emmy and BAFTA-winning BBC2 production about the internet, *The Virtual Revolution*.

Stan Smith, Professor Emeritus in English at Nottingham Trent University, is the author and editor of many books on modern and contemporary poetry, including a study of the Anglo-Welsh poet Edward Thomas (1986). Recent work includes an Introduction to a new edition of Raymond Williams's *The Country and the City* published by the Russell Press. He is a member of the editorial board of *Key Words*.

Abigail Ward is Senior Lecturer in Postcolonial Studies at Nottingham Trent University. She is the author of *Caryl Phillips, David Dabydeen and Fred D'Aguiar: Representations of Slavery* (2011) and has essays on postcolonial literature published in a range of books and journals. In 2009, she co-edited a special issue of the journal *Atlantic Studies* (6:2), entitled 'Tracing black America in black Britain'. Her current project explores representations of Indian indenture in contemporary literature from Trinidad and Guyana.

Benjamin Ware is a Postdoctoral Research Fellow in the Department of English and American Studies at the University of Manchester and a Visiting Research Fellow at the Institute of English Studies, School of Advanced Study, University of London. He is currently working on a project provisionally entitled 'Ethical Turns in Modernist Literature'.

Daniel G. Williams is Senior Lecturer in English and Director of the Richard Burton Centre for the Study of Wales at Swansea University. He is the author of *Ethnicity and Cultural Authority: from Arnold to Du Bois* (2006) and is editor of a collection of Raymond Williams's writings on Wales, *Who Speaks for Wales? Nation, Culture, Identity* (2003) and a collection of essays on contemporary Welsh poetry, *Slanderous Tongues* (2010).

Yuzo Yamada is Associate Professor at the Graduate School of Language and Culture, Osaka University, Japan. He was also Visiting Associate Professor at the Osaka Study Centre of The Open University of Japan for adult education between 2003 and 2008. He has written extensively about popular drama and British cultural studies, including *Writing under Influences: A Study of Christopher Marlowe* (1999) and *Kanjo no Cultural Studies: from the age of* Scrutiny *to the New Left's movement* (2005). He also co-published an anthology of cultural studies for Japanese readers, *How to Read Cultures* (2008), in which he edited and annotated Raymond Williams's *Television* and 'Culture is Ordinary'.

Raymond Williams Foundation (RWF)

The RWF aims 'to commemorate the works of Raymond Williams, in particular in the sphere of adult education for the benefit of the public'. Its objectives include 'support for adult education through partnership with the Workers Educational Association (WEA) and other organisations'. RWF has a close relationship with the Raymond Williams Society and there is potential to consolidate this relationship given the particular strengths of each body.

The centrepiece of RWF activity in recent years has been an annual Raymond Williams weekend held in May at Wedgwood College in Staffordshire. The 2011 weekend was the 23rd, with the keynote lecture given by Richard Wilkinson, co-author (with Kate Pickett) of *The Spirit Level*, whose thesis is summarised in its sub-title: *Why More Equal Societies Almost Always Do Better*. Tristram Hunt, now the Labour MP for Stoke-on-Trent Central, opened the course with a lecture on 'The Idea of Equality', using his biography of Engels to illustrate the theme entertainingly. The lecture can be accessed on the RWF website.

The main thrust of RWF work continues to be linking such residential events to the growing network of informal pub/café/bar discussion circles. Philosophy in Pubs (PiPs) is closely associated with RWF and PiPs held its first (and very successful) residential at the Adelphi Hotel, Liverpool, in June 2011. A new initiative is the RWF Residential Library – Reading Retreat scheme. This was launched with the participation of sixteen venues across Great Britain, with aims of supporting and developing library collections and promoting residential reading room 'retreats' with grants from the RWF where needed.

In the last year, the RWF has attracted increasing interest from across the globe, in the form of academics seeking information but also applications for funding. An RWF partnership with RUWON in Nepal has been established with RWF grants assisting women and families with desperate economic and educational needs. Similar applications from Southern India and Central Africa were recently approved.

Details of all RWF activities can be found on the website:
www.raymondwilliamsfoundation.org.uk

Derek Tatton
RWF Administrator and RWS Executive Committee member

Style Notes for Contributors

Presentation of Copy
Key Words is an internationally refereed academic journal. In the first instance typescripts for prospective publication should be submitted to the Contributions Editor (details may be found on the inside back cover with Dr Catherine Clay, School of Arts and Humanities, Nottingham Trent University, Clifton Campus, Nottingham NG11 8NS, catherine.clay@ntu.ac.uk). Articles should normally be no longer than 6,000 words; reviews should typically be between 1,500 and 2,000 words. Articles should be double spaced, with generous margins, and pages should be numbered consecutively. For matters of style not addressed below, please refer to *The Chicago Manual of Style*, 15th ed. or http://www.chicagomanualofstyle.org/contents.html. Contributors who fail to observe these notes may be asked to revise their submission in accordance with them.

Provision of Text in Electronic Format
Key Words is prepared electronically. Consequently, contributors whose work is accepted for publication will be asked to supply a file copy of their work (either on disc, CD-ROM or by electronic mail) to the Contributions Editor. The preferred word processing format is Microsoft Word (any version).

References and Bibliographic Conventions
Citations in *Key Words* appear as endnotes at the conclusion of each contribution. Essays presented for prospective publication should adopt this style. Endnote markers should be given in arabic numerals and positioned after, not before, punctuation marks, e.g. '.[1]' rather than '[1].'. With no bibliography, full details must be given in a note at the first mention of any work cited. Subsequent citations can then use the short form or a cross-reference. Headline-style capitalisation is used. In headline style, the first and last words of title and subtitle and all other major words are capitalised. Titles of books and journals should be formatted in italics (not underlined).

Please cite books in the following manner:

On first citation: Raymond Williams and Michael Orrom, *Preface to Film* (London: Film Drama, 1954).

On subsequent citations: Williams and Orrom, *Preface to Film*, 12.

Please cite journal articles in the following manner:

> Patrick Parrinder, 'Politics, Letters and the National Curriculum', *Changing English* 2, no. 1 (1994): 29.

Chapters in books should be referenced in the following way:

> Andrew McRae, 'The Peripatetic Muse: Internal Travel and the Cultural Production of Space in Pre-Revolutionary England', in *The Country and the City Revisited: England and the Politics of Culture, 1550–1850*, ed. Gerald MacLean, Donna Landry, and Joseph P. Ward (Cambridge: Cambridge University Press, 1999), 41–57.

For internet articles:

> Raymond Williams Society Executive, 'About the Raymond Williams Society', Raymond Williams Society, http://www.raymondwilliams.co.uk/ (accessed 26 March 2009).

Please refer to newspaper articles in the following way:

> John Mullan, 'Rebel in a Tweed Suit', *The Observer*, 28 May 2005, Features and Reviews section, 37.

A thesis should be referenced in the following manner:

> E. Allen, 'The Dislocated Mind: The Fictions of Raymond Williams' (PhD diss., Liverpool John Moores University, 2007), 22–9.

Conference papers should be cited in the following style:

> Dai Smith, 'Translating Raymond Williams' (paper presented at the Raymond Williams's Culture and Society@50 conference, Canolfan Dylan Thomas Centre, Swansea, 7 November 2008).

Quotations
For quotations use single quotation marks, and double quotation marks for quotations within quotations. Punctuation is used outside quotations. Ensure that all spellings, punctuation, abbreviations etc. within a quotation are rendered exactly as in the original, including errors, which should be signalled by the authorial interpolation '(*sic*)'.

Style Notes for Contributors

Book Reviews

Book reviews should open with full bibliographic details of the text under review. These details should include (in the following order): in bold type, first name(s) and surname(s) of author(s), or first name(s) and surname(s) of editor(s) followed by a parenthetic '(ed.)' or '(eds)'; in italics, the full title of the volume followed by a period and a hard return; then, in regular type, the place of publication, publisher and date of publication; the page extent of the volume, including front papers numbered in Roman numerals; the price (where available) of the supplied copy and an indication of 'pb.' or 'hb.'; and the ISBN of the supplied copy. For example:

Dai Smith, *Raymond Williams: A Warriors Tale.* Cardigan: Parthian Books, 2008. xviii + 514 pp. £24.99 hb. ISBN 978 1 905762 56 9.